Something Seems Strange

Something Seems Strange

Critical Essays on Christianity, Public Policy,
and Contemporary Culture

Anthony B. Bradley

WIPF & STOCK · Eugene, Oregon

SOMETHING SEEMS STRANGE
Critical Essays on Christianity, Public Policy, and Contemporary Culture

Wipf & Stock
An Imprint of Wipf and Stock Publishers
199 W. 8th Ave., Suite 3
Eugene, OR 97401

www.wipfandstock.com

PAPERBACK ISBN: 978-1-4982-8390-8
HARDCOVER ISBN: 978-1-4982-8392-2
EBOOK ISBN: 978-1-4982-8391-5

Manufactured in the U.S.A.

To Joshua Cunningham, Alexander Bouffard,
and Benjamin George

Contents

Acknowledgements | ix
Introduction | xi

Section One—The Church and the Christian Life | 1
Section Two—Politics and Economics | 136
Section Three—Education | 194
Section Four—Contemporary Culture | 211

Bibliography | 269
Subject Index | 281
Scripture Index | 285

Acknowledgements

THIS BOOK WOULD NOT exist if it were not for colleagues and students at The King's College in New York City. Many of these essays emerged from my conversations and classroom interactions with some of the most dynamic and inspiring friends I have ever had. I must thank for Kris Mauren and the Rev. Robert Sirico, co-founders of the Acton Institute for the Study of Religion and Liberty in Grand Rapids, Michigan, where I have worked as a research fellow since 2002. The Acton Institute has provided me a platform and multiple international opportunities to speak and write about issues reprinted in this volume from my work at Acton. My principle content and style editor has been my friend and colleague Dr. Kevin Schmeising, also a research fellow at the Acton Institute. I credit Kevin with single-handedly making me sound more intelligent and coherent than I actually am. John Couretas, Acton's communication director, has masterfully worked to add the finishing touches on these essays and to disseminate them all over the world. Many of the essays in this volume were originally written for various web platforms at WORLD Magazine. I owe the continuation of my teaching career to Dr. Marvin Olasky, the editor-in-chief of WORLD. He believed in me and gave me opportunities when few others were willing to do so. Mickey McLean served as my most excellent editor at WORLD News Group and I am indebted to his fine work at making my writing better. I would also like to thank Davis Campbell, my research assistant at The King's College, for his expert formatting and editing work on this volume. This book would not have happened without Mr. Campbell's work. Dr. Charlotte Kent worked tirelessly to edit the footnotes and bibliography. Dr. Kent lives in New York City where she works as a writer and editor, finessing her own and others' sentences, footnotes, web content, etc. She can be found at scriptandtype.com or The National Arts Club. Mr. Campbell and Dr. Kent were the perfect editorial team. Christian Amondson, Matthew

Wimer, and the team at Wipf and Stock were very gracious to work with me again on this project and I am thankful for their patience as we brought this book to print. Finally, I take full responsibility for any and all mistakes found in this book.

Introduction

THIS BOOK SERVES AS a sequel to my first book with Wifp and Stock, *Black and Tired* (2011). Since 2011, I had the wonderful pleasure of earning a Master of Arts degree from Fordham University in Ethics and Society. As I studied more psychology, legal philosophy, Christian social thought, natural law, and economic theory in the program my writing changed. I am definitely more deliberate about writing from the intersection of several Christian principles, including principled pluralism, sphere sovereignty, subsidiarity, solidarity, personalism, apophatic theology, and theosis.

Since I arrived at The King's College in 2009, I have had the honor and privilege of teaching religious studies which allows me to reflect publicly on current events with the aim of intersecting economics, psychology, political philosophy, sociology, cultural criticism, African American studies, and moral theology. As I've said before, contemplating social and political life from a theological perspective is nothing new; we find such reflections throughout the entire biblical narrative, from Genesis to Revelations. As I did in back in 2011, what follows in this book are theological and moral reflections on some of the social issues affecting our local, national, and global communities. The topics range from church life, to presidential politics, to public school education policy, and more—all examined from a theological perspective.

These essays are a form of public theology in the sense that they wrestle with this generation's issues, bringing theology to life and demonstrating God's relevance in a post-everything world.

This book explores the intersection of race, politics and economics, social trends in culture, and trends in education by integrating the following justice principles from the Acton Institute.[1] They include:

1. See "Acton Institute Core Principles," Acton Institute.

(1) Dignity of the Person—The human person, created in the image of God, is individually unique, rational, the subject of moral agency, and a co-creator. Accordingly, he possesses intrinsic value and dignity, implying certain rights and duties both for himself and other persons. These truths about the dignity of the human person are known through revelation, but they are also discernible through reason.

(2) Social Nature of the Person—Although persons find ultimate fulfillment only in communion with God, one essential aspect of the development of persons is our social nature and capacity to act for disinterested ends. The person is fulfilled by interacting with other persons and by participating in moral goods. There are voluntary relations of exchange, such as market transactions that realize economic value. These transactions may give rise to moral value as well. There are also voluntary relations of mutual dependence, such as promises, friendships, marriages, and the family, which are moral goods. These, too, may have other sorts of value, such as religious, economic, aesthetic, and so on.

(3) Importance of Social Institutions—Since persons are by nature social, various human persons develop social institutions. The institutions of civil society, especially the family, are the primary sources of a society's moral culture. These social institutions are neither created by nor derive their legitimacy from the state. The state must respect their autonomy and provide the support necessary to ensure the free and orderly operation of all social institutions in their respective spheres.

(3) Human Action—Human persons are by nature acting persons. Through human action, the person can actualize his potentiality by freely choosing the moral goods that fulfill his nature.

(4) Sin—Although human beings in their created nature are good, in their current state, they are fallen and corrupted by sin. The reality of sin makes the state necessary to restrain evil. The ubiquity of sin, however, requires that the state be limited in its power and jurisdiction. The persistent reality of sin requires that we be skeptical of all utopian "solutions" to social ills such as poverty and injustice.

(5) Rule of Law and the Subsidiary Role of Government—The government's primary responsibility is to promote the common good, that is, to maintain the rule of law, and to preserve basic duties and rights. The government's role is not to usurp free actions, but to minimize those conflicts that may arise when the free actions of persons and social institutions result in competing interests. The state should exercise this responsibility according to the principle of subsidiarity. This principle has two components. First, jurisdictionally broader institutions must refrain from usurping the proper functions that should be performed by the person and institutions more immediate to him. Second, jurisdictionally broader institutions should assist individual persons and institutions more immediate to the person only when the latter cannot fulfill their proper functions.

(6) Creation of Wealth—Material impoverishment undermines the conditions that allow humans to flourish. The best means of reducing poverty is to protect private property rights through the rule of law. This allows people to enter into voluntary exchange circles in which to express their creative nature. Wealth is created when human beings creatively transform matter into resources. Because human beings can create wealth, economic exchange need not be a zero-sum game.

(7) Economic Liberty—Liberty, in a positive sense, is achieved by fulfilling one's nature as a person by freely choosing to do what one ought. Economic liberty is a species of liberty so-stated. As such, the bearer of economic liberty not only has certain rights, but also duties. An economically free person, for example, must be free to enter the market voluntarily. Hence, those who have the power to interfere with the market are duty-bound to remove any artificial barrier to entry in the market, and also to protect private and shared property rights. But the economically free person will also bear the duty to others to participate in the market as a moral agent and in accordance with moral goods. Therefore, the law must guarantee private property rights and voluntary exchange.

(8) Economic Value—In economic theory, economic value is subjective because its existence depends on it being felt by a subject. Economic value is the significance that a subject attaches to a thing whenever he perceives a causal connection between this thing and the satisfaction of a present, urgent want. The subject may be wrong in his value judgment by attributing value to a thing that will not or cannot satisfy his present, urgent want. The truth of economic value judgments is settled just in case that thing can satisfy the expected want. While this does not imply the realization of any other sort of value, something can have both subjective economic value and objective moral value.

(9) Priority of Culture—Liberty flourishes in a society supported by a moral culture that embraces the truth about the transcendent origin and destiny of the human person. This moral culture leads to harmony and to the proper ordering of society. While the various institutions within the political, economic, and other spheres are important, the family is the primary inculcator of the moral culture in a society.

My opinions and the scholarly yet accessible style in which I express them owe much to the work of Thomas Sowell, one of the most cogent and lucid of American socio-economic analysts. I learned from Sowell the importance of supporting my propositions with incontrovertible evidence and irrefutable facts. Unlike my previous collection of essays, I decided to include footnotes and add a selected bibliography. Because this is not a standard academic text, I only included the footnotes and bibliographic references that I believed were particularly vital as they pointed to important and controversial data. As such, many specific citations were omitted intentionally as to not bog down readers with hair splitting detail and to avoid needlessly adding extra pages to the volume. As my writing and understanding continue to grow and mature, I recognize that I do not represent "the last word" on any of these issues. I hope, however, that the following essays will advance national and international conversations about the common good and make the world, in some small measure, a better place. Treat this book as an exercise of me thinking out loud. I invite constructive engagement as we all seek to pursue, unlock, and discover the truth.

Anthony B. Bradley

The King's College
New York, NY

The Church and the Christian Life

The New Legalism

Is Paul's urging to live quietly, mind your own affairs, and work with your hands (1 Thessalonians 4:11) only for losers? Do you feel that you're wasting your gifts if you "settle" into an ordinary job, get married early and start a family, or live in a small town or suburb? Acton Institute Power Blogger Anthony Bradley has some provocative thoughts on the "new legalism."—Marvin Olasky

BACK IN 2013 I made the following observation on Facebook and Twitter:

> "Being a 'radical,' 'missional' Christian is slowly becoming the 'new legalism.' We need more ordinary God and people lovers (Matt 22:36-40)."

This observation was the result of a long conversation with a student who was wrestling with what to do with his life, given all of the opportunities he had available to him. To my surprise, my comment exploded over the internet with dozens and dozens of people sharing the comment and sending me personal correspondence.

I continue to be amazed by the number of youth and young adults who are stressed and burnt out from the feelings of shame and inadequacy they experience if they happen not to be doing something unique and special. Today's millennial generation is being fed the message that, if they don't do something extraordinary in this life, they are wasting their gifts and potential. The sad result is that many young adults feel ashamed if they "settle" into ordinary jobs, get married early and start families, live in small towns, or as 1 Thessalonians 4:11 says, "aspire to live quietly, and to mind [their] affairs, and to work with [their] hands." For too many millennials, being an ordinary person, who works a non-glamorous job, lives in the suburbs, and has nothing spectacular to boast about, is a fate to be avoided at all costs.

Here are a few thoughts on how we got here.

Anti-Suburban Christianity

In the 1970s and 1980s, the children and older grandchildren of the builder generation (born between 1901 and 1920) sorted themselves and headed to the suburbs to raise their children in safety, comfort, and material ease. And now millennials (born between 1977 and 1995), taking a cue from their baby boomer parents (born between 1946 and 1964) to despise the contexts that provided them their advantages, have a disdain for America's suburbs. This despising of suburban life has been inadvertently encouraged by well-intentioned religious leaders inviting people to move to neglected cities to make a difference, because, after all, the Apostle Paul did his work primarily in cities, cities are important, and cities are the final destination of the Kingdom of God. They were told that God loves cities and they should, too.[1] The unfortunate message became that you cannot live a meaningful Christian life in the suburbs.

Missional Narcissism

There are many churches that are committed to being what is called missional. This term is used to describe a church community where people see themselves as missionaries in local communities. A missional church has been defined, as "a theologically formed, Gospel-centered, Spirit-empowered, united community of believers who seek to faithfully incarnate the purposes of Christ for the glory of God," says Scott Thomas of the Acts 29 Network.[2] The problem is that this push for local missionaries coincided with the narcissism epidemic we are facing in America, especially with the millennial generation.[3] As a result, living out one's faith became narrowly celebratory only when done in a unique and special way, a "missional" way. Getting married and having children early, getting a job, saving and investing, being a good citizen, loving one's neighbor, and the like, no longer qualify as virtuous. One has to be involved in the arts and social justice activities—even if justice is pursued without sound economic or social

1. "God Loves Cities," Christiantoday.com.
2. Frazier, "What Does 'Missional' Mean?"
3. Twenge and Campbell, *The Narcissism Epidemic.*

teaching. I actually know of a couple who were being so "missional" decided to not procreate for the sake of taking care of orphans.

To make matters worse, some religious leaders have added a new category to Christianity called "radical Christianity" in an effort to trade-off suburban Christianity for mission. This movement is based on the book *Radical* by David Platt and is fashioned around "an idea that we were created for far more than a nice, comfortable Christian spin on the American dream. An idea that we were created to follow One who demands radical risk and promises radical reward."[4] Again, this was a well-intentioned attempt to address lukewarm Christians in the suburbs, but because it is primarily reactionary and does not provide a positive construction for the good life from God's perspective, it misses "radical" ideas in Jesus' own teachings like "love."

The combination of anti-suburbanism with new categories like "missional" and "radical" has positioned a generation of youth and young adults to experience an intense amount of shame for simply being ordinary Christians who desire to love God and love their neighbors (Matthew 22:36–40). In fact, missional, radical Christianity could easily be called the "new legalism." A few decades ago, an entire generation of baby boomers walked away from traditional churches to escape the legalistic moralism of "being good," but what their millennial children received in exchange, in an individualistic American Christian culture, was shamed-driven pressure to be awesome and extraordinary young adults expected to tangibly make a difference in the world immediately. But this cycle of reaction and counter-reaction, inaugurated by the baby boomers, does not seem to be producing faithful young adults. Instead, many are simply burning out.

Why is Christ's command to love God and neighbor not enough for these leaders? Maybe Christians are simply to pursue living well and invite others to do so according to how God has ordered the universe. An emphasis on human flourishing, ours and others', becomes important because it is characterized by a holistic concern for the spiritual, moral, physical, economic, material, political, psychological, and social context necessary for human beings to live according to their design. What if youth and young adults were simply encouraged to live in pursuit of wisdom, knowledge, understanding, education, wonder, beauty, glory, creativity, and worship in a world marred by sin, as Abraham Kuyper encourages in the book *Wisdom and Wonder*? No shame, no pressure to be awesome, no expectations of fame but simply following the call to be men and women of virtue and inviting their friends and neighbors to do the same in every area of life.

4. "The Movement," Radical the Book.

w millennials will respond to the "new legalism," but it
rent trend of young Christians leaving the church after
60 percent. Being a Christian in a shame-driven "mis-
hurch does not sound like rest for the weary. Perhaps the
iese pendulum swings and fads is simply to recover a ma-
ng of vocation so that youth and young adults understand
ake important contributions to human flourishing in any
sphere or... cause there are no little people or insignificant callings in
the Kingdom.

Poor Whites Need Jesus and Justice, Too

If you want to hear crickets in a room full of educated, missionally minded, culture-shaping evangelicals, ask this question: "What are you doing to serve the needs of poor white people?"

A recent seminary graduate, who is white, asked me what he needed to do to prepare to plant a church in a small lower-class town that is 76 percent black and 21 percent white. He was rightly cautious after reading in *Aliens in the Promised Land* about Rev. Lance Lewis' call for a moratorium on white evangelicals planting churches in black areas because of evangelicalism's cultural obtuseness and patriarchal disposition toward ethnic minorities. Since most black communities in the South are already saturated with churches, I asked this young man why he was not interested in planting a church among the lower-class whites in his county. His humble response: "It had not occurred to me to plant a church among lower-class whites."

While urban, justice-loving evangelicals easily shame white, suburban, conservative evangelicals for their racially homogenized lives, both communities seem to share a disdain for lower-class white people. "Rednecks," "crackers," "hoosiers," and "white trash" are all derogatory terms used to describe a population of lower-class whites who have suffered centuries of injustice and social marginalization in America, especially from educated Christians.

Even though lower-class whites comprise the largest percentage of America's welfare recipients and the largest percentage of those living below the poverty line, evangelicals remain largely focused on poverty among African-Americans and Hispanics. The imagery conjured by "social justice" and "mercy-ministry" rhetoric is a collage of underprivileged African-American and Hispanic kids living in "da hood." When evangelicals are challenged to relocate to poor areas for the sake of the being "missional," small towns and rural areas with high concentrations of lower-class whites, like Springfield, MO, or Troy, NY, do not normally make the list. While Christian colleges and seminaries across America are teeming with "urban ministry" programs, there is only one large, accredited seminary in America that has a degree program targeted specifically for rural ministry: Duke Divinity School in Durham, N.C., a seminary founded and supported by the United Methodist Church.

One common excuse for the lack of focus on white poverty is how disproportionately worse poverty is in black and Hispanic communities. There is no argument there. African-Americans have a poverty rate of 25.8 percent, Hispanics/Latinos 17.1 percent, whites 11.6 percent, and Asian-Americans 5.3 percent. But, in terms of absolute numbers, there are more poor whites in the United States than any other group. More than 19 million whites fall below the poverty line for a family of four, which is nearly twice the number of blacks. Therefore, whites account for more than 41 percent of the nation's poor, argues author Mark Rank in *Chasing the American Dream*. Furthermore, the Congressional Budget Office calculates that whites receive 69 percent of U.S. government public welfare benefits.[5] In other words, when you hear words like "poor" or "welfare queen," which conservatives coined in the 1980s, the image that *should* come to mind is that of a single, white female.

The fact of white poverty raises new questions. For example, why are these 19 million people not reflected in the American evangelical discourse on poverty and social justice? Why do college-educated white evangelicals seem to have a preference for lower-class ethnic minorities in inner cities? Who are the pastors and justice advocates representing the needs of lower-class whites? In fairness, there are several churches and ministries serving in poor white communities across the country but their numbers pale in comparison to urban and inner-city efforts. Why is this?

Perhaps the root of the problem is that middle-class evangelicals are content maintaining the narrative that they have come to save the world's people of color from themselves. "American society is completely dependent upon a worldview that places white Christian-Americans at the top of the hierarchy, with African-Americans falling into the lowest place" observes Kirsten Hemmy, formerly an associate professor of languages and literature at Johnson C. Smith University in Charlotte, N.C. This view of whites at the social peak, she says, is a part of "our collective imagination— informed by art, culture, media, and history" that is "just as important as reality."[6] Hemmy also believes that evangelicalism's paternalistic history and

5. Applebaum and Gebeloff, "Who Benefits from the Safety Net?"
6. Hemmy, Personal Email Correspondence, March 14, 2015.

condescension with people of color fuels disinterest in helping poor whites. "Poor white people should be able to fend for themselves, so mission work and ministry is focused on the black community, as though poor black people, because they are black, cannot fend for themselves."

"You can feel good about helping a black family in the projects, because you can easily identify a few basic problems and leave,"[7] says Robert Fossett, pastor of First Presbyterian Church (Presbyterian Church in America) in Greenville, Ala. "No one expects you to live there unless you are intending to gentrify the neighborhood and turn it into your own image.[8] But when it comes to poor whites, i.e., 'white trash,' while there is also a deep cultural disconnect with white evangelicals—poor whites tend to be on the boundaries of towns and cities in rural populations. . . . The assumption is that poor whites are where they are because they are inbred, lazy, and un-educated, and they choose to live like this. And as everyone knows, you can't fix lazy, degenerate, immoral white trash. Besides, it's far easier to mock a trailer park than it is to plant a church there."

Fossett's comments, in fact, fit the long history of disgust and con-tempt educated whites have had toward poor whites in America for nearly 250 years. In *Not Quite White: White Trash and the Boundaries of White-ness*, Matt Wray, a sociology professor at Temple University in Philadelphia, quotes South Carolina Anglican minster the Rev. Charles Woodsman ex-pressing such contempt toward the white underclass in 1766: "They delight in their present low, lazy, sluttish, heathenish, hellish life, and seem not de-sirous of changing it."[9] The so-called "white trash," says Wray, "reveals itself as an expression of fundamental tensions and deep structural antimonies: between the sacred and the profane, purity and impurity, morality and im-morality, cleanliness and dirt."[10] To be white in America was not simply a racial category. "Whiteness" identifies a class of people who view themselves as culturally superior and more advanced than others like poor whites, blacks, Native Americans, and so on. White is something lower-class im-migrant groups like the Irish had to become, as David R. Roediger explains in *Working Toward Whiteness: How America's Immigrants Became White*. To not live up to the cultural expectations of whiteness, regardless of one's actual skin color, was to invite utter disdain by the educated class. Including Christians.

7. Ibid.
8. Ibid.
9. Wray, *Not Quite White*, 22.
10. Ibid., 2.

According to Wray, by the 1760s, elites in the colonies viewed lower-status whites as a "distinct, inferior social group." From the 17th to the early 19th century, poor whites were lumped in with Indians and blacks as "immoral, lazy, and dirty." These stigma-types were particularly fitting given the fact that lower-class whites worked, and sometimes even lived, among Native Americans and freed blacks. "Crackers," "white trash," "rednecks," and the like were considered objects of Christian mission because their perceived laziness was understood as a moral problem that led to their material poverty and corruption. Elites sought to redeem the lives of poor whites during the Colonial era by instilling in these lowly people the virtues of hard work, the Christian life, and good hygiene.

By the late 18th century, as landowning elites in the British colonies preferred African slave labor, Wray writes that lower-class whites found themselves "pushed aggressively and violently into the western trans-Appalachia frontier"—the upper Ohio River Valley, Virginia, the Carolinas, and Georgia. These poor whites were increasingly known as "crackers"—as first used in a 1766 administrative letter from Gavin Cochran, a Colonial officer, to the Earl of Dartmouth in Great Britain. Crackers are backwoods people who Wray says are known to be "ill-mannered, arrogant, treacherous, and cruel, stealing from Indians and propertied white colonists alike." Wray explains that "cracker" was not so much a term that stirred contempt, but a word that served as a clear cultural marker between God-fearing colonists and other not quite whites. "Cracker" remained in use through the Revolutionary era into the new republic and by the early 19th century was joined by the phrase "poor white trash."

Poor white trash, often shortened to "white trash," debuted in written form in Baltimore in 1833, as black domestic workers distinguished themselves from whites doing similar jobs. Middle-class and elite whites added the phrase to their lexicon as way to stigmatize those who were not living up to the standards of "real whiteness." By the antebellum period, white elites in the Southern states had concluded that white trash inhabitants were degenerate because of some kind of genetic disorder that could not be cured merely by adjusting their circumstances. The era's fascination with social Darwinism pushed this biological explanation of white poverty to the fore: Poor whites were naturally inferior, and they needed strong leadership to curb their uncivilized ways.

Whites in the North held similar views. Wray quotes Quaker-raised public figure Bayard Taylor saying in 1861 that "the white trash of the South represented the most depraved class of whites I have ever seen. Idle, shiftless, filthy in their habits, aggressive, with no regard for others."[11] As America transitioned into the 20th century, the accepted solution to the white trash problem was extinction via eugenics.

The use of eugenics—a program to improve the genetic fitness of society by controlling who can procreate—is commonly associated with Nazi Germany, or Margaret Sanger's justification for opening abortion centers in Harlem, N.Y. But most Americans are unaware that both of these programs were modeled after an effort in the United States to outlaw reproduction of lower-class whites. From 1906 to 1927, more than 8,000 white women were forcibly sterilized, a practice protected by state law so that poor whites would not continue to populate regions in the Midwest, the Ohio River Valley, the South, and Appalachia. Eugenics supporters traveled across the country chronicling the lives of poor whites to make the case that they should not procreate with each other, their relatives, or other minorities like blacks or Native Americans.

Their program of forced sterilization was enshrined in law in a landmark 1927 Supreme Court Case, *Buck v. Bell*. Carrie Buck protested her involuntary 1924 commitment to the Virginia Colony for Epileptics and Feeble-Minded. After giving birth out of wedlock, Buck was declared "feeble-minded," as were many other poor whites at the time. She was institutionalized and slated for involuntary sterilization. Buck objected, lost the case, and was sterilized. In an eight-to-one majority, Oliver Wendell Holmes Jr. opined, "It is better for all the world, if instead of waiting to execute degenerate offspring for crime, or to let them starve for their imbecility, society can prevent those who are manifestly unfit from continuing their kind. The principle that sustains compulsory vaccination is broad enough to cover cutting the Fallopian tubes. Three generations of imbeciles are enough."[12] By 1923, the American Eugenics Society had recruited prominent clergy in advisory roles, such as Massachusetts Episcopal Bishop William Lawrence and New York's Harry Fosdick, along with J.W. Eliot, head of social service work of the Northern Baptists, and leading Quakers like Rufus Jones.

The long tradition of racism in this country includes white-on-white contempt. Elite Christians have consistently been complicit in this rancor. Does the line of elite visceral tension running through American history lead all the way up to evangelicalism's neglect of lower-class whites in 21st century America? Today it seems that "the least of these" includes more than 19 million poor whites who are just the wrong color for gospel ministry and mission. As educated evangelicals turn a blind eye to 41 percent of

---

11. Ibid., 59-60.

12. Nemeth, *Criminal Law*, 6.

the nation's poor, are they more driven by a white messianic narrative than by an indiscriminate love for neighbor?

Anthony Bradley vs. Evangelical Tribalism

Ideological tribalism: How evangelicals go about social ethics

I recently had an exchange with a Duke Divinity School student regarding many of the things I've written at the Acton Institute over the past 12 years. The student said this about me:

> When it comes to speaking comfort to power and castigating the most vulnerable in our society, there is perhaps no public theological voice more eager than that of Anthony Bradley's. His body of work is a textbook in blaming the victim and reducing problems to pathology.

Not only had the student actually not read most of the things that I have written but the comment exposes something that Jonathan Haidt explains well that I've talked about before: ideological "tribalism."

Evangelicals generally develop perspectives on justice down tribal ideological and political lines because they normally do not source the Christian social thought tradition when constructing perspectives on justice. It turns out I was simply being criticized by a card-carrying, bona fide political progressive who is also a Christian. In this light, I was not surprised by the content of the critique. I do not hold the same presuppositions about creation, the implications of the fall, natural law, human dignity, the role of the state, the authority of Scripture, and so on, as progressives do, so naturally progressives are going to see calls to personal moral virtue and challenges to the patriarchy, soft bigotry, and the historic tendency for coercive government to make things worse off for those on the margins through the welfare state as "speaking comfort to power and castigating the most vulnerable."

The exchange provides a clear example of how evangelicals, ignorant of the Christian social thought tradition, go about the business of addressing social issues. It goes something like this:

Step 1: For a variety of well-intentioned reasons, choose a preferred political ideology you believe is the right one and will adequately address the differentiated problems in society. As David Koyzis explains, it could be libertarianism, socialism, nationalism, conservatism, progressivism, or democracy.[13]

---

13. See Koyzis, *Political Visions and Illusions.*

Step 2: Read your preferred political ideology into the Bible in such a way that it becomes a tool for interpreting and applying the Bible to social issues. That is, your political ideology becomes your hermeneutic for "biblical" views on justice.

Step 3: Cherry-pick Bible verses (often ignoring their context) and repackage them to make the case that your preferred, tribal, political ideology is indeed "biblical," "follows the teaching of Jesus," is "Christian," and so on. Here the goal is to prove that God must obviously be on your tribe's side.

Step 4: Now that you have baptized your political ideology by pouring on a random assortment of Bible verses, you are ready to declare your ideological tribe and those who agree with you "right." As a result, any other tribe that does not read the Bible through your ideological lens is not only wrong, they also are the enemy and a threat to the church and the world.

Step 5: Issue a call for all other Christians to embrace your tribal ideology. Now that your tribe is "right" you are free in the blogosphere, for example, to declare all of those who are "not like us"—that is, not in our tribe—to be "wrong." Those in the other tribe (i.e., the enemy tribe) need to change their views so that they can more closely adhere to what your tribe believes the Bible teaches and, therefore, advance to the right side of Truth. Your tribe's truth.

Those are the basic steps in evangelical tribalism when applying theology to social issues, and many millennials in recent years have freely adopted this approach. One of the best examples of a polarizing tribal progressive millennial is Rachel Held Evans. Anytime she writes anything critiquing "conservative" evangelicals it is because, to her, people like Owen Strachan do not embrace the presuppositions and methods of progressive Christianity and poorly represent Christianity. For reasons that are puzzling to many, Evans wants men like John Piper and Al Mohler to join her tribe's ideological progressivism. Progressive leaders like Jim Wallis want the same.

Again, both conservative and progressive evangelicals can live tribally. For example, from the conservative world, someone like Gary North will proof text free-market economics as the Bible's economic system, and progressives like Jim Wallis will proof text the Bible to support the Democratic Party's ideological platform invoking his concern for "the least of these."[14]

In the Protestant ideological tennis match, progressive evangelical Christians and mainline Protestant liberals do have this in common: They both believe that Christians who embrace the inerrancy, infallibility, and final authority of the Bible are the wrong kinds of Christians. But there is a key difference between them. Protestant liberals are open and honest about

14. See "Interview with Jim Wallis," PBS.org.

their theological and methodological presuppositions. Mainline Protestants, for example, will tell you that they are liberals and do not believe the Bible to be the final authority, reject atonement theology, and so on. But progressive evangelicals tend not to be so forthright, it seems. Progressives present themselves as being objective representatives of the teachings of Jesus, as historic-yet-advanced evangelicals. Progressive evangelicals, like their liberal mainline cousins, have simply traded off, in many cases, the tools in the Christian social thought tradition for the analytical tools of the social sciences and the humanities (critical race theory, feminist theory, etc.). For progressive evangelicals, the social sciences are authoritative and are often above critique.

For most evangelicals, principles in the Christian social thought tradition—like natural law, solidarity, subsidiarity, sphere sovereignty, personalism, and so on—do not provide the raw material for helpful discourse, because the only thing that matters is whether or not one's tribal understanding is supported, defended, and promoted. Evangelicals are left with an ethical framework derived from individualist biblicism. Most do not even use a confession of faith as a starting point. This is classic Christian postmodern tribalism, because the goal is to prove that God is on your tribe's side and not theirs.

In recent years it's become apparent that conservative evangelicalism has raised a generation of millennials who have left their orthodox and traditional evangelical circles and have fully embraced ideological progressivism. They have no tradition and no tested, authoritative texts. The conservative versus progressive tribal discourse, while it may get students graduate degrees and professors tenure, is doing nothing to advance the Christian social thought tradition, nor is it providing Protestants a credible voice in the public square.

In conclusion, the Acton Institute makes its case from within the Christian social thought tradition, and these are the principles worth debating. Instead of tribalism, perhaps we should be asking, "Are we being consistent and rightly applying the tools of the Christian tradition?" Are we rightly applying subsidiarity and sphere sovereignty? A lively discourse about the right application of Christian principles within the Christian tradition is far more fruitful and interesting to me than engaging in a tribal war that tries to prove whose tribe best represents Jesus. Mainline Protestant liberals and conservative evangelicals understand this and no longer really engage one another. Progressive evangelicals, on the other hand, believe they are above the fray but seem to be lost in their own self-deception. Progressive Christians, one might argue, are simply mainline Protestant liberals attempting to wear "evangelical" tribal clothing. It does not seem to be working, and secularists seem to enjoy declaring Christianity irrelevant by pitting conservative and progressive Christians against one another. Can we not do better than this?

Waning Evangelical Influence

By most accounts, evangelicalism began with the influence of the Great Awakenings of the 18th century, which provided a set of social norms and values that has shaped much of American life and public policy for nearly three centuries. But those days may be over.

The 2012 Republican Party platform, which embraced many of those norms and values, was clearly rejected by more than half of the American electorate. I am no futurist, and I am open to being wrong, but to me it appears that evangelical influence in American political and cultural life is quickly coming to a close. In fact, before too long, it wouldn't surprise me to see the Republican Party begin to distance itself from conservative evangelical Christians.

Just look at the data from the election. According to the exit polls from the New York Times, Barack Obama received 55 percent of the female vote, 60 percent of the millennial generation vote, 52 percent of the Generation X vote, 93 percent of the black vote, 71 percent of the Hispanic/Latino vote, and 73 percent of the Asian vote.[15] The only majority Mitt Romney held was among white men and white women. In fact, the constituencies that predominantly voted for President Obama are the exact same groups that conservative evangelical churches and denominations have been unsuccessful at reaching.

Our country's changing demographics also speak to this point. According to census data from 2012, more than half of all children recently born (under 1 year old) were minorities.[16] But these minorities do not even come close to making up half the births in evangelical churches across the country. Given these numbers, are conservative evangelicals even relevant to the Republican Party in future elections?

The GOP also keeps missing opportunities.

Republicans who have chosen unhelpful rhetoric on immigration policy continue to alienate many Latinos who tend to embrace traditional family values and free-market economies. To many of them, immigration is the most important issue above all others.

15. "President Exit Polls," The New York Times.
16. "Most Children Younger than Age 1 are Minorities," United States Census Bureau.

With black voters, Republicans continue to be at a disadvantage, as they battle the "racist" label Democrats attach to the party and its candidates. The GOP also needs to understand that many in the black community care more about entitlement programs than they do about abortion.

The millennial generation, many of whom have been raised in a culture of divorce and single-parenthood, experience a disconnect when they hear Republicans touting the value and importance of "traditional families."

With these cultural dynamics, Republicans, in order to take back the White House, are going to have to start appealing to their new actual base: deistic fiscal moderates.

And here's a valuable lesson for conservative evangelicals from last Tuesday's election results: If your church, college, seminary, denominational annual meeting, etc., looks like Romney's concession speech audience, you likely will be unable to transform, influence, or engage America. To do so, you'll need to start including minorities and women as executive leaders and thought leaders who will help chart institutional direction.

Taken altogether, then, could it be that Americans are now saying, "Farewell evangelicals. It was a good run"?

Raising Super-Christians

After teaching college for a few years, I've realized two things: (1) how young adults sincerely want to make their parents proud, and (2) how parents communicate, directly or indirectly, that their children are failures. A previous generation of parents was happy having kids who simply were "good," but today's parents want kids who are good *and* "successful." And students who have grown up in conservative evangelical churches are not immune from this parental pressure.

Young Christian adults know, of course, that their parents love them, that grace is better legalism, and that they are not rebels, yet they wonder if their parents' praise depends on whether they are athletically, academically, and professionally successful. Even though good books like *Age of Opportunity* by Paul Tripp and *Give Them Grace* by Elyse Fitzpatrick and Jessica Thompson have rightly challenged a generation of parents to deal with the perils of legalism, rebellion, and moralism, today's narcissistic and individualistic Christian culture has resulted in increased pressure on youth to be the "Tim Tebow" of whatever vocation they choose.

Two moms I know offered possible explanations for this performance-parenting trend. One said, "I think a great deal of the anxiety young people face comes from carrying the burden of their parents' own unfilled dreams and lack of joy." Another explained, "First, kids are a reflection of [their parents]. What better way to elevate parenting than the success of the children? It really can be nothing more than satisfying the parent's sense of success and accomplishment of which the child contributes. Second, it's the issue of how we've defined success among Christians, which typically has translated into doing big things for God or achieving notoriety in some way. That's nothing more than the infiltration of the American dream culture into the church, which is quite different from God's paradigm. It's why in general we love megachurches and celebrity pastors."[17]

Are these moms correct? It seems that over-praising and telling kids how "special" they are oddly puts pressure on children to fulfill impossible expectations. I wonder what would happen if America had a culture that simply taught children that doing something big for God and His Kingdom is nothing more and nothing less than loving God and neighbor.

Raising super-Christians hardly seems to be what the Bible intends as it commands us to "Train up a child in the way he should go; even when he is old he will not depart from it" (Prov 22:6).

An Incomplete Theology

One of the realities of being a white Protestant in America is the historic freedom from needing a theological framework to confront structural and institutional forms of injustice due to race. Race continues to be a heavy burden for people of color in America. As such, a theological framework primarily oriented toward issues of personal salvation and morality is sufficient to address the questions of the dominant white culture. However, for blacks and Latinos, who not only have to wrestle with personal questions regarding sin and salvation but also evil from the outside because of their race, they need the Cross to provide hope that God intends to relieve the burdens and liabilities of being a subdominant minority. These burdens range from stereotypes and racial discrimination to issues of identity in light of Anglo-normativity and sociopolitical wellbeing. Blacks and Latinos need a comprehensive theology that deals with the cosmic scope of God redeeming every aspect of the creation affected by the Fall through the work and person of Christ.

Dr. Vincent Bacote, associate professor of theology at Wheaton College and an UrbanFaith contributor, presents a comprehensive theological framework in his chapter in a book I edited titled *Keep Your Head Up: America's New Black Christian Leaders, Social Consciousness, and the Cosby*

17. Personal correspondence, October 6, 2012.

Conversation. Bacote discusses the themes of Creation, Fall, Redemption, and Renewal (CFRR). CFRR reminds us of the following: God created the world good, it was corrupted by the Fall's introduction of sin and brokenness into the world, but God has a unique plan to renew the entire creation through the work and person of Jesus Christ. That is, the entire creation formed and shaped by Christ will also be renewed by Christ and reconciled unto Him (Col. 1:15-23).

CFRR not only tells us who we are, it also gives Christians a vision of the implications of the kingdom of God. Christians are not passive bystanders but are called to be leaders in the business of reconciliation until Christ returns to bring finality to the process of renewal that he inaugurated at his death and resurrection in ways never before realized in human history (Rom. 8:12-25).

For those seeking to preach the Good News of what was accomplished in the work and Person of Jesus Christ to blacks and Latinos, the application of biblical texts cannot be limited to personal issues of salvation and sanctification. Subdominant minorities who are immersed in a world of white privilege need to hear hope that God also intends to relieve them of the complex burdens of being a minority—burdens that whites do not encounter in their day-to-day lives in America. This is one reason why minority teachers are vitally important in ethnic church contexts. Otherwise, applying the gospel to the realities of white privilege will likely not be addressed regularly. Now, by *white privilege* I simply mean the privilege, special freedom, or immunity white persons have from some liability or burden to which non-white persons are subject in America.

A team of authors led by Fordham University psychology professor Celia B. Fisher and others provides an excellent list of issues that blacks and Latinos need to reconcile with the Truth. In an article titled "Applied Developmental Science, Social Justice, and Socio-Political Wellbeing," Fisher and her team remind us that when evil entered the world it created a context for the following burdens experienced by Native Americans, blacks, and Latinos in America: (1) societal structures, policies, and so on that limit access for minorities, (2) the persistence of high-effort coping with the reality of marginalization that produces high levels of stress, (3) psycho-political wellbeing and validity concerns which address the ways in which minorities apply human dignity to themselves within a context of Anglo-hegemony, (4) communities that accept dysfunctional behaviors as behavioral norms in the shaping of one's personhood, (5) institutional racism which examines the "institutional structures and processes passed on from generation to generations that organize and promote racial inequity throughout the culture,"[18] (6) proactive measures intended to dismantle racism, and (7) contexts to provide healing for those who have experience major and minor encounters with racist attitudes, beliefs, or actions.

The revivalist impulse by many evangelicals rightly understands that ultimate social change comes when members of society become followers of Christ. However, American history has clearly proven that personal salvation does not stop people from being racists nor from setting up social institutions and policies that deny others access to the means of liberty and human dignity. If evangelism alone were effective for social change, Christians would never have participated in the trans-Atlantic slave trade, been slave owners, created apartheid in South Africa, or allowed Jim Crow laws to come into existence.

Theologians like Abraham Kuyper remind us that, because of God's common grace, evangelism is not necessary to persuade people to treat others with dignity and respect—after all, the law of God is written on the heart (Rom. 2:15) even though it merits them no favor with God. Therefore, work at both. We must morally form individuals and dismantle cultural norms of racism that become structural.

I suspect that this is one of the major reasons why many whites are unsuccessful at reaching blacks and Latinos. If the gospel is not being applied to issues of the heart *and* issues that require outside, structural justice, we will miss areas in need of biblical application. Blacks and Latinos in America do not have the privilege of *not* talking about the issues addressed in the Fisher article, because all minorities experience aspects of those issues in various ways.

If we believe that the Bible speaks to the questions of the day, then we have to do a better job of developing the cultural intelligence that applies the Truth to issues of the heart and to the cultural spaces minorities inhabit as subdominant races.

That's What Friends are For

For several years now, two friends and I have convened annually in South Florida for a time of sharing, lamenting, thankfulness, praise, challenge, rebuke, encouragement, celebrating, and much needed sleep. Why do we do this? Because we need each other. I think God made us to be in relationships with others. It's a part of what it means to be human. I consider myself blessed to have good friends.

18. Fisher et al., "Applied Developmental Science," 55–59.

The Bible explains the value of good friendships. When David heard of Jonathan's death he lamented poetically, "I am distressed for you, my brother Jonathan; very pleasant have you been to me; your love to me was extraordinary, surpassing the love of women" (2 Samuel 1:26). Friendships among God's people in the ancient Near East are so foreign to the way Americans live life that most churches would probably throw men out for uttering words like David's.

Since I started publishing articles, op-eds, appearing on national media platforms, and so on, I've come to understand two verses from Proverbs the hard way. First, Proverbs 18:24 reminds us, "A man of many companions may come to ruin, but there is a friend who sticks closer than a brother." Secondly, "A friend loves at all times, and a brother is born for adversity" (Proverbs 17:17). I have had various seasons of being attacked in painful ways, and it's been revealing to see which of my so-called "friends," who at one time pledged care and commitment, disappeared when the hate mail, phone calls, and vicious slander started to pour in. Needless to say, I learned a tough lesson.

You know who your *real* friends are when the bottom falls out and disaster visits your life. As the Bible teaches, mere "companions" provide no comfort net when "the going gets tough." Friends, on the other hand, are there to walk with you through the storm. Present, committed, and unmoved. As I get older, I experience in new ways that the book of Proverbs is not only good but also true. Thank God for good friends.

Christianity's Non-European Future

If European cultural trends are a precursor to the future of Western culture, American Christians might find themselves discouraged. According to the Pew Research Center's Forum on Religion and Public Life, Europe is home to only about one-quarter of the world's Christians, compared to two-thirds just a century ago.[19] Christianity began as a Middle Eastern religion and had its theological scaffolding establish primarily by Africans. Moving into Europe, Christianity had a culturally dominant role for centuries until the Enlightenment slowly loosened the grip of faith in that culture. Today, it seems that the Enlightenment is the dominant "religion" of Europeans.

The Pew report observes:

> About one-quarter of the global Christian population can now be found in sub-Saharan Africa, while 37 percent live in the

19. "Global Christianity," PewResearchCenter., 9.

Americas and 13 percent reside in the Asia-Pacific region. Brazil has twice as many Roman Catholics as Italy, while Nigeria has more than twice as many Protestants as Germany, where the Protestant Reformation began.[20]

While Christianity has a minor presence in Europe, according to the report, Christians are still the world's largest religion, with nearly 2.2 billion claiming faith. Muslims remain the second-largest group, with 1.6 billion people.

What does this mean for Christians in America? Two thoughts come to mind:

1. We must recognize that ultimately these trends remind us of the sovereignty of God and of divine providence. Despite our efforts, we recognize that the Spirit moves wherever the Father wills. God has proven to work this way throughout the entire biblical narrative and Christian history. Where and why the Spirit works in the world continues to be a mystery.

2. European Christianity should be studied more closely as a model of what *not* to do in terms of how the church interacts with cultural change. How did Europe lose its Christian faith? What happened? What responsibility did church leaders and theologians have in becoming increasingly irrelevant to the culture? Is it possible that reading European theologians to strengthen Christianity in America might be unwise given the fact they didn't tarry in Europe? These are important questions.

Admittedly, I'm not an historian and don't know the answers to all these questions but if *You Lost Me* author David Kinnaman is right about nearly 60 percent of American young people involved in church life as teens dropping out after high school, American Christians will need to look to Africa, Latin America, and Asia for leaders in the future.

Did Christians Give Marriage Away?

American common law definitions of marriage were historically shaped by the influence of Christianity. In *God's Joust, God's Justice: Law and Religion in the Western Tradition*, John Witte Jr. does an excellent job of explaining the formation of marriage law, writing that what defined marriage for centuries in the West was its emphasis on procreation and fidelity, and the

20. Ibid., 9–10.

institution's sanctity, civil use in curbing vices and establishing the foundation for education, and usefulness in maturing a couple's Christian faith. This understanding no longer exists in our culture, and some argue that when Americans began divorcing in high numbers, redefined marital sexuality via contraception use, and reduced marriage to mere commitment, it set the stage for our current same-sex marriage debate.

Because church-going evangelicals divorce at high rates, this community of believers has lost its moral authority to defend the indissoluble nature of marriage. For example, I recently gave a lecture at New York University explaining the traditional view of marriage and was asked: "Then why is the divorce rate among conservative Christians so high?" It was a great question. I wish the divorce rate for believers was 0 percent. I couldn't say much in defense. It seems that many Christians have forgotten that the Lord hates divorce (Malachi 2:16).

Because of the work of Howard Kainz, professor emeritus at Marquette University, many argue that married couples using contraception redefine sex in ways that render same-sex marriage unobjectionable. Kainz observes:

> [I]f you believe you have a right to non-procreative sexual intercourse, you have no right to criticize non-procreative sex by others—for example, by a gay couple. You may justify your personal practices on the basis of your genuine mutual love and commitment to lifelong fidelity. But homosexuals may be even more intensely in love with each other and even more firmly committed to mutual fidelity. They may even be more open to procreation than you are, through adoption or through in vitro fertilization. To want to have sex without the possibility of offspring, and condemn others for similarly non-procreative sex, would be blatantly inconsistent.[21]

Because of the sex/children connection, George Mason School of Law professor Helen Alvaré explains in two articles why American marriage historically did not divorce itself from children.[22]

Lastly, the reduction of marriage to a mere contract between consenting adults has stripped marriage of its sanctity and its family-forming utility in shaping the common good, as John Calvin would encourage.

As a result, I'm beginning to wonder if the alternative marriage debate is not already lost. Christians do not provide a model of marriage in practice that makes a persuasive case against changing the traditional definition. A theologian friend says that the marriage debate in America is doomed

21. Kainz, "If Contraception," paragraph 6.
22. Alvaré, "Traditional Family Law," paragraphs 1-12.

unless it is defined as "a sexuality-based social institution for the union of the couple and the procreation and nurture of children." Otherwise, marriage will continue to be defined by utilitarian moral relativists.

Freedom From Miserable Christianity

In his new book *Forever: Why You Can't Live Without It*, Paul Tripp does a fantastic job of explaining why believers and nonbelievers alike misunderstand what Christianity is all about.[23] There has been a tendency in our culture to pitch Christianity as a means of achieving personal peace and affluence (as Francis Schaeffer often tried to counter). But Tripp points out that if we were honest, we'd find thousands of sad, defeated, disappointed, doubting, and soon to be cynical Christians out there. Why? Because we forget about what Jesus accomplished for His people. As such, many Christians simply go through the motions of faith. The life is gone. Faith doesn't make much sense. And many believers are left feeling miserable.

According to Tripp, here are signs of a miserable faith:

- Disappointment with God. Thinking that God has not given us the life that He has promised.

- Lack of motivation for ministry. A passion for ministry is not a result of training but comes out of a deep conviction that God is who He says He is.

- Numbing. When we're disappointed with our lives, we'll find ways to escape and self-medicate.

- Envy of others' lives. Miserable faith focuses on the joys of the lives of others that we believe we deserve.

- Letting go of the habits of faith. If faith isn't working out like we want, then why pray, worship, read the Bible, etc.

- Greater susceptibility to temptation. If God's not doing His part, miserable people believe that they should not do theirs.

Alternatively, a vibrant faith, Tripp suggests, hinges on properly understanding the role of grace in pointing us to the eternal implications of the resurrection as described in 1 Corinthians 15. Without the resurrection Christianity makes no sense. In fact, the resurrection provides the catalyst for life-giving faith. For Tripp, the resurrection of Jesus and the hope of forever accomplish the following: (1) They tell us what is really important

23. Tripp, *Forever*, 1.

in life; (2) they have the power to radically change the way we approach the responsibilities, difficulties, and opportunities of daily life; and (3) they teach us delayed gratification.

Without the resurrection pointing us to eternal life, Christians will lose hope to persevere to the end and will fail to properly align life's realities with expectations. Tripp's *Forever* is a wonderful reminder of what really matters in the Christian life so that we don't turn our faith into an empty religion that neither glorifies God nor frees us to live life to the fullest (John 10:10).

Teaching Long-Term Kingdom Thinking

If you want to radically change the lives of men and women in low-income neighborhoods, then emphasize the kingdom in your teaching. Over the past few years I've had the opportunity to mentor young people from low-income neighborhoods and broken families. In that work I've found that the biggest conceptual hurdle was not the gospel but helping young people graduate from short-term thinking to long-term thinking. When you have no money and no hope for the future you are likely to spend all of your energy thinking about gratifying desires today.

"Eat, drink, and be merry, for tomorrow we die," says the fool. This is the motto of short-term thinking. Paul challenges this way of thinking by focusing on the believer's future resurrection (1 Corinthians 15:32). There is more to life than this life. Moreover, our ultimate satisfaction with life cannot even be found in this life but in the one to come for those who are united to Christ.

Jesus teaches us not to store up treasures on earth but to think about our lives in light of heaven (Matthew 6:19-21). In fact, Jesus' teaching on the kingdom (Matthew 6:33) helps condition us to embrace long-term thinking and delayed gratification. We are to seek first the kingdom of God and all that that entails, and rest in the sovereign providence of God for what we need today and tomorrow. This is not only good practical theology, but it also liberates us from the short-term thinking that dominates low-income communities and keeps people from making wise choices.

In *Gospel of the Kingdom: Scriptural Studies in the Kingdom of God*, George Ladd rightly stresses the importance of the kingdom this way:

> The Kingdom of God is the redemptive reign of God dynamically active to establish his rule among men, and that this Kingdom, which will appear as an apocalyptic act at the end of the age, has already come into human history in the person

and mission of Jesus to overcome evil, to deliver men from its power, and to bring them into the blessings of God's reign. The Kingdom involves two great moments: fulfillment within history, and consummation at the end of history.[24]

If the kingdom is not the central theme when working in low-income communities we may not be helping people as much as we think. The ability to practice the virtue and wisdom of delayed gratification in this life is primed to perfection by the gospel of Jesus Christ, which orients our lives toward the priorities of the kingdom to be consummated at the end of history.

Who Will Lead a Third Great Awakening?

As American mainstream culture continues to enshrine the religion of secular humanism in our meta-modern world, there is hope that someday there will be another Great Awakening in this country. Preachers like Jonathan Edwards and George Whitefield led the first one, while James McGready and Charles Finney were at the forefront at the second. A possible Third Great Awakening will only come about if the laity leads it, because too many of today's pastors are caught up in celebrity pastor narcissism.

The seduction of becoming a famous, celebrity pastor is too much of a temptation for those who have fallen prey to the belief that the only way to be effective is to build an empire and legacy around oneself. The explosion of conferences and events built around particular pastors' personalities to gain a following could be evidence of this seduction. As such, many pastors are so caught up in gaining Twitter followers, writing fluffy books, and making a name for themselves as an "author, speaker, teacher, pastor" that they have disqualified themselves to lead cultural renewal.

An example of a lay-led movement is the Cal-Pac Prayer and Repentance conferences emerging in the United Methodist Church on the West Coast. In the spirit of the Methodist-influenced Second Great Awakening, lay leaders like Eaar Oden are on a mission to lead his church to revival on the basis of gospel-driven repentance and prayer. On the movement's Facebook page you'll find references to J.C. Ryle, Charles Spurgeon, R.C. Sproul, and Bible quotes from the ESV.

Oden explains the importance of these conferences this way:

> Two-hundred and thirty-four years ago in 1767, John Wesley preached a sermon titled 'the Repentance of Believers,' where

24. Ladd, *Presence of the Future*, 218.

he preached on the continual need for repentance, beyond the initial repentance unto salvation. These are his words: 'There is also a repentance, which is required after we have believed the gospel, and in every subsequent stage of our Christian walk, or we will not be able to run the race which is set before us. And this repentance and faith is as necessary to continue to grow in grace as the former faith and repentance were to enter into the Kingdom of God.'[25]

Such conferences led by the laity are not for the purpose of hosting celebrity pastors to speak. Instead, participants spend 80 hours of interrupted Bible reading and prayer, followed by a total of two hours of listening to speakers, culminating in a huge fellowship meal.

We live in an American culture that breeds narcissistic celebrity pastors who want a following (1 Corinthians 3:4), so if any Holy Spirit-driven movement is going to bring about revival, it's going to happen among those who are not exalted (Matthew 23:11-12). Perhaps it will be regular, non-famous women and men who simply read the Bible, pray together, and follow the leading of the Holy Spirit. Imagine the possibilities.

The John 3:16 Discount

Would you recite a Bible verse for a discount on an oil change? If so, Charlie Whittington, owner of a Kwik Kar Lube & Tune in Plano, Texas, has a deal for you. He's offering oil changes for $19.95 to customers who bring in a coupon and recite John 3:16. Whittington has come under fire for the promotion, with some alleging that he is discriminating against nonbelievers and profiting from religion.

Some customers refused and paid a higher price. Marshall Wei, a Chinese immigrant, objected, asking, "Why should I be compelled to quote something I do not feel comfortable to quote?"[26] But Whittington remains committed to the promotion because he says it's a privately owned franchise and he can do whatever he wants to with it. "If I'm standing for what I believe, so be it," he said. "Bring it on."

Is it discrimination? I would be inclined that say "no" on the basis that coupons are not compulsory and no customer is turned away from the business because he or she refuses to recite the verse. Customers like Wei are not compelled to have their oil changed at this particular Kwik Kar. He could

25. http://www.methodistrepentance.com/ (website no longer active). October 19, 2011.

26. "'For God so Loved the World' for a $19.99 Oil Change?" CBS News.

have easily taken his business elsewhere. Wei chose not to recite the verse and paid full-price (about $46). In the end, the market will either reward or punish Whittington for mixing the Bible with his business. I say let him bear the consequences of his actions.

But is this a proper use of the Bible? On one hand, you could argue that is it not good to use the Bible as an incentive to make a profit. Mixing Jesus with money can undermine the purpose of Scripture to point people to the work of the Trinity. On the other hand, you could argue that this approach encourages people to think about and discuss Scripture—and *anything* that gets people to do that is good to some degree.

No matter where you comes down on this issue, I think we can all agree that what makes America great is that Whittington has the freedom to bear the market consequences of mixing his religion with a private business, and for that I am grateful.

No More Drive-By Youth Ministry

Inner-city life is hard. The complexities of life in "da hood" should encourage those seeking to serve inner-city youth to approach individuals with humility and long-term relationships. For years, I have been bothered by drive-by "mercy ministry" approaches by those who pull up in vans from outside low-income neighborhoods to "do ministry" as if those complexities do not exist. Granted, intentions are good and many are thankful that real concern is evidenced, but drive-by ministries are under the delusion that spending a few hours with inner-city youth from difficult circumstances is actually helping them in the long-run. The truth is that "making a difference" in the life of youth from difficult circumstances takes years of personal care and discipleship, not just a few hours of games, Bible stories, and listening to testimonies every month. Many of the problems in "da hood" are systemic and generational because the chain of child trauma has not been intercepted and healed.

Child trauma is devastating and is one of the ways in which sin and evil destroy the lives of many people early in life, igniting a life of self-destruction and hurting others. Children who experience trauma become teens who present typical reactions like impaired cognitive function, impaired academic performance, feelings of depression, anxiety, irritability, despair, apathy, irrational guilt, easy and frequent crying, increased feelings of insecurity, social isolation, sleep difficulties, and acting out or anti-social behaviors that may lead to juvenile delinquency, substance abuse, sexual promiscuity, fatigue, hypertension, psychosomatic and somatic symptoms, and the like.

In *Ten Things Every Juvenile Court Judge Should Know About Trauma and Delinquency*, from the National Council of Juvenile and Family Court Judges, Kristine Buffington, Carly Dierkhising, and Shawn Marsh offer a highly informative perspective that I argue is just as needed for those working with inner-city youth from difficult circumstances. The authors make the following points trauma exposed children:

1. **A traumatic experience is an event that threatens someone's life, safety, or well-being.** Trauma can include a direct encounter with a dangerous or threatening event, or it can involve witnessing the endangerment or suffering of another living being. A key condition that makes these events traumatic is that they can overwhelm a person's capacity to cope, and elicit intense feelings such as fear, terror, helplessness, hopelessness, and despair. Traumatic events include: emotional, physical, and sexual abuse; neglect; physical assaults; witnessing family, school, or community violence; war; racism; bullying; acts of terrorism; fires; serious accidents; serious injuries; intrusive or painful medical procedures; loss of loved ones; abandonment; and separation.

2. **Child traumatic stress can lead to Post Traumatic Stress Disorder (PTSD).** Rates of PTSD in juvenile justice-involved youth are estimated between 3 percent to 50 percent making it comparable to the PTSD rates (12 percent-20 percent) of soldiers returning from deployment in Iraq.

3. **Trauma impairs a child's development and health throughout his or her life.** Exposure to child abuse and neglect can restrict brain growth especially in the areas of the brain that control learning and self-regulation. Exposure to domestic violence has also been linked to lower IQ scores for children. Youth who experience traumatic events may have mental and physical health challenges, problems developing and maintaining healthy relationships, difficulties learning, behavioral problems, and substance abuse issues.

4. **Complex trauma is associated with risk of delinquency.** In fact, about 72 percent of youth that enter the juvenile justice system have diagnosable psychiatric and psychological disorders. Moreover, research shows that youth who experience some type of trauma of any kind are at elevated risk of entering the juvenile justice system. Even worse, about 50 percent of the male victims of child maltreatment later became juvenile delinquents.

5. **Traumatic exposure, delinquency, and school failure are re-lated.** Success in school requires confidence, the ability to focus and concentrate, the discipline to complete assignments, the ability to regulate emotions and behaviors, and the skills to understand and negotiate social relationships. When youth live in unpredictable and dangerous environments they often, in order to survive, operate in a state of anxiety and paranoia often expressed through "abnormally increased arousal, responsiveness to stimuli, and scanning of the environment for threats."[27] according to the Dorland's Medical Dictionary for Health Consumers.

6. **Trauma assessments can reduce misdiagnosis, promote positive outcomes, and maximize resources.** Often, trauma-exposed children are misdiagnosed as hyperactive, having attention deficits, or general behavior disorders when, in fact, there are deeper issues present.

7. **There are mental health treatments that are effective in helping youth who are experiencing child traumatic stress.** As much as I be-lieve in biblical counseling, because of the physical damage done to the brain of trauma-exposed children, there needs to be more openness for some youth to get clinical help.

8. **There is a compelling need for effective family involvement.** Youth who do not have helpful and consistent family support are at higher risk of violence and prolonged involvement in the court system.

9. **Youth are highly resilient.** Resiliency is the capacity for human beings to thrive in the face of adversity like trauma. Research suggests that the degree to which one is resilient is influenced by a complex interaction of risk and protective factors that exist across various domains, such as individual, family, community and school. Research on resiliency suggests that youth are more likely to overcome adversities when they have caring adults in their lives.

10. **The juvenile justice system needs to be trauma-informed at all levels**—and so should church youth workers serving kids from difficult circumstances.

What Buffington, Deirkhising, and Marsh present above is the beginning of a shift in how we think about urban ministry. Low-income children from broken families living in rough inner-city neighborhoods are at risk of exposure to multiple traumas in ways that middle-class youth are not. Not

---

27. Dorland, *Dorland's Illustrated Medical Dictionary*, 898.

to understand the pervasiveness of trauma is not to take "da hood" seriously as a potential trauma zone.

The inference should not be that *all* inner-city kids are trauma victims, but that trauma must be a variable in considering how to help those in need and assessing whether or not current programs are capable of dealing with root issues. I am guilty of making this mistake in the past. I could have been far more helpful and patient had I been a trauma-informed inner-city church worker.

In the final analysis, I would argue that only healthy local churches are capable of bringing the kind of holistic community required to address urban pain and dysfunction. Only a committed community of believers can provide the long-term care, compassion, and discipleship needed to increase resilience and heal trauma-exposed communities.

While drive-by mercy ministry is great for PowerPoint presentations and fundraising brochures, holistic liberation driven by the Greatest Commandment (Matt. 22:34-40) requires a long-term commitment to loving relationships.

Culturally Rebellious Christian Living

The most radical, counter-cultural, rebellious thing a young adult can do in America today is join a Christian church and commit his or her life to the pursuit of holiness as described in the Bible.

We live in an America where the norms of society are dominated by narcissism, individualism, consumerism, materialism, and moral relativism. These "isms" are our culture. To believe that moral truths are subjectively relative, to pursue a life of utilitarian consequentialism, and to adopt happiness as the greatest personal virtue is to simply be like everyone else, a cog in a morally vacuous culture. This is what it means these days to be average, common, even boring. It's the newest tradition inaugurated by our nation's baby boomers.

But if you want to reject contemporary Western societal norms and live a rebellious and dangerous life as a young adult, then commit your life to moral virtue (Philippians 4:8). Who would have thought that we'd ever live in a society where joining a church and adopting Christian values as a way of life would be considered swimming upstream for young adults?

In a recent *New York Times* opinion piece, David Brooks lamented the individualistic moral relativism that rules the day and its deleterious effect on young adults:

> In most times and in most places, the group was seen to be the
> essential moral unit. A shared religion defined rules and prac-
> tices. Cultures structured people's imaginations and imposed
> moral disciplines. But now more people are led to assume that
> the free-floating individual is the essential moral unit. Morality
> was once revealed, inherited and shared, but now it's thought
> of as something that emerges in the privacy of your own heart.

What is so troubling about this individualistic moral relativism is that
it ignores basic human needs. For example, people still need something to
give meaning to their lives, to give them a sense of belonging, and be able to
find common ground with others.

In America, Christianity—with its emphasis on loving God and loving
neighbor (Matthew 22:36-40) and its celebration of the church as a place
to form virtue for the common good—has provided meaning, identity, and
community. But in a culture where individualistic moral relativism is the
norm, there is fierce competition to fill that void, because, in a capitalist
context, wherever your heart is, there goes your money. As such, Americans
get lost in the futile search to find meaning and belonging in professional
sports, careers, recreational activities and organizations, etc., to an extent
that has never been seen before in American history. The truth is, these
things cannot deliver on their promises to deliver fulfillment because human beings were not designed to find satisfaction in such pursuits. As a result, many will die bitter and angry, protesting that they were robbed of joy.
But the truth is, they wasted a lot of time looking for it in the wrong places.

For thousands of years the same realities that provide meaning, belonging, and solidarity with others—namely, being in relationship with God
and His people while orienting one's life toward the mission of God—continue as the way to live well. In today's culture, following Jesus has become
the American rebel's way of life.

Holy Spirit Apologetics

I was recently reading John Warwick Montgomery's classic article "Christian
Apologetics in the Light of the Lutheran Confessions" and was struck by his
emphasis on the fact that only the Holy Spirit can change someone's heart
and mind so that one accepts the Gospel. What a relief! It's not the persua-
siveness of our speech, the cleverness of our philosophical arguments, or the
piling on of historical evidence or data that does the real work. In fact, those
are all means that God uses to challenge a person's worldview but ultimately

it is the work of Holy Spirit that acts to change the heart. Apologetics, then, must be considered a wholly Trinitarian endeavor.

Interest in apologetics has surged in recent years, but I'm beginning to wonder if many Christians who engage skeptics, antagonists, and those who are apathetic about the claims of Christ see themselves, first and foremost, as a part of the means that God might use to persuade their friends about the Gospel. Warwick observes:

> Salvation is a gift, and is brought home to the heart only by the sovereign work of God the Holy Spirit. . . . [T]he confessional apologist will see himself not as a Holy-Spirit-substitute but as a John the Baptist in the wilderness of a secular age, preparing the way of the Lord, making the paths intellectually straight which lead to the Lamb of God—to the only One who can take away the sins of the world.[28]

Does this mean that Christians should do nothing? Absolutely not! The Holy Spirit normally works through the explaining of the Scriptures to impart belief, so there is a need for His people to do the work of explaining, clarify, and challenging. Montgomery says, "[T]hough only the Holy Spirit can apply Biblical texts in a salvatory way to human hearts, believers can and should employ Scripture to convince unbelievers of the nature and truth of God's message."[29]

Sometimes we forget what the Bible actually teaches on the subject. I have found the following passages to be a helpful orientation in the work of engaging non-Christians in discussions:

"Jesus answered, 'Truly, truly, I say to you, unless one is born of water and the Spirit, he cannot enter the kingdom of God. That which is born of the flesh is flesh, and that which is born of the Spirit is spirit'" (John 3:5-6).

". . . For the Spirit searches everything, even the depths of God. For who knows a person's thoughts except the spirit of that person, which is in him? So also no one comprehends the thoughts of God except the Spirit of God. Now we have received not the spirit of the world, but the Spirit who is from God, that we might understand the things freely given us by God. And we impart this in words not taught by human wisdom but taught by the Spirit, interpreting spiritual truths to those who are spiritual" (1 Corinthians 2:10-13).

"You know that when you were pagans you were led astray to mute idols, however you were led. Therefore I want you to understand that no one

28. Montgomery, "Christian Apologetics," 266.
29. Ibid., 268.

speaking in the Spirit of God ever says 'Jesus is accursed!' and no one can say 'Jesus is Lord' except in the Holy Spirit" (1 Corinthians 12:2-3).

What do these passages reveal? They demonstrate that explaining Christianity to those who do not accept its claims is an exercise in prayerfully requesting the presence of the Third Person of the Trinity. This wonderfully takes the pressure off of those who feel incompetent to be apologists with polished arguments or theologically sophisticated answers. The Holy Spirit is more than capable of using our imperfections and limitations to explain Christian truth, because ultimately God defends and reveals Himself.

So the next time you are attending a conference on apologetics and there is no emphasis on the necessity of the Holy Spirit, it may simply be a gathering of people who enjoy being quarrelsome and argumentative instead of a group seeking the active work of the God to bring people in loving union with His Son, and it might be a waste of your time.

Hopkins, Homework, and the Gospel

I have been called many names over years, but to have my race and Christianity questioned reaches a new intellectual low. Dwight Hopkins, professor of theology at the University of Chicago Divinity School, recently penned a review of my book *Liberating Black Theology* that raises such questions.

Black liberation theology became familiar to most Americans because of the preaching of the Rev. Jeremiah Wright, President Obama's former pastor at Trinity United Church of Christ in Chicago. From what I understand, Hopkins continues to attend that church, so it is not too surprising that he might suggest that, not only am I possibly not black and unfamiliar with the black church, but also that I might not even be a Christian.

Hopkins asks:

> To what country does [Anthony Bradley] belong (i.e., Germany, Greece, etc.)? Is he a Christian or a member of a church? What is his group of accountability—Black liberation theologians, pastors, lay people, clergy, or administrators? Is he familiar with Black church ministries?[30]

Granted, I'm not famous but most of those questions could have been answered simply by searching "Anthony Bradley" on Google. Why does Hopkins believe me to be a possible white outsider, someone unfamiliar with the black church subculture, and possibly not even a Christian? Because I believe that people sin and need to repent of sin because we have all

30. Hopkins, "Liberating Black Theology," 117.

been corrupted by the fall of Adam and Eve (Genesis 3). Therefore, we all need to be united with Christ for liberation.

Moreover, I believe that Marxism, as a system, eventually destroys human dignity and undermines human flourishing.[31] As a result, Hopkins protests my "belief in the religion of US monopoly capitalism, a gospel of individualism, and faith in the Fall."[32] Perhaps this is the new definition of a non-Christian, Uncle Tom.

The phrase "monopoly capitalism" is a Marxist reference to something that no one with a good understanding of free markets would actually promote. In this phrase, Marxists rightly object to a capitalist economy being controlled be a few elites. I agree. That's not free market capitalism. In fact, monopolies are only possible when government interferes in the market to protect companies from competition. The best example of this would be the current U.S. economy, which is highly controlled by government, or government-created monopolies like the U.S. Postal Service, or government control of market transactions through regulatory agencies. This explains why we have lobbyists swarming all over Congress today.

I won't comment on what a "gospel of individualism" means because there does not exist a logical referent to what that means in my book or anything I have ever written.

What Christians of all races should find troubling is a seminary professor who would object to someone believing that sin entered the world at some point in human history. For over 2,000 years, Eastern and Western Christianity has affirmed various aspects of the Fall. Thankfully, God's redemptive mission announced in Genesis 3:15 introduced the framework for His solution through the promise of a Messiah.

Lastly, even though Hopkins has several academic degrees and has written several insightful scholarly books and articles, his assertion that I am a black man "unfamiliar with Black American churches" is nonsensical given the fact that I am the grandson of a black Baptist preacher from rural Alabama; was raised in a black United Methodist Church pastored by graduates of the Interdenominational Theological Center, an all-black seminary in Atlanta; was first licensed to preach in an inner-city African Methodist Episcopal Church, an all-black denomination; have worked in inner-city churches in places like Baltimore and Chattanooga, Tenn.; and am a member of Alpha Phi Alpha, America's first black fraternity. In fact, it is *because* of my commitment to black liberation that this brand of black liberation theology needs to be critiqued.

---

31. See John Paul II, *Centesimus Annus*, 12-21.

32. Hopkins, "Liberating Black Theology," 118.

The moral of the story is this: Even scholars need to do their homework. What Hopkins puts on the display is that there are real theological tensions killing the black church in America. Unfortunately, for someone like me to believe the classical 2,000-year-old truths of global Christianity brands me an outsider. But if my theology represents the dominant global and historic Christian confession, it seems that we may need to ask new questions regarding who the outsiders actually are.

Be the First to Love

One of the profound distinctions between Islam and Christianity is that Christianity is centered on the chief command to love. But is this how Christianity in America is known? I wonder how a commitment to cultivating a Christian culture of love would affect the way believers are received in a Western world that's increasingly hostile to classical Christian ideas. What if the operating system of the Christian life was "be the first to love?"

When encouraging Christians to love others first, I find that some immediately want to jump to discussions about God's justice and holiness. Others will use silly aphorisms like "hate the sin, love the sinner." But I find these to be excuses for how to not show love. What if conservative Christians operated under the principle to show love first when engaging target adversaries like political liberals and progressives, practicing homosexuals, and pro-abortion advocates? What if "progressive" Christians on the left used the principle of "be the first to love" when engaging conservative Christians who hold to classical Christian commitments? Progressive Christians claim to be different than the "mean conservative Christians"— until you read their books, blogs, tweets, and Facebook postings about the "Christian right."

The greatest commandment God gives His people is to be a people of love. Jesus makes this really clear as He summarizes the Law in Matthew 22:37-40:

> You shall love the Lord your God with all your heart and with all your soul and with all your mind. This is the great and first commandment. And a second is like it: You shall love your neighbor as yourself. On these two commandments depend all the Law and the Prophets.

The entirety of the Christian life is to apply God's Word within the context of loving God and loving others. The greatest commandment is not social justice. It's not even to "share the gospel." One can be committed to social justice and evangelism and not be committed to love. It's quite easy. I can share the gospel out of guilt, pride, condescension, anger, self-righteousness, and the like, and do it in such a way that does not demonstrate love. I can be committed to social justice and help others out of a narcissistic self-love that makes me feel good about how much better I am than others.

To take it one step further, Jesus told his followers, "Love your enemies and pray for those who persecute you, so that you may be sons of your Father who is in heaven" (Matthew 5:44-45). This is crazy talk, right? Looking at the Christian blogosphere and other social media platforms, it seems that believers justify personal attacks of Christians and non-Christians by name because some unlovable other "deserves it." The thinking goes something like this: "I don't have to show love first because that person says or does unlovable things" (i.e., things that I don't personally like). But it seems that loving people first—and even praying for people you don't like—is the stuff that makes one a recognizable member of the people of God.

Christians love first because God loved them before they knew Him. "We love because he first loved us," writes John the Apostle (1 John 4:19). Moreover, Paul reminds Jesus' followers that "faith, hope, and love abide, these three; but the greatest of these is love" (1 Corinthians 13:13). Since it appears that the goal and motive of the Christian life should be love, why does American Christianity tend to raise successive generations of men and women who are on crusades to attack either the rich and powerful or liberals?

I am not convinced that Christianity is becoming irrelevant in Western society because churches aren't committed to "the gospel" or that Christians are ignoring the poor and the oppressed. The real problem might be those committed to various practical commands in Scripture do not practice their faith in light of what God says about love. After all, love never fails (1 Corinthians 13:8).

Atheists Question Christian Division

Because all Christians do not agree on doctrine and are not a unified body in one denomination, many atheists reject the gospel. Legitimate questions atheists could ask include: "How do I know what to believe about Jesus if Christians themselves do not agree?" or "Which denomination has the truest form of Christianity and how does one choose the right church?" Admittedly, these are good questions.

At the website Ask the Atheist, schisms that create denominations are explained this way:

When a religion splits into two denominations, it's called a schism (pronounced 'SKIZZ-um'). People in the same denomination may argue a great deal, but when a particular dispute over religious practice, doctrine or dogma spreads far enough the two factions officially declare each other to be wrong in the eyes of their deity. That moment is when the schism happens, and afterwards the two groups are referred to using different names.

The Atheist goes on to explain that denominations exist because there are "no real Christian theocracies left, and no denomination is able to force dissenters into line the way the Church once could."

An example of divided fellowship is the relationship between Lutherans and Calvinists, two of the world's oldest post-Roman Catholic traditions. At The Gospel Coalition website, Kevin DeYoung, senior pastor at University Reformed Church in East Lansing, Mich., writes about the absence of Lutherans "in the big tent of evangelicalism." DeYoung's evangelicalism (which is primarily Calvinistic) does not encounter many confessional Lutherans. In response, Jonathan Fisk, a Lutheran pastor posted a video that generated nearly 3,000 views in a few weeks. Why? Because, as the atheists point out, there are real, substantial differences between Christians.

Fisk holds that Christians are divided into the four main fellowships: Eastern Orthodox, Roman Catholic, Reformed, and Lutheran. He argues that all denominations are, in the end, connected to one of these four. Each of these fellowships believes that the others are wrong on essential doctrines.

The Atheist understands this:

> If the Christian God exists, He probably would want Christians to unite under a single banner, and Christians of all denominations likely realise this. However, they reason, if the wrong denomination wins out and all Christians embrace the wrong doctrine, then nobody will really be doing God's will at all. Those of each denomination think they've got the right one, and most often decide that Christian unity ultimately isn't worth abandoning the 'true' faith. It's their way or nothing. Of course, this leaves all Christians at a gigantic impasse.

Are the four fellowships at an impasse? Fisk explains that the continuation of divisions in Christianity is not unique because "we're sinful human beings who prefer people like ourselves to anyone who would challenge the status quo, and you find that everywhere." Even the atheist has to admit that there are different kinds of atheists who do not agree about what atheism means. Division reveals something about human nature.

The DeYoung/Fisk conversation raises several questions in my mind. How should Christians respond to the atheist question about division? Will the Gospel Coalition ever have Lutheran speakers at its conferences? Will Lutherans invite Reformed speakers or Catholics to theirs? Does schism undermine the truth of Christianity to nonbelievers? Do those four fellowships constitute different Christianities? Are there beliefs that all Christians, regardless of fellowship, upon which all Christians agree?

I certainly do not have all the answers but the answers matter a great deal. There is much work ahead of the Church, because how these questions are answered bears witness to the truth of the gospel call to a watching world.

Libel is not Love

One sign of the declining state of Christianity in America is the way in which believers publicly slander one another, which can do violence to love and undermine the witness of the Church to nonbelievers. An example occurred in 2011 when a Christian blogger took offense to a comment made by a prominent pastor, and then, sadly, the blogger's rant went viral on the internet.

Granted, the pastor, Seattle's Mark Driscoll, seems to draw controversy like a magnet, mainly because of his willingness to speak out boldly against feminism in our society and paganism in the media, his unvarnished challenges to men to "be men" instead of soft and "effeminate," his staunch defense of the inerrancy of Scripture, and his belief that the pastorate is reserved for men and that women should stay home to nurture their children.

But what stirred up the blogger was a Facebook post by Driscoll, who caustically asked, "So what story do you have about the most effeminate anatomically male worship leader you've ever personally witnessed?" After receiving more than 600 comments, Driscoll deleted the post, but the cat was already out of the bag. I am not here to defend Driscoll's post and would personally challenge him over what he wrote. My concern is how Christians handle conflict with other Christians in public.

That's where Rachel Held Evans and her blog post, "Mark Driscoll is a bully. Stand up to him," come in. There is nothing loving about calling a pastor a "bully"—"a blustering, quarrelsome, overbearing person who habitually badgers and intimidates smaller or weaker people." That is a serious charge. In her post, Evans describes why she believes Driscoll to be a bully, implying that he, his teachings, and the elders at his church are not functioning in ways consistent with Scripture.[33] While it is more than reasonable to understand why someone would take issue with Driscoll's post, Evans' way of responding cannot and should not be encouraged. What was even more disturbing was the way in which many other believers jumped on the slander bandwagon to feed on the carnage once it went viral.

Jacob W. Ehrlich, in *The Holy Bible and the Law*, explains that because of the oral culture of the world of the Bible there is no difference between slander and libel in Christianity. And according to the International Standard Bible Encyclopedia, slander in the Bible is understood as an "accusation maliciously uttered, with the purpose or effect of damaging the reputation of another. As a rule it is a false charge (compare Mt 5:11); but it may be a truth circulated insidiously and with a hostile purpose (e.g., Dan 3:8, 'brought accusation against,' where Septuagint has diaballo, 'slander'; Lk 16:1, the same Greek word)."[34]

Evans' slanderous post also represents one of the things that God finds detestable, "a false witness who pours out lies and a person who stirs up conflict in the community" (Proverbs 6:19). Additionally, the Bible teaches that if someone offends us we should go to the person directly first (Matthew 18:15-20).

Christians publicly defaming the character of other Christians by name is not the way of love (1 Peter 4:8, Romans 12:9-10).

Thanks to the dissension that has now been stirred up, atheist websites are applauding Evans' response to Driscoll. What type of Christianity are we displaying before the world if slander is our response to the words of leaders we find offensive? Evans maintains that "Mark's bullying is unacceptable," and I would add that so is ungodly public speech against another Christian.

Wesleyan Honesty

In the Protestant Reformation, *sola scriptura* was meant to make the case that the Bible is the ultimate and final authority on matters related to salvation and faith. This often gets misunderstood as the Bible being the only authority Christians use for matters of faith in the Christian life. But as R.C. Sproul teaches in *What Is Reformed Theology*, the doctrine properly understood means that only the Bible has the authority to bind the conscience of believers.

While the Bible is the primary and final authority of Truth and the Christian faith, our faith is also mediated, explained, and delivered through

33. Evans, "Mark Driscoll is a Bully."
34. "Slander," International Standard Bible Encyclopedia Online.

a particular tradition and perspective. For centuries Protestants have recognized the authority of their confessions of faith. These confessions, which remain subordinate to what is plainly taught in the Bible and are open to questioning in ways the Bible is not, are regularly used to evaluate pastoral candidates and church membership on the basis of subscription to those documents. For example, Presbyterians use the *Westminster Confession of Faith*, Lutherans use the *Augsburg Confession of Faith*, and Anglicans use the *Book of Common Prayer*.

The Wesleyan tradition takes a different approach, challenging the sola scriptura misapplications and pointing to what Christians do *in practice*, namely, follow Jesus while negotiating the authorities of Scripture, tradition, reason, and experience. Wesleyans call these authorities the Wesleyan Quadrilateral; I call it "honesty."

Wesleyans do not teach that these four authorities are all equal but that they describe the actual sources Christians use to situate faith in subordination to the primacy of the Bible. For example, we use our rational faculties (reason) to interpret and apply what we read in the Bible as well as the guidance provided by our particular traditions. We use reason to test what tradition teaches according to what is plainly revealed in the Scriptures. We use experience, as Steve Wilkens and Mark L. Sanford explain in *Hidden Worldviews*, not as something subjective but with the understanding that "an idea passes the test of experience if its claims are consistent with the facts, observations and actual life events."[35] Experience, then, complements the Bible and our God-given reason.

The Wesleyan approach has led Don Thorsen, a professor at the Haggard Graduate School of Theology at Azusa Pacific University, to prefer *prima gratia*, *prima fide*, and *prima scriptura* instead of the *sola gratia*, *sola fide*, and *sola scriptura* celebrated from the Protestant Reformation. Thorsen believes that the Latin word prima ("primarily") "makes more sense in describing the complex understanding of Protestant Reformers and their nuanced articulation of salvation and religious authority."

Thorsen continues:

> Although the *sola* principles remain important for understanding the history of Protestant Christianity, they are best understood theologically from a Wesleyan perspective as representing *prima* principles because Protestants—past and present—think that salvation and religious authority include more than grace, faith, and scripture alone. Salvation should be thought of in terms of *prima gratia*—initiated primarily by

---

35. Wilkens and Sanford, *Hidden Worldviews*, 213.

God's grace—and *prima fide*—accepted primarily through faith. Likewise, religious authority should be thought of in terms of *prima scriptura*; scripture represents the primary religious authority of Protestantism but not its exclusive religious authority. Church tradition, logical reflection, and relevant experience all play important and authoritative roles in the founding and continuation of Protestantism.[36]

While much of this may seem to be merely semantics, it seems that Thorsen is seeking ways to bring better unity among Christians by putting on the table what Christians do *in practice*. Claiming that your church or denomination's teaching is "biblical" and according to the Bible alone while another group's is not is neither intellectually nor historically honest according to a Wesleyan perspective. No church or denomination uses the Bible as its *only* authority, and unfortunately it seems that only some are willing to admit that.

Perhaps being honest about our sources of authority, and how we use them, could foster a type of solidarity and humility that could unite Christians in what we share in the Kingdom instead of glorifying the distinctions that can create a posture of arrogance and pride about being "right."

A Call for a Trinitarian Missional Alliance

The Bible is primarily, exclusively, and essentially about the work of God the Father, Son, and Holy Spirit. Christianity, by extension, is a religion of this Triune God. Sadly, the Trinitarian doctrine that helped to unify Christians in the early church has lost its appeal as a point of alliance for Christians today. Thankfully, Philip Ryken and Michael LeFebvre have provided what I consider to be a way forward in unifying Christians to see that church fulfills her calling in *Our Triune God: Living in the Love of the Three-in-One*.

The authors remind readers that to know God is to know the Creator as Triune: "We praise the Father, Son, and the Holy Spirit for having equal, divine majesty, while at the same time honoring each Person's unique personality."[37] The first chapter explains that the plan of salvation requires the active engagement of every Person of the Trinity (Ephesians 1:3-14). Many Christians forget that no one comes to Christ without the active intervention of the Holy Spirit to respond the good news about God the Father and Son (1 Corinthians 12:3). Moreover, it is the Triune God who sanctifies and perseveres believers to the end.

36. Crawford, *Continuing Relevance of Wesleyan Theology*, 201.

37. Ryken and LeFebvre, *Our Triune God*, 13.

In chapter two, readers are reminded that the Trinity is a mystery, like many of the truths of Christianity. God's Triune nature is beyond the comprehension limits of created and finite human beings and has puzzled Christians from the beginning. But the entire Bible bears witness to God's Triune nature.

Chapter three encourages Christians to employ Trinitarian thinking in practical day-to-day spirituality. The saints are loved and cared for by all three persons of the Trinity and all three can be prayed to and worshiped daily.

The fourth chapter rightly exalts the Triune God as the source of Christian joy, worship, celebration, and mission. The Christian life is one of joyous gratitude for the work of God the Father, Son, and Holy Spirit.

If there is going to be another Great Awakening in America it will only happen through a Christianity united in mission around the work of the Triune God. Currently there is no place for Bible-believing, gospel-centered, Christ-exalting, mission-driven churches to partner locally or nationally for the movement of the Kingdom.

Gospel-focused American Christianity remains divided: The Neo-Calvinist and Reformed churches rally around groups like The Gospel Coalition, Together for the Gospel, and Acts 29; gospel-centered Lutherans mostly remain among themselves in denominations like the Lutheran Church-Missouri Synod and the Wisconsin Evangelical Lutheran Synod; traditional Wesleyans remain clustered in denominations like The Wesleyan Church and the Church of God (Holiness); Pentecostals flourish in denominations like the Assemblies of God and the Church of God in Christ; and Southern and National Baptist conventions are worlds unto themselves. And the list goes on. The church in America needs something that puts Jesus' prayer for unity in John 17 on display before the nations for the sake of Kingdom mission.

Christians of all stripes would do well to rally around the Trinity because it encourages each communion to bring forth its strengths, and challenges each tradition to be humble about the mysteries of faith that divide us yet do not constrain the greatest commandment of all Christians to love God and to love their neighbors (Matthew 22:36-40). Moreover, a Trinitarian center would be multi-ethnic, economically diverse, geographically dispersed, and truly represent the possibilities of Revelation 7:9.

Evangelism, social justice, apologetics, charity, and the like are held in good tension when centered on the Trinity. The Trinity keeps us from extremes. The possibilities are endless. Ultimately, there would be nothing more honoring to the Triune God than to have the people of God in an alliance around all three Persons. The Ryken-LeFrebvre book is good place for this alliance to begin.

Are We Institutionalizing Missional Narcissism?

Idolatry is tricky: Something that is otherwise good can quickly rule us. For example, while loving oneself is actually a good thing, as Jesus teaches (Matthew 22:39), inordinate or excessive love of self leads into the quicksand of narcissism. Because narcissism affects individuals, it can end up polluting the institutions we construct and lead in our own sin-tainted image. I'm afraid that some well-intentioned Christians, in the quest to have the most unique church ever, could be inadvertently contributing to the demise of Christianity in America.

In a 2008 article, "Organizational Narcissism," from the journal *Organizational Dynamics*, Dennis Duchon and Michael Burns explain how institutions can become narcissistic in the quest for uniqueness. According to the authors, these organizations become "self-absorbed and focus[ed] on protecting an identity" and are preoccupied with themselves.[38]

As self-absorption becomes habit, a narcissistic organization uses its inflated self-importance to justify all sorts of activities that inadvertently lose touch with those they intended to reach and end up hurting people along the way. Moreover, narcissistic organizational leaders will not admit that their organizations have limited knowledge and capabilities. They believe that they can figure out how to do whatever they set their minds to. They are blind to their organization's weaknesses and never mention them in public. Duchon and Burns describe the self-loving organization as "attention-grabbing" with "hip, fashionable" leaders who project the "illusions of control" while highly valuing an entrepreneurial style of leadership that shoots down contrary opinions and gathers "yes people" who are "celebrated as team players."[39]

The institutional narcissism prevalent in some corners of missional evangelicalism is worth book-length treatment. Having said that, let me offer just one example of the inadvertent power of missional narcissism. The Rev. Tim Keller is quoted as saying:

"If you and your church were to disappear off the face of the earth tomorrow, would anyone in the unbelieving community around you notice

---

38. Duchon and Byrns, "Organizational Narcissism," 354.

39. Ibid., 356.

you were gone? And if they did even notice would they say, 'We are really glad they are gone,' or 'Gee, we're going to miss them.'"[40]

While Keller makes an excellent point about the gospel footprint that Christians should have in their communities, missional narcissists pervert such a statement to justify the self-aggrandizing quest to be the most unique and accomplished church in town, maybe ever—a church with programs, preaching, and music like no other church. Narcissists take Keller's principle and apply it to their quest to be nostalgic. The result is that intended groups are not reached and many folks in the church become collateral damage.

Jesus prayed for Christian unity (John 17:6-26), but missional narcissists focus on division and separation from other Christians who may not be as "cool" or accomplished. In many inner cities, for example, some missional narcissists arrive proclaiming their unique and special presence while neither following the lead nor listening to the black and Latino church leaders already there. Missional narcissists encourage "fantasies of success," explain Duchon and Burns, which tempt some into the self-deception that his congregation has the knowledge and competencies to transform the entire town or even the world.[41] Moreover, missional narcissists cannot understand why *everyone* is not attending their church. They believe that they are so awesome that everyone should want to be there. Narcissist leaders struggle to accept the fact that they have severe limitations in their ability to lead people who are not like them.

The list of applications of the Duchon and Burns article to missional narcissism is quite long, but in the end, the authors argue for a self-confident realism. That is, instead of narcissism, organizations should move forward with humility and honesty about their strengths and limits. A self-confident, realistic Christianity, then, is successful because of its faithfulness to Scriptures, not because it is unique and special. What makes Christianity different is Jesus, not the uniqueness of any local church, so boasting about your group's special awesomeness is simply inconsistent with the historic spread of Christianity around world and is unnecessary.

Evangelicalism's Narcissism Epidemic

Researchers believe that today's 20-somethings are not only the most narcissistic generation in American history, but are also drowning in an American culture that feeds their narcissism. In *The Narcissism Epidemic*, psychology professors Jean Twenge and Keith Campbell explain that American

---

40. This quotation, and many others, can be found at http://timkeller.info/quotes/

41. Duchon and Burns, "Organizational Narcissism," 358.

individualism has denigrated into an obsession with "me, me, me," adding that "Americans love to love themselves."[42]

The authors go on to define a narcissist as someone who has an "over-inflated view of his own abilities," and is simply "overconfident" and sees himself as fundamentally superior, special, entitled, and unique. Narcissists want to feel important even when they are not. Moreover, they often use other people in a "grand game of deception," the authors note, adding, "If you do this well-convincing yourself and everyone else that you are as terrific as you think you are-you can be a winner in the game of self-admiration."

As I read through the book, I began to wonder if some aspects of evangelical culture actually spiritualize narcissism in the following ways:

1. By having parenting priorities that coddle children and deceive them into thinking they are unique and special and, by extension, placing unrealistic and unbiblical performance expectations on them to be basically perfect, sinless, athletic, academically successful, and accomplished in order to live a fairy-tale life of comfort and ease. To make matters worse, some place expectations on young people to do "awesome things for God someday," "change the world," "make a difference," etc. "Move to the inner city or go into missions so you can do something substantial with your life," we tell them. "And don't get married too early. Marriage and kids could mess up all the cool things you can do for God." But the Apostle Paul seems to suggest that Christians "aspire to live quietly, and to mind your own affairs, and to work with your hands" (1 Thessalonians 4:11). Maybe one of the most radical things your child will do in this life is stay married and raise kids who love God.

2. By buying into business marketing strategies that feed narcissistic temptations for local congregations to be unique and special by crafting vision and missions statements that go beyond biblical teachings like "loving God and loving neighbor" (Matthew 22:36-40). Isn't *love* big enough to be a "big hairy audacious goal"?[43] What could be more profound, revolutionary, and directional than love? Perhaps love is not radical, sexy, or glamorous enough in an age of narcissism.[44]

3. By accepting the idea that you need to be important and have your name recognized in your community and the nation. In other words, be a part of an influencer church with one of those influential, famous

42. Twenge and Campbell, *The Narcissism Epidemic*, 13.

43. See Collins and Porras, *Built to Last*.

44. For an example see Platt, *Radical*.

book-writing pastors who speak at conferences. A church on the move! Twenge and Campbell have an entire chapter that describes the narcissist craving for attention that challenges me to question what I am reading when I see posts on Facebook or tweets on Twitter about what unique and awesome thing a church is doing abroad or domestically. I wonder if God is impressed with influential churches. "Hey look at how awesome we are; God sure is working!" But isn't your church "da bomb" if it's working to love God and love your neighbor? What else would you want in a church to do and to be? And, by the way, your little local congregation is not going to "redeem your city." Changing cities is the Holy Spirit's job (Acts 2).

I hate to sound overly simplistic, but I am beginning to wonder if we undermine the mystery of the Christian life by adding extra tasks, missions, and principles that are not in the Bible and burn people out in the process, making Christianity a burden. Maybe the way to live radically in a culture that craves attention is to live in such a way that points people to mystery of the Trinity and not to our institutions or ourselves.

Between Four Worlds

A few years ago I was scolded by a woman in an evangelical church for not having read much of C.S. Lewis' work as a child. While I watched her shake her head I was shamed into thinking that my Christian upbringing was deficient. I suppose there was an expectation that every "good Christian" kid raised in the church should know Lewis. But her assumption was offensive to me because it ignored the simple fact that I was raised in the black church where the writings of C.S. Lewis are largely unknown. I wonder, would this woman have had a different attitude had she understood that many blacks who now attend evangelical churches were not raised in white evangelical churches? The truth is, black evangelicals have the difficult burden of having to navigate between four worlds: the several hundred-year-old, well established black church universe; the evangelical church subculture; mainstream black culture; and mainstream Anglo-oriented American culture.

When I am around my black friends and family in the black church I get weird looks if I am unaware of what is happening in the black gospel music scene or if I'm unfamiliar with the latest teachings of one of the black megachurch pastors. I am expected to be able to sing along with Fred Hammond, Hezekiah Walker and LFC, Vanessa Bell-Armstrong, Lisa Page-Brooks, Kirk Franklin, and others. I am expected to be familiar with the ministries of pastors like Dr. H. Beecher Hicks, the late Bishop G.E. Patterson, Bishop Charles Blake, E. Dewey Smith, and so on.

Black evangelicals are also expected to be well acquainted with white evangelical subculture icons like C.S. Lewis, Charles Spurgeon, John Piper, Tim Keller, and books like *Pilgrim's Progress*. There are also the hymns and contemporary artists with whom blacks are expected to at least be familiar with, like "Fairest Lord Jesus," "Come, Thou Fount of Every Blessing," Twila Paris, Michael Card, Michael W. Smith, Natalie Grant, Third Day, and so on—even if they do not necessarily like them.

Mainstream black culture is a completely different world, in which blacks are expected to be well aware of the latest issues raised by Tavis Smiley, Cornel West, Kevin Powell, and TheRoot.com; the latest buzz on either the Tom Joyner or Steve Harvey morning radio shows; or the latest film by Spike Lee. Not to mention that recent television shows like *Are We There Yet?*, *The Great State of Georgia*, and *Let's Stay Together* should remain in the cultural awareness holding tank just in case you're at a party.

American pop culture is much easier to navigate, because, regardless of one's racial subculture, we're all saturated with the music and films that emerge from Hollywood. Most everybody saw *Black Swan*, *The Fighter*, *Inception*, and *True Grit*, right? And we are all familiar with Lady Gaga, Lady Antebellum, Katy Perry, Justin Bieber, and Ray LaMontagne, right?

But for black Christians, navigating between these four worlds can be time-consuming and challenging. Even thinking about all this makes me tired. In the end, I am making a public plea for patience and grace for blacks coming into evangelical circles, because what many evangelicals consider standard and normal for *all Christians* simply is not. Black Christians should not be shamed because they were raised in a world, a very different one than the evangelical mainstream, and have to spend time navigating between four worlds concurrently. At times, it's simply exhausting.

The Christian Life as Apologetics

In one portion of the apologetics of Tertullian (ca. 160-225), we find a defense of the faith on the basis of how differently Christians live from their neighbors. The Christian life is intended to be lived in such a way that it puts on display the glory of God. In the early church, what made Christians stand out were the ways in which they were different from the surrounding culture in pursuing a virtuous and holy life. Being different is a struggle for American Christians who often find it desirable to be as much like our society in every way except for the occasional Sabbath from culture for religious activities. But the Bible is a book describing how and why God's people are supposed to live differently (Leviticus 20:23, Colossians 3:1-17, 1 Thessalonians 4:5).

Tertullian takes this principle even further in his *Apology* by explaining what happens when people commit their lives to Christ. Following Christ changes everything about one's life and family. Given the positive consequences of the Christian life, Tertullian wonders why those who attack Christianity spew so much venom:

> [Some attackers], in the case of persons whom, before they took the name of Christian, they had known as loose, and vile, and wicked, put on them a brand from the very thing which they praise. In the blindness of their hatred, they fall foul of their own approving judgment! 'What a woman she was! how wanton! how gay! What a youth he was! how profligate! how libidinous!-they have become Christians!' So the hated name is given to a reformation of character. Some even barter away their comforts for that hatred, content to bear injury, if they are kept free at home from the object of their bitter enmity. The wife, now chaste, the husband, now no longer jealous, casts out of his house; the son, now obedient, the father, who used to be so patient, disinherits; the servant, now faithful, the master, once so mild, commands away from his presence; it is a high offense for anyone to be reformed by the detested name.

Struggles with one's "reformation of character" are not only difficult during young adulthood. Because the temptations of youth are more visible, young people often get picked on for struggling with sin and idolatry more than their parents. But with older adults the temptations are much more subtle.

Could your pastor make a defense of the faith by pointing to the lives of the people in your church? Moreover, how would the "reformation of character" affect the divorce rate within Christian churches, Christian parents raising children for academic success instead of Kingdom success, those Christian families that regularly skip church for youth sports activities, car and house purchases, hoarding material possessions under the guise of "stewardship," gluttony, spending patterns, and so on? This is very difficult because we often yield to idols without even realizing it until it is too late. But the Bible is very clear that Christians are to live differently and to invite people to live a life of virtue transformed by the Triune God. Peter reminds Christians to "live such good lives among the pagans that, though they accuse you of doing wrong, they may see your good deeds and glorify God on the day he visits us" (1 Peter 2:12). My guess is that if Christians in America were committed to this, in principle, it could change the disposition that non-Christians have toward those who hold closely to the teachings of the Bible.

Our Only Comfort in Life and Death

On Feb. 9, 2011, my 85-year-old aunt went to be with the Lord. As the oldest sibling in a family of eight children, Elizabeth Durant Swinson was affectionately known as "sister." The nieces and nephews called her "Aunt Sister." When I heard the news of her passing I was immediately struck by all of things she experienced from 1925 to 2011.

My aunt was born into a Jim Crow-ruled Goldsboro, N.C. My grandfather was a bricklayer and my grandmother, like many black women of that era, performed domestic work for white families. My aunt experienced her fair share of racial slurs by God-fearing whites in North Carolina over the years as well as the humiliation of having to drink from "colored" water fountains and being served from the rear of restaurants. Even against these odds she managed to graduate from college with a Bachelor of Science degree in education and had a 35-year teaching career in the very community in which she was raised.

A life-long member of the Mount Calvary Missionary Baptist Church, my aunt's faith in Christ and His church was so vital in being able to deal with the challenges of the Great Depression, social racism, the turmoil of the Civil Rights Movement, and the normal struggles of life that come with 56 years of marriage. I was almost brought to tears looking at the faces of her friends at the funeral who simply looked tired, and rightly so. Theirs is a generation that suffered greatly to open doors and create opportunities for blacks like me to accomplish things in America that my great-grandparents would not have thought possible. Moreover, I am sure my aunt never would have imagined as a child that the United States of America would, in her lifetime, have a black president.

Regrettably, I missed the opportunity to ask her directly about her thoughts on all the technological advances she had seen in America since the 1920s. Indoor plumbing, air-conditioning, landing on the moon, home computers, microwaves, the internet, cell phones, and the like are all things that could not have been in the imagination of 5-year-old in 1930.

Although the funeral was difficult, my family was able to celebrate God's faithfulness to my aunt and His covenant faithfulness throughout the generations of our family. I had the privilege of speaking at the funeral, where I reminded the audience, from the Heidelberg Catechism, that in this life of laughter and tears the only comfort for Christians is the knowledge that we belong to the Triune God. Looking back at Aunt Sister's life it was good to see an 85-year-old witness to that truth.

From the Heidelberg Catechism:

> Question 1. What is thy only comfort in life and death?

> Answer: That I with body and soul, both in life and death, am not my own, but belong unto my faithful Saviour Jesus Christ; who, with his precious blood, has fully satisfied for all my sins, and delivered me from all the power of the devil; and so preserves me that without the will of my heavenly Father, not a hair can fall from my head; yea, that all things must be subservient to my salvation, and therefore, by his Holy Spirit, He also assures me of eternal life, and makes me sincerely willing and ready, henceforth, to live unto him.

Are Evangelicals Too Republican?

Are evangelicals too closely associated with the culture of conservative politics? I was really challenged by this question after reading Bill Bishop's *The Big Sort: Why the Clustering of Like-Minded America Is Tearing Us Apart*.[45] The book explains how Americans have clustered and isolated themselves geographically and socially by political affiliation. Liberals live and socialize with liberals and conservatives live and socialize with other conservatives. We no longer mix. To my surprise, Bishop expands the discussion by reporting that evangelicalism is now a place where being a Christian and a registered Republican are synonyms for Christian orthodoxy.

Bishop frames the narrative this way: Beginning in the 1970s Americans sorted themselves into neighborhoods and social networks with those sharing similar political views. The conservatives moved to the suburbs and the liberals stayed closer to the city. This sorting also determined the growth of suburban evangelical churches on the principle that "like attracts like." According to Bishop, the "real white flight" of the past two generations was not simply racial but ideological, which created communities and neighborhoods that were more or less either Republican or Democratic. It became more and more the norm by the 1980s for neighbors to share similar political agendas and perspectives. Using voting data, Bishop demonstrates that these neighborhood-based trends hold true today as well.

45. Bishop, *The Big Sort*.

48 SOMETHING SEEMS STRANGE

The "big sort," as Bishop describes in Chapter 7, resulted in evangelicals becoming more and more associated with Republican politics, especially upper-income Christians, rather than distinct theological positions. As evangelical churches were planted in the suburbs, combined with rise of megachurches, it's not too surprising that in the past two generations the Republican Party has experienced its largest growth among middle and upper-class suburban Americans. In 1960, 60 percent of evangelicals identified themselves as Democrats, but by 1988 that number was down to 40 percent. What happened?

Bishop suggests that churches today promote themselves as socially and politically tribal. That is, "You'll like this church. There are people like you already there." Churches are safe spaces to have one's personal social and political values affirmed.

Bishop isn't the only one asking questions about whether or not conservative politics too closely defines Christian orthodoxy. Here are a few other books that have been recommended to me:

- *The Rapture of Politics: The Christian Right as the United States Approaches the Year 2000*, by Steve Bruce, et al.

- *White Protestant Nation: The Rise of the American Conservative Movement*, by Alan Lichtman.

- *Right Face: Organizing the American Conservative Movement, 1945-65*, by Niels Bjerre-Poulson.

- *Suburban Warriors: The Origins of the New American Right*, by Lisa McGirr.

- *Millennial Dreams and Apocalyptic Nightmares: The Cold War Origins of Political Evangelicalism*, by Angela Lahr.

These books raise interesting questions for me. For example: Does the conflation of faith and politics explain why evangelicalism's 20-somethings seem bitter to some? Is it possible that evangelicalism's children born in the 1980s and '90s don't know how to be a Christian without being a Republican? If you can be a pro-choice Republican, can you be an anti-abortion Democrat and still be a faithful follow of Jesus Christ? Does being a Christian mean that one should limit one's social network and place of residence to communities dominated by Republicans and social conservatives? Moreover, does this explain, in part, why evangelicalism is so isolated from Christians in the black and Hispanic communities who are not Republicans? Has the GOP taken advantage of the "big sort" in the past? There are more questions to ask for sure, and I'm not certain what all the answers are either, but it's clear that conservative social clustering is causing many to question whether or not evangelicalism seeks to make disciples of Jesus Christ or to grow the GOP.

Defending Christianity Through the Centuries

It's been said, "The more things change, the more they remain the same." In the area of Christian apologetics, this is most certainly the case.

Looking back at the Christian leaders who defended the Bible's teachings in the past, we are reminded that the profession of the truth of redemption has remained the same even as cultures have changed. Irenaeus (A.D. 120-202/3), one of the earliest apologists for Christianity, found himself defending the truth claims of the Bible in a culture that was idolatrous and mixed Christianity with other philosophies and religions in various cults. He gave a powerful refutation of the religions of his day by stating the ways in which those religions were illogical, making clear the truth-claims of the Bible story. It's a simple yet beautiful story.

Irenaeus tackled gnosticism as well as Marcionism, which said that Christianity was different from and in opposition to Judaism. Marcionites rejected the entire Old Testament and said that the God of the Old Testament was a lesser demiurge (a godlike entity) who had created the earth but was also the source of evil. In 2011 we may not have "heresies" in the exact same form, but we do have our fair share of pagan philosophies and religions that mix Christianity with other beliefs, like the Nation of Islam, for example.

In Chapter 10 of his treatise *Against Heresies*, Irenaeus set the record straight by pointing out the theological errors in the prevailing views of his time and by clearly stating the timeless truths of Christianity that Christians hold dear nearly 2,000 years later. What Irenaeus confessed reminds the Christians of today of our connection to an ancient tradition of women and men professing work of the Triune God:

> The Church, though dispersed throughout the whole world, even to the ends of the earth, has received from the apostles and their disciples this faith: [She believes] in one God, the Father Almighty, Maker of heaven, and earth, and the sea, and all things that are in them; and in one Christ Jesus, the Son of God, who became incarnate for our salvation; and in the Holy Spirit, who proclaimed through the prophets the dispensations of God, and the advents, and the birth from a virgin, and the passion, and the resurrection from the dead, and the ascension

into heaven in the flesh of the beloved Christ Jesus, our Lord, and His [future] manifestation from heaven in the glory of the Father "to gather all things in one," and to raise up anew all flesh of the whole human race, in order that to Christ Jesus, our Lord, and God, and Saviour, and King, according to the will of the invisible Father, "every knee should bow, of things in heaven, and things in earth, and things under the earth, and that every tongue should confess" to Him.[46]

Is apologetics really that simple? In some ways, yes. We are called to give a reason for the hope that we have in Christ (1 Peter 3:15). We are stating what unites us as Christians today, yesterday, and forever. The defense of the faith in the second century is not all that different from what we need to communicate today. Like Irenaeus, our job is analyze the prevailing religions and philosophies of our day, point out the errors of those views—with gentleness and respect—and tell the same story that Christians have been telling for centuries: The incarnate Son of God has come to save sinners and redeem his world. We should never underestimate the power of that confession. That was Irenaeus' story and I'm sticking to it.

Evangelicalism's Bitter 20-Somethings

Is it me or does it seem that many kids reared in affluent conservative evangelical communities become bitter people in their 20s? I've recently read blog posts and articles by 20-somethings reared in suburban evangelicalism that seem to be committed to doing one thing: attacking the very community that raised them and doing it bitterly. I call them "the Bitters."

How the Bitters communicate fits Ronald Inglehart's thesis from the early 1970s about post-materialist young people. Inglehart wrote that when children grow up in abundance, like many suburban evangelical kids, they are more concerned as young adults with "self-expression" than with hard work and survival—the concerns of those who grew up struggling with scarcity.[47]

Adding to that, Bill Bishop, in *The Big Sort: Why the Clustering of Like-Minded America Is Tearing Us Apart*, writes that children of abundance become post-materialist young adults who lose interest in organized religion and become increasingly focused on personal spirituality. Economic growth and military security decline in political importance and are replaced by issues like personal freedom, abortion rights, social justice, and the

46. *Against Heresies*, Book I, Chapter 10.
47. See Inglehart, "The Silent Revolution in Europe," 991–1017.

environment. These young adults are less inclined to obey central authority and lose trust in hierarchical institutions. Finally, they harbor resentment for the big organizations that created America's modern, industrial society: big business, traditional church denominations, traditional family structures, and so on.

The Bitters, who tend to gravitate toward Christian hipster culture,[48] are on a mission to expose the "conservative conspiracy" wherever they can find it (or create it) under the guise of "healthy critique." Bitters define themselves by what they are not. If their parents are Republicans they become staunch Democrats. If their parents are in a conservative church, Bitters will find a more liberal church. Bitters choose "the left" because it's not "the right." There is no greater sin for Bitters than sounding like you might be "conservative."

To define one's identity in terms of being "not like them" seems cowardly. The longing for self-expression Inglehart discussed in his thesis may be a longing to be heard and affirmed, because many kids of affluence are ignored in homes where meaningful participation in family life is communicated as optional. Bitters likely feel deeply insignificant, like they don't matter. They probably weren't "cool" in high school. Craving affirmation, Bitters want someone to pay attention to them—finally. The easiest way get attention is to protest things dear to the hearts of their elders. "You're paying attention now aren't you," the Bitter protests. The great irony is that Bitters still want connection to their formerly conservative communities. If you're really "done" with something, then you don't waste time attacking it; you just ignore it and leave it alone. I could be wrong about the Bitters. I hope so. But what I do see is a group of 20-somethings wasting their time on a quest that will never deliver the revolution that it promises. You are what you are, not what you are not.

The American Church and Adoption

How can a country have Christian churches and 115,000 orphans? It shouldn't be possible, but it is the case in America, with a sizable group of Christian families in all 50 states and true orphans lingering in foster care year after year. But what would happen if more pastors and church leaders would adopt orphans or model orphan care in their personal lives? Pastors tend to preach and teach about their interests and practices. And American Christians tend to apply the Bible to real life issues *after* a pastor or recognized leader stirs up interest. So if church leaders would cast a

48. See McCracken, *Hipster Christianity*.

practice-driven vision for orphan care, churchgoers likely would be challenged to participate in one of the most ancient practices of God's covenant people (Exodus 22; Deuteronomy 14, 16, 24).

If a church considers itself a comprehensively "biblical" one, then it should foster a culture of adoption and orphan care as a practice of "true religion" (James 1:26–27). Historically, orphan care has distinguished redeemed people from other people groups in the world. In fact, no other religion in the world has made orphan care a normal aspect of spiritual life like Christianity. A God that has made a series of successive covenants to redeem His entire creation through the work of His Son uniquely has positioned His people to put salvation on full display through redemptive acts like adoption.

On a trip to Atlanta several years ago, I was reminded of the adoption problem as I watched a special Christmas edition of "Wednesday's Child" on the local Fox 5 television. The program profiles orphaned children who have been permanently severed from their families, and over the years there have been about 600 Atlanta children featured but only about half of them have been adopted. The adoption of 300 children is great news, but placements could be better in a city with such a high concentration of large evangelical churches. In fact, Atlanta Christians alone could adopt all of Georgia's 1,800 true orphans.

I wonder what would happen if Christians thought of family beyond its sometimes idolatrous, biological constraints? My guess is that adoption would become a part of normative church culture. American orphan statistics would plummet. Several years ago I worked in a church where adoption was a part of the pastor's practice, as well as the practice of the congregational leaders, and it became a part of the church's culture. Adoption was on display in the pews on Sundays. It was beautiful to witness.

I certainly do not want to make orphan care any type of new legalism, nor a litmus test for church leadership, but I am convinced that orphans will continue to linger in foster care until more pastors and leaders begin to adopt and teach about their experiences. I'm neither a pastor nor a church leader, but if I were, and were married, I'd be, without question, an adoptive parent and this practice would become a regular part of my teaching and, Lord willing, my church's culture.

I also recognize that every family cannot adopt orphans for various reasons. But the United States only has 115,000 true orphans. Is the American church so dead that we cannot find 115,000 Christian families willing to adopt? Or maybe churchgoers are simply following their leaders.

Black Church Solidarity

Just before Thanksgiving in 2010, the leadership of the nine largest historically black denominations announced the launch of The Conference of
National Black Churches (CNBC). These evangelical and mainline denominations, representing nearly 30 million churchgoers and 50,000 congregations in the United States, have joined forces to address a myriad of issues
in the black community. The CNBC held its first annual consultation titled
"For the Healing of Our People," Dec. 7–10 that year in Washington, D.C.

While there are individual churches and denominations and faith-
based organizations doing good work in local neighborhoods in America,
the CNBC sees itself as filling a void. Some problems are simply too big for
one church or denomination to address alone, so the CNBC plans to offer
much needed cross-denominational coordination in an effort to serve African-Americans and other underserved populations in the areas of health,
education, social justice, and economic empowerment.

But what about black evangelicals who align themselves with predominantly white denominations and churches and their issues? What role, if
any, do they have in initiatives like this? Many blacks in these churches tend
to distance themselves from black churches and black communities, but the
CNBC could provide them with a unique opportunity to remain involved
at some level. That involvement could take the form of them encouraging
their own denominations to direct more human capital toward issues like
the black marriage crisis, the HIV/AIDS crisis among black women, public
education deficiencies, and juvenile incarceration rates.

I'm not sure what the answers are, or how the logistics of something
like this could work in practice, but the ability of black evangelical and
mainline denominations to work together on social issues could encourage
new vistas for all Christians across racial and denominational lines to be co-
belligerents in addressing multiple issues for the common good in America
while maintaining distinct biblical and theological commitments.

Ignored Black Evangelical Scholars?

Protestant mainline churches seem to be far more interested in tapping into
the resources of African-American theological scholars in ways that evangelicalism seems unwilling or incapable of doing.

For example, Eddie Glaude Jr., who holds a Ph.D. from Princeton University and is a professor of Religion and chair of the Center for African

American Studies at Princeton, is regularly tapped for his perspective on Christianity and culture, including contributions on The Huffington Post.[49]

Then there's Josef Sorett, who earned his Ph.D. at Harvard University and is an assistant professor of Religion and African-American Studies at Columbia University. He writes frequently at CNN.com and in various scholarly publications.

Are there black evangelical scholars, with completed Ph.D.s, who are recognized within evangelicalism in the same way that Glaude and Sorett are within other Protestant circles? If not, why not? Is there something different about evangelicalism?

Black theological scholars are able to offer unique contributions to the practice of faith and applications of the biblical text, given the knowledge that our experience of the Trinity is shaped sociologically as well as biblically. Context matters.

Perhaps not recognizing that social context influences how one reads and applies the biblical text keeps many Asian, Latino, and Native American theologians from being asked to contribute within evangelicalism. Perhaps evangelicalism simply lacks such black scholars. But a brief survey of a few large Christian institutions paints a much different picture.

Here are just a few examples:

- Dr. Vincent Bacote (Ph.D., Drew University) is an associate professor of Theology and the director of the Center for Applied Christian Ethics at Wheaton College. Dr. Bacote is an expert on ethics, orthopraxis, and Abraham Kuyper, and is the author of *The Spirit in Public Theology: Appropriating the Legacy of Abraham Kuyper*.

- Dr. Eric Washington (Ph.D., Michigan State University) is an assistant professor of History at Calvin College and researches the black church from its development in the late 18th century through the 19th century with respect to Calvinism.

- Dr. Bruce Fields (Ph.D., Marquette University) is an associate professor of biblical and systematic theology at Trinity Evangelical Divinity School in Deerfield, Ill. and has taught there since 1988. He is the author of *Black Theology: Three Crucial Questions for the Evangelical Church*.

- Dr. Ralph Watkins (Ph.D., University of Pittsburgh) Dr. Ralph C. Watkins Associate Professor of Evangelism and Church Growth, Religion at Columbia Theological Seminary. He is author of several books

49. You can find his contributions at http://www.huffingtonpost.com/eddie-glaude-jr-phd/

including the forthcoming *Hip-Hop Redemption: Finding God in the Music and the Message.*

- Dr. J. Kameron Carter (Ph.D., University of Virginia) graduated from Dallas Theological Seminary and is now an associate professor in Theology and Black Church Studies at the Duke University Divinity School. He has written a groundbreaking book, *Race: A Theological Account.*

- Dr. Craig Mitchell (Ph.D., Southwestern Baptist Theological Seminary) is an Associate Professor of Philosophy, Politics, & Economics and Director of the Criswell Institute for PPE at Criswell College and the author of a few books, including *Charts of Philosophy and Philosophers.* Mitchell is perhaps one of the most academically accomplished theologians in all of evangelicalism, holding six different academic degrees.

In addition to these examples, there are many more black evangelical scholars in theology that I could list at schools all across America.

Xavier Pickett, co-founder of Reformed Blacks of America, is completing a Ph.D. in Theology at Princeton Theological Seminary after graduating from Westminster Theological Seminary in Philadelphia. Pickett and I were recently wondering why black evangelical scholars seem to be ignored. Among the reasons could be that they do not publish as much their mainline counterparts. Or that evangelicals seem to prefer the theological reflection of black pastors instead of black scholars at academic institutions.

Mainline Protestants seem to do the opposite. Pickett and I do not have all the answers but it seems that the top Christian websites like ChristianityToday.com and Crosswalk.com may be ignoring black scholars to the detriment of evangelicalism. Again, we're not certain. Black evangelical scholars are all over America and hopefully they will be able to start contributing to conversations about the direction of evangelicalism.

Tweeting a Shibboleth Gospel

I need a Twitter-gospel break.

The new trend of provocatively restating "the gospel" on Twitter may be inadvertently keeping Christians on spiritual milk. Social media is a wonderful tool for communication and has multiple good uses, but like anything else, it has limits which its users need to recognize. Twitter is the new roadside church sign where corny quips go viral. I speak for many who are worn out on the Twitter-gospel.

The Twitter-gospel attempts to reduce the Good News to a 140-character "tweet" that will make readers think it is good enough to be endlessly retweeted, because each retweet builds up the sought-after coolness affirmation for some. It's the "slam dunking" of the Bible. I am even beginning to wonder if a few of these Twitter-gospelers are trying to tweet their way to fame.

Something so important seems hardly reducible to a clever one-liner. The gospel seems clear. *The Dictionary for Theological Interpretation of the Bible* defines is as "the good news of salvation in Jesus Christ." *The New International Dictionary of the Bible* defines it as "the Good News that God has provided a way of redemption through his son Jesus Christ." But the Twitter-gospel can frustrate the simplicity of the message, as examples found by Jake Belder provide:

"Legalism says achievement leads to approval, the gospel says that approval leads to achievement."

"The gospel obliterates, annihilates, and disembowels any notion of wage earning as a basis for our acceptance with God."

"The Gospel makes us stop asking: What have I done for God? And makes us ask: What's the Lord done through/in/despite me?"

I fully understand that many of these tweets are intended to encourage the faithful to persevere, because for those of us who struggle with idolatry and sin (Romans 7) we need to hear the gospel daily. We get it. So tell us, then, what the gospel actually is instead of collaborating with weak attempts at imaginativeness to reformulate something people have actually died to communicate. Unlike the Bible, the Twitter-gospel has no context, and unless you're a Christian you might not get the point without some sort of theological background.

While it gives the appearance of sophistication, much Twitter-gospel is gospel milk. It reminds me of a couple passages from Hebrews: "Anyone who lives on milk, being still an infant, is not acquainted with the teaching about righteousness. But solid food is for the mature, who by constant use have trained themselves to distinguish good from evil" (5:13-14), and "Therefore let us leave the elementary teachings about Christ and go on to maturity, not laying again the foundation of repentance from acts that lead to death, and of faith in God, instruction about baptisms, the laying on of hands, the resurrection of the dead, and eternal judgment" (6:1-2).

The Twitter-gospel is for über-church Christians who retweet the "elementary teachings" repeatedly, and thanks to that, "the gospel" may be on its way to becoming a shibboleth. Moreover, the individualistic nature of the Twitter-gospel cannot be all that the Good News implies for the Christian life, right? So for all of us who want to uphold the meaningfulness and sanctity of the message of the Good News of salvation in Jesus Christ, will the Twitter-gospelers please give "the gospel" a Twitter Sabbath?

'Social Justice' Has Christian History

While the term "social justice" means different things to different Christian and other religious organizations, an historic use of the concept in theological ethics was conjoined to a discussion of the common good that sought to explain the importance of private property, free enterprise, and the threat of big government.

On May 15, 1931, Pope Pius XI issued *Quadragesimo anno* (QA) to commemorate the 40th anniversary of Pope Leo XIII's encyclical *Rerum Novarum*. As explained by Christine Fiber Hinze in a commentary of QA, Pope Pius XI has been credited with introducing the term "social justice" into the lexicon of Christian ethics.[50] When Protestants started using the term will require more research, but the Catholic usage was fairly easy to trace.

According to Hinze, Italian theologian Luigi Taparelli D'Azeglio introduced the term into Catholic social ethics in the mid-1800s to rearticulate potentially misunderstood concepts like "legal justice" and "general justice." Gustav Gunlac and Oswald von Nell-Breuning were particularly influential in inserting the language into QA. The concept was officially described later in 1937 in the encyclical *Divini redemptoris*, which attacked atheistic communism:

> [T]here [is] social justice with its own set obligations, from which neither employers nor workingmen can escape. Now it is of the very essence of social justice to demand for each individual all that is necessary for the common good. But just as in the living organism it is impossible to provide for the good of the whole unless each single part and each individual member is given what it needs for the exercise of its proper functions. . . . If social justice be satisfied, the result will be an intense activity in economic life as a whole, pursued in tranquillity and order.[51]

For Pius XI in QA, social justice referred to the central and necessary set of conditions where each person makes free, non-government-coerced contributions to the common good. It included keeping in check the power of the State and the freedom of Christians to form their own institutions

---

50. See Hinze, "*Quadragesimo Anno*," 151–74.

51. Pius XI, *Divini Redemptoris*, Sec 51.

in civil society. It ensured that economics and morality were not alien to one another in concept or in practice. Social justice according to Pius XI referenced the necessity of private property against the tenets of socialistic thinking, because the right of private ownership not only enabled individuals "to provide for themselves and their families but also that the goods which the Creator destined for the entire family of mankind may through this institution truly serve this purpose."[52] It mentioned the importance of wealth creation to provide a basis for charity and prohibitions against arbitrary wage demands by third-parties "which a business cannot stand without its ruin and consequent calamity to the workers."[53] Pius XI's definition of social justice included the importance of subsidiarity and a return to moral formation so that people would not confuse freedom to do good with passions that have been disordered because of original sin.

Social justice as a concept has not been a problem per se, but rather the problem lies in how it is defined. What we can say, based on historical reflection, is that any Christian articulation of social justice that seeks to hand the poor over to government for dependency and control is antithetical to the concept of justice within the history of Christianity.

Practicing True Diversity

Some argue that American evangelicalism is in the midst of a cultural identity crisis. When the term "evangelical" is used, it commonly references white suburban contexts. This is why the key leaders who speak at most evangelical conferences are mostly white males, with the exception of the exact same black guys—Tony Evans, Thabiti Anyabwile, Voddie Baucham, and a couple of others—who are, at times, used to show "diversity." There are usually no Asians or Latinos represented.

Many hope that evangelicalism in America would reflect more of the global realities of Christianity, and Soong-Chan Rah is emerging as an evangelical leader poised to help evangelicals think more about the new racial diversity realities for American Christianity. Rah is the author of *Many Colors: Cultural Intelligence for a Changing Church*, which is the follow-up to the award-winning *The Next Evangelicalism: Freeing the Church from Western Cultural Captivity*.

The United States is currently undergoing the most rapid demographic shift in its history. By 2050, white Americans will no longer make up a majority of the population. As the American population demographics

52. Pius XI, *Quadragesimo Anno*, Sec 45.

53. Ibid., paragraph 72.

shift, the demographics of the American church shifts as well, meaning that American Christianity is becoming more and more ethnically and cultur- ally diverse.

The church in American is at a crossroads. Like the early church in Acts 15, we are challenged by the intersection of gospel and culture. Drawing from Scriptural truths and real life examples, Rah calls for the development of cultural intelligence to address new social-cultural realities.

Many Colors follows up with a challenge to churches to develop skills, attitudes, and approaches to ministry that equip churches to engage the new cultural dynamics. The book explores the need to learn about our (often- times negative) cultural and racial histories, to learn about different power dynamics at work, to explore ranges of cultural expressions, to develop ways of thinking beyond the linear, and to develop cultural intuition. The book also offers practical suggestions to seek ways to honor the presence of God in the different cultures found in the American church.

Many Colors is designed to spur individuals, churches, and parachurch ministries toward more effectively bearing witness to the gospel of Jesus Christ, the Good News for people of every racial and cultural background. Its message is positive; its potential impact, transformative.

From Boys to Men

With a trembling coffee mug filled with water, I walked into a classroom of ninth-graders in the fall of 1999 completely unaware that my life would never be the same. I was in graduate school and accepted a part-time po- sition teaching the Old Testament at Philadelphia-Montgomery Christian Academy near the City of Brotherly Love. I don't usually use language like this, because it is the worst of "Christianese" and is terribly cheesy, but my opportunity to walk closely with eight young men in the years that followed was definitely "a God thing" and has profoundly influenced my life and career.

What we initiated is probably only possible within the context of a Christian school. A ninth-grade history teacher and I decided to create a men's Bible study for our students because we noticed that the feminization of church was churning out a generation of "nice guys" who were not capable of leading, had no sense of why God created them to be men—other than have a family and a nice job—and were oddly passive. The ninth-grade boys would walk the halls with heads bowed and shoulders slouched as if they were carrying 80-pound weights in each hand as their bodies were carried along by an airport terminal moving sidewalk. As teachers, we decided to do something because these guys represented the future of the church.

We announced that there was an open meeting for a men's Bible study to talk about what it meant to be a Godly man. We envisioned that the room would be bustling with boys from broken families and fatherless homes who knew they needed help. To our utter surprise, after a couple of weeks of conversations about piety, purity, and perspiration over the complexities of life, what remained were about eight guys who were sons of pastors, elders, and churches leaders. Solid families. Godly families. Churched beyond belief. Confused, passive, and without vision.

We met every Friday during the school year for three years straight during lunch. We frequently got together during the summers as well. Unlike youth ministry, the other teacher and I were with these guys every day in the classroom, in the hallways, at sports practices, etc. I moved away after their junior year, but these young men continued to meet for accountability and prayer on Saturday nights on their own initiative during their senior year of high school. To this day, I've never encountered high school guys with that sort of dedication. High school senior guys meeting on Saturday nights for Christ? Who does that?

Since 1999 I have had the privilege of remaining in close contact with these men. For example, some of us met up for a reunion weekend at the Jersey Shore. At that point they averaged 25 years of age, and I couldn't have been more proud of the men that they've become. I've been blessed to walk with them through the soul-searching college years, a few weddings, new questions and confusions about their faith, major career decisions, and more. Over that weekend I told them how much I have been blessed because of their presence in my life. Nearly all of my research and writing about the church being what God intends her to be derives from my walking through life with them since 1999.

I had no idea that walking into a classroom to teach students about the character of God in the Old Testament 11 years ago would lead to me having stuffed clams and fried Oreos on the boardwalk in Seaside Park, N.J., in 2010 with the same men who are now showing me that God's precepts are true, alive, and active. Christian community is amazing.

Progressive Christianity

After appearing on Glenn Beck's Fox News program in July 2010, I received a considerable amount of criticism from "progressive" Christians for appearing on a show hosted by a man challenging Christianity's connection to a particular type of socialistic understanding of social justice. Black liberation theology certainly had its historical moment, but many assume that critics miss that point because they are too traditional. For example, on the Union Theological Seminary blog, Preston Davis criticized Beck (and me) by arguing that liberation theology should be appreciated because of its historic influence:

> Most of us understand that Christianity and any religious expression comes into contact with historical contexts. Glenn Beck doesn't. I won't spend this time arguing with his simplified, antiquated form of Christianity he learned from the Acton Institue[sic] and its Anthony Bradly[sic].[54]

Perhaps my "antiquated" form of Christianity does not have space in a seminary community that, some would argue, sees one part of Christian engagement to be the whole of Christian identity. For example, the mission of Union Theological Seminary is stated as such on their website:

> Union Theological Seminary in the City of New York is a seminary and a graduate school of theology established in 1836 by founders 'deeply impressed by the claims of the world upon the church.' Union prepares women and men for committed lives of service to the church, academy, and society. A Union education develops practices of mind and body that foster intellectual and academic excellence, social justice, and compassionate wisdom. Grounded in the Christian tradition and responsive to the needs of God's creation, Union's graduates make a difference wherever they serve.[55]

After reading this my first question was, "What role does the Bible play?" Thankfully, educating leaders for the church ought to be a dominant part of the mission of any school calling itself a seminary. But the work of "social justice" is an expectation of the church only in juxtaposition with the teaching of the gospel. I don't know any Christians who support injustice, but it's important that we define justice. What are the elements of justice? Social justice is a natural consequence of the movement of the Kingdom of Jesus Christ through His church in society. What is antiquated, it seems to me, is seeking to pursue justice broadly and not have it grounded it anything transcendentally authoritative. The "Christian tradition" is not enough.

54. This text can no longer be found online, as the Union Theological Seminary Blog no longer exists. July 21, 2010.

55. "Mission & Vision." Union Theological Seminary.

By way of comparison, the mission statement of Westminster Theological Seminary, my alma mater, is a truly progressive approach oriented around the revolutionary and culturally subversive power of the Bible for the whole person and all of life: "Westminster Theological Seminary exists to form Christian leaders to proclaim the whole counsel of God throughout a changing world."

To achieve the mission, Westminster is committed to the core values that have changed the world and provided the basis for the liberation of millions from the power of the devil as well as structural oppression, including:

- "The triune God, Father, Son, and Holy Spirit, is worthy of the worship of *all people in all places of His dominion* and this fact must be the fundamental motive for every human activity."

- "Scripture, as *the very Word of God written,* is absolutely authoritative and without error."

- "A fundamental mandate of the church, discipling the nations for the glory of Christ, requires culturally sensitive, theologically competent ministers who have both the ability and the passion to apply *the eternal word* of Scripture to *the changing world*" in which God has placed us."

- "A learned ministry set in the lifestyle of humble and *holy affection* for Jesus Christ is essential in today's church and world and must be modeled by the board, administration, faculty, and students."[56]

Proclaiming "the whole counsel" of God with these commitments means that Christian leaders are compelled to orient all of life according to God's revelation of Himself for our personal lives as well as for society. The whole counsel of God includes more than the book of Exodus, the prophetical books, chapter 2 of Acts, and the gospels. If we truly want to do justice to humanity as Christians we must preach to the whole person and the whole society the entirety of God's Word as it was delivered to us. The whole counsel of God is about loving God with all one's being and loving one's neighbor. The whole counsel is for the whole person's heart, mind, soul, and strength. This is progressive Christianity.

56. "Mission Statement," Westminster Theological Seminary, lines 10-30.

White In-flight Hipsters vs
White Flight Suburban Evangelicals

Young evangelicals have made their initial descent into urban areas all over America, bringing their hipster culture and paternalism toward minorities along with them. Brett McCracken's book *Hipster Christianity: When Church and Cool Collide* presents an overview of these baby-boomer hipster children and their vision for Christianity.[57] Writers like McCracken and Soong-Chan Rah remind us that the hipster Christian movement may not be as cutting-edge and progressive as it sounds. Instead of avoiding minorities—as suburbanites are often charged with doing—hipster Christians are simply colonizing them.[58]

There seems to be much celebration about new church plants in "the city," but it doesn't really seem like much is actually changing in terms of how these new churches look demographically. For example, suburban church parishioners are said to have fled the city to get away from minorities, i.e., "white flight." Hipster Christians talk about wanting to live among minorities but are gentrifying the neighborhoods in the process and really don't care. Both groups mainly worship with other whites just like them. White "in-flight" is purging the city of minorities and driving the underclass to the suburbs. These white in-flight Christians often have paternalistic visions bringing redemption to the poor little brown natives who currently inhabit neighborhoods with houses needing renovation. And their inflated hipster egos portray the city as a place that needs them desperately.

White flight church pastors may be clean-cut white males wearing khakis pants and sweater vests. White in-flight hipster pastors are also white males who might have piercings (or at least had them at some point) and maybe even a tattoo. They drink high-end alcoholic beverages and occasionally smoke cloves or imported cigars. They still may be surfers or skateboarders and at one time played in an indie band before a growing appreciation for folk and international music developed.

White-flight suburban churches may sing hymns exclusively or appreciate Nashville's contemporary Christian music scene. The suburban worship leader is a soft-spoken white guy playing music that seems to be nothing more than love ballads to Jesus, asking Him to "hold us close" or confessing Jesus' beauty. White in-flight worship leaders are also soft-spoken white guys (or gals) with slightly unkempt hair and tight jeans of various colors, and are all about "liturgy." Horned-rimmed glasses, scruffy

57. See Olasky, "Notable Books."
58. For further reading, see Rah, *Next Evangelicalism*.

beards, and plaid shirts abound, while they lead the congregation in Christian songs to an indie-rock cadence.

White flight churches served as a refuge for the middle class. White in-flight churches are destinations for formerly suburban young evangelicals fleeing Wal-Mart and Target country only to bring Trader Joe's, Whole Foods, organic coffee shops, and organic grocery stores to "da hood." They are also middle class. White in-flight Christians move into black and Latino neighborhoods, and instead of joining churches that are already there, hipsters plant churches—for "theological" reasons—for people who are just as cool as they are. Suburban churches are built around the family. Hipsters are too into birth-control for family, so children are traded-off for "justice," "the arts," and "serving the poor."

I could go on, but suffice it to say that suburban Christians should not accept the finger-pointing by the cool, hipster Christians who are, in fact, living out the same sociology in a different ZIP code. Hipster churches are just as culturally homogenous as their parents' churches but with a twist of "cool." Protestants are skillful fad chasers. We need a vision of remaining in neighborhoods regardless of who moves in or out. Jesus, come quickly.

When Wounds Layer

A very wise man told me recently that at some point in life most people experience pain inflicted by others. Some experience being hurt deeply multiple times. My sage friend cautioned me against the idea that forgiving those who hurt me makes the pain disappear. It's quite the opposite, he says. Past wounds hurt us. They affect us deeply. Over time we get better at handling pain, but it is rare that offenses that hurt us are simply forgotten. To make matters worse, new offenses at the hands of others stack on top of past hurts. The layering of wounds can lead to hypersensitivity or callousness. Time does not heal all wounds. Not even "the Gospel" makes the pain disappear. The presence of the Trinity, however, is actively at work to give a proper framework for living with pain caused by others.

The wounds we receive eventually develop scabs in most cases. These scabs, however, are so fragile that additional experiences of pain can set us off when they irritate past hurtful experiences. We can respond irrationally and often fail to connect the dots between our reactions and our past. Because this wound layering happens to all of us, if we're honest, it gives us permission to see people who hurt us in a new light. Perhaps the person who hurt you acted out in sinful response to past pain. This is not an excuse but it may help render the offending person not to be as gutless as imagined.

"I'm not your mother so don't direct your anger at me," calmly says Sarah, Brent's wife. Sarah and Brent were in the middle of an argument about something relatively minor. Brent, becoming increasingly angry and irrational, began to yell at his wife. Knowing that her husband was raised in a home with an emotionally abusive mother, she looked at him and reminded him that his overreaction was tied to his unresolved anger toward a mother who hurt him repeatedly. He was yelling at his mother by yelling at Sarah. Sarah did not get angry. This is an amazing woman. She saw her husband in light of his layered wounds. In submission to his wife he confessed to her accuracy, apologized, and repented.

This wise friend helped me see that the severity of my reactions to new hurts inflicted by others are related to old ones, just like Brent's initial reaction to his wife. My problem is that I often pursue a sinful response rather than a response that drives me to God. David, for example, was a man wounded and betrayed many times over. In Psalm 69:29, David simply prays, "I am in pain and distress; may your salvation, O God, protect." David's words encourage us to place our wounds in His hands. God's sovereignty over life's issues brings freedom.

Mishandling Twenty-somethings

Most churches have no idea what to do with spiritually mature men in their 20s, so they wrongly direct them to seminary or to a ministry with kids, hoping these guys will rub off on the youth and keep them coming to church and out of trouble. The consequences of this mishandling have been dire. On the one hand, the ones sent to seminary graduate and move on from formal ministry within five to seven years to do what it was they really wanted to do before the confusion started. On other hand, you have guys who are sent into youth ministry having no discernible gifts, training, or experience in discipling younger brothers and sisters in the faith. This tends to result in these young men functioning as nothing more than "babysitters." They are charismatic, like to hang out, play guitar, and are available. That's good enough for many churches. Both scenarios, however, can represent poor stewardship.

I am pained, for example, by the number of guys directed to seminary or formal ministry who never should have been because church communities were confused about what is normal for men in the church. I have several friends from my seminary days who are now not only out of vocational ministry altogether but also working in vocations that are completely disconnected from the church. Many are finally, at nearly 40 years old, working in vocations that they originally set out to do before they were misdirected by the whispers of church people who confuse spiritual maturity and vibrancy in young men with a "call to ministry." This trend actually reveals the sad state of an American evangelical gynocentric church: Spiritually interested young men are the exception rather than the expectation. These men tend to stand out because their twentysomething male peers are generally absent in most churches and many of the others present are going through religious motions, attending because of parental legalism, or because of girlfriend or wife pressure. This vocational mismatch is actually not good for the church because it can put leaders in positions they should not be in and usually negatively affects the entire church community in the long-run. We can avoid this.

When a younger brother says to me that "he feels called to ministry," I usually understand that to mean that he craves and needs validation and would like to use the church to make him feel good about himself. Or even worse, as Leon Podles explains in his book *The Church Impotent: The Feminization of Christianity*, many young men feel called to the church because uninitiated men find the church to be "a safe field, a refuge from the challenges of life and therefore attracts men who are fearful of making a break with the secure world of childhood dominated by women."[59]

Whatever the reason, it would be great to see local churches so healthy and full of twentysomethings that the presence of spiritually vibrant twentysomething men would be so normal that we would have better criteria for sending men into ministry beyond being "on fire for Christ" and having a desire to teach and serve. That should be simply normal for any man following Jesus.

Is Your Church Rah Certified?

Christianity in America is declining among whites but flourishing in ethnic and immigrant communities. This mirrors an international trend. Soong-Chan Rah, the Milton B. Engebretson associate professor of Church Growth and Evangelism at North Park Theological Seminary in Chicago, is preparing American evangelicals for a future global Christianity that will primarily be led by Asians, Africans, and Latin Americans. In his book, *The Next Evangelicalism: Freeing the Church from Western Cultural Captivity*, Rah argues that Christianity has shifted from the white and Western culture to Africa, Asia, and Latin America. As such, unless white Christians begins

59. Podles, *The Church Impotent*, xiv.

to embrace multi-ethnicity as the new paradigm for the local church, their churches will not survive another generation.

I call the embracing of this global reality as concomitant with "Rah certification." I fully understand that many people live in homogeneous communities where multi-ethnicity is not as easily realized as it is near large cities. Rural communities tend to not be as diverse as urban ones. For others, however, living in or near cities and not having multi-ethnic church leaders and members may be a recipe for extinction. In 1900, Europe and North America accounted for 82 percent of the world's Christian population. By 2005, that number was down to 39 percent. To date 60 percent of world's Christians are in Africa, Asia, and Latin America. Moreover, by 2023, half of America's children will be non-white. As these trends continue, America will likely have a white minority by 2050.

Rah notes in his book, and on video,[60] that today's evangelical church became enmeshed in the last 50 years or so with secular values like individualism, consumerism, and racism. According to Rah, in the last 50 years or so evangelicals have turned Christianity into a "me-centered" faith where people concerned primarily with their personal relationships with Jesus and their individual families while ignoring the social dimensions of the gospel's work in local communities. Evangelicals tend to embrace a materialistic and consumerist expression of faith, where families church hop to find the best youth programs or pursue the idols of comfort, ease, and professional success in comfortable church buildings. From the 1950s through 2000, evangelicalism grew significantly on the heels of "white flight" away from "liberals" and minorities. Suburban Christian schools grew. Suburban churches grew. Some churches even moved entire congregations out of cities to the suburbs to get away from minorities.

Because of the changing demographics in America, the death of Christianity in Western Europe, the steady decline of Christianity among whites in America, Rah certification means that your church and denomination needs to abandon an individualistic, consumerist, materialistic, white flight-oriented vision of the gospel to one that seeks to develop multi-ethnic leaders and congregations wherever possible in light of the church's future (Revelation 5:9). Rah certification means that you pray and hope for your church and denomination to have multi-ethnic leaders in the near future and you are willing to invest in that reality. Rah's is an important concern: Are white Christians in the United States and Europe ready to submit to the spiritual authority of Africans, Asians, and Latin Americans or immigrants,

60. Rah, "The Next Evangelicalism," 1:00:41.

Asian Americans, Latinos, or African Americans? According to Rah, they should get ready, because the future is now.

If Platt's *Radical* was Radical

Is it really "radical" to encourage Christians to not be attached to their stuff, preach the gospel, and give to the poor? Or do these topics really represent the "milk" described in Hebrews (5:12-14)? Is evangelism and helping the poor the new legalism? I asked these questions after reading David Platt's good book *Radical: Taking Back Your Faith From the American Dream.*

Using Christianity as a means of achieving comfort, safety, ease, and professional success has certainly poisoned the missional spirit of many Christians. But while Platt rightly calls this syncretism sin, in the end readers are left with nothing more than a "compassionate revivalist" Christianity that fails to radically call Christians to live in harmony with God's desire to redeem the entire creation. The book seems to be a sampling of the revivalist Shaker movement during the Second Great Awakening, which called Christians to renounce material attachments for an "authentic Christianity."[61]

Admittedly, I am biased. I'm a Reformed theologian who understands the biblical story in terms of creation, fall, redemption, and restoration.[62] Revivalist Christians understand the Bible's chief narrative in terms of sin, repentance, faith, and disciple-making, and Revivalism is usually associated with American fundamentalism. Reducing the mission of the Kingdom to evangelism tends to discourage Christians from pressing the claims of Christ into renewing and creating culture.[63] For example, many revivalist evangelical preachers of the 19th and 20th centuries engaged in powerful evangelism while neglecting to fight against racial segregation after slavery was abolished.

Platt takes an appropriate sledgehammer to Christians who have refashioned Jesus into a middle-class, comforting and loving nice guy who hides in suburbia to avoid Samaritans, as well as to those who ignore the needs of the poor and serve the idols of self-advancement, self-esteem, individualism, materialism, and universalism. He nails the deadly consequences of these trends. However, if Platt wants to launch a radical movement, the following issues, at minimum, need attention:

---

61. For more see Rah and Streich, "Second Great Awakening."

62. For more see Wolters, *Creation Regained.*

63. For more see Crouch, *Culture Making.*

1. Christians are called to be more than disciple-makers. The fall of Adam and Eve affected more than people. The effects of the fall are seen in the entire creation (Genesis 3:14-24). The whole creation is active in the drama of sin entering the world. As such, Jesus came to reconcile all things in creation to himself (Romans 8:19-22; Colossians 3:15-20). In fact, Mark quotes Jesus as telling the disciples, "Go into all the world and proclaim the gospel to the whole creation" (Mk 16:15). Disciple-making is a major part of the cosmic redemptive mission of God, but the work of the Kingdom transforms people, places, and things. Redemption in Christ reaches as far as the Fall in terms of culture and the arts, business, education, politics, law, entertainment, and so on. Platt fails to call Christians to press the claims of Christ wherever the devil is working.

2. Materialism is not exclusively a middle-class problem. It's universal. Rich and poor alike struggle with ungodly attachments to stuff. Materialism is a condition of the heart not endemic to any particular socio-economic class. A homeless person can be just as materialistic as a wealthy person. The prosperity gospel would neither be attractive to wealthy people nor poor people if *all people* did not struggle with viewing blessings in material terms. In fact, materialism can be the very thing that drives frugality. Therefore, a Gnostic avoidance of material enjoyment, combined with the reduction of serving the poor to cutting one's own consumption, does not create the conditions for a radical Christianity that shapes social mores.

3. "White Messiah" Christianity? Inadvertently, Platt encourages the "White Messiah" neo-paternalism common among justice-oriented younger evangelicals. Nearly all of Platt's illustrations of living radically to help the poor are of white evangelicals going to the "inner-city," or some developing country of non-Caucasians, to find the helpless brown, yellow, needy, and ignorant natives who need white Christians to solve their problems. A truly radical approach would also send Christians to wherever the devil is destroying God's good creation (1 John 3:8)—in trailer parks, Western Europe, Australia, rural America, and the suburbs. Christians follow Christ wherever the curse is found. For example, according to census data from 2014, 73 percent of America's poor population is white while 18 percent is black,[64] but you wouldn't know that from reading Platt.

64. DeNavas-Walt and Proctor, "Income and Poverty in the United States, 2013," 12.

4. Aid and charity do not help the poor in the long-run. Platt encourages Christians to cap their lifestyles and give aid to causes and organizations that are gospel-centered, church-focused, and specific. Creating wealth in poor countries, however, demands economic and political reform as well. Giving aid while not applying the gospel to social structures will not help the poor holistically. A more radical approach encourages Christians to work at all levels of sustainable economic development because evil exists in those sectors as well. Short-term visions are not radical. Platt's simplistic connection of the gospel to poverty does not address the differentiated issues connecting the poor to God's will on earth as it is in Heaven.

5. Where's the love? I was hoping that the language of love would permeate the book since Jesus named love as the greatest commandment (Matthew 22:36-40). What releases people from loving the American Dream is radical obedience motivated by love in order to love others justly. Before going to the "inner city" we must be challenged to articulate what it means to love God and others to avoid hurting people we intend to help. Also, Platt mentions the role of baptism in connection to radical obedience, but what truly demonstrates the radical scope of missional love are the implications of the Lord's Supper for Christian engagement with culture.

The book concludes by encouraging readers to live radically for one year but does not provide readers with a model of sustainable spiritual formation in the primary forms of love, like justice, mercy, and faithfulness (Matthew 23:23), nor the cardinal virtues like prudence (James 1:5), fortitude (1 Corinthians 16:13), self-discipline (2 Timothy 1:7), and humility (1 Peter 5:5). God calls us to live radically for cosmic redemption, but to do so with wisdom and discernment. To be fair, Platt's book is not intended to be a theology textbook and seems intended to be an introduction. A book this short will miss a lot by virtue of its length. My above critiques notwithstanding, *Radical* will remain a powerful revivalist challenge to those of us who are Reformed and tend to get so caught up in restoring creation that we forget that Jesus does expect us to spread the gospel in word as well as in deed.

The Suburbanization of Social Justice

The social justice Christians flocking to cities may be too late. Where were they in the 1960s, '70s, and '80s? By 2008, the suburbs had become home to the largest and fastest-growing poor population in the country, according to a 2010 Brookings Institution study.[65] In the near future, the more progressive justice-oriented Christians will be in the suburbs, rather than in the city. Perhaps American Christians concerned about the poor should stop chasing poverty, plant themselves in whatever neighborhood they find themselves, and love whomever comes and goes as housing trends change over time.

Many Christians equate poverty with "inner city" or "urban" areas populated by black people, which is nothing less than factually inaccurate, patronizing, and, some would argue, racist. This wrongheaded caricature overlooks the reality that poverty in America is predominantly suburban, rural, and white. According to census data from 2014, 73 percent of America's poor population is white while 18 percent is black. Why then does "the poor" have a black or brown face? Even though a larger percentage of the black population is poor compared to whites, for poverty to be associated primarily with blacks in the inner city may suggest a latent white-messiah, neo-paternalist mentality among those who believe their "whiteness" is what black people in the inner city need. Because there are rarely, if ever, calls for Christians to flock to suburban and/or rural contexts to help "the poor," one wonders if all this justice talk has more to do with race patronization than "poverty," as some would argue.

I'm not saying that cities do not have real needs or that these trends are seen equally in every major city in the United States at the moment. Sound economic thinking, however, reminds us that supply and demand follow people with disposable income, hence the reality of gentrification and the suburbanization of poverty. Organizations like the Christian Community Development Association will need to radically rethink their rhetoric about social justice and its "relocation" principles in an America where poverty is suburban, rural, and white.

Is it not likely that many evangelicals flocking to cities for justice are actually going there as consumers, using "justice" as an excuse to live in "cool" places? Loving the city is different than loving the actual people in that city. City governments prefer yuppies and hipsters to the poor, so new housing, retail, and entertainment opportunities are making former "ghetto" neighborhoods attractive, while shifting lower income people to the suburbs. According to Brookings:

> Between 2000 and 2008, suburbs in the country's largest metro areas saw their poor population grow by 25 percent— almost five times faster than primary cities and well ahead of the growth seen in smaller metro areas and non-metropolitan

65. For more see Garr and Kneebone, "The Suburbanization of Poverty."

communities. As a result, by 2008 large suburbs were home to 1.5 million more poor than their primary cities and housed almost one-third of the nation's poor overall.[66]

This new trend teaches us that "relocation" as a principle of justice is not necessary and may not always be what is most needed. It also tends not to consider the long-term economics of poverty trends nor the generational housing pattern shifts. Moreover, "the poor" never represent a static community. People move in and out of poverty, and Christians constantly moving to find them could discover rehabbed apartments, Whole Foods, Starbucks, and sushi restaurants right where the poor used to reside.

In end, if you're a suburban social justice-minded Christian, you don't need to move to the city to find "the poor," because they are coming to an apartment complex, trailer park, or other subsidized form of housing near you. Are suburbanites ready to receive them? Moving to the city is great and you don't need to appeal to justice to sanctify it. Seriously. What's wrong with moving to the city for the consumption of cultural options and opportunities, to save on auto expenses, and to live more efficiently? Besides, most cities could use the beautification and economic face-lift that gentrification brings.

The Elements of Social Justice

There is much rhetoric about social justice, but few frameworks for sustainable economic empowerment and liberation for the truly disadvantaged. Whatever one's conception of justice is, it must be applied in a way that does not do more harm in the name of "doing good." Without an integrated synthesis of theology, anthropology, and economics, as Abraham Kuyper explained in 1891 in *The Problem of Poverty*, our conceptions of justice will dehumanize the poor. What I am proposing is a basic structure for social justice that can move us toward sustainable empowerment.

1. Love. It is not random that Jesus' first word when he was asked about the greatest commandment was "love." Jesus makes a simple, yet profound re-statement (Deuteronomy 6:5; Leviticus 19:18) that a human's greatest vocation is to love God and his neighbor as one loves himself. Love properly orders our affections, desires, and actions so that we seek the good. Love, then, must be the presupposition of social justice so that our conception of justice is in harmony with the will of the Triune God. (Matthew 22:36-40)

66. Garr and Kneebone, "Suburbanization of Poverty," lines 1-7.

2. Human dignity. There will be no justice for the truly disadvantaged without a commitment to human dignity. In Genesis 1:26, God says, "Let us make mankind in our image." The image of the Trinity is imprinted upon every human. When you see another person, you see the goodness of being made in the image and likeness of God. The truly disadvantaged should be directed toward realizing the freedom and responsibility, the spirituality, the excellence of character and holiness, the expected contribution to the social good, and the application of creativity and rationality in the arts and culture that are necessary consequences of bearing the image of the Triune God.

3. Solidarity. Solidarity reminds us that we are all in this together. We are truly responsible for each other's wellbeing. There is no "us" versus "them." There are only "we" and "us." The *Compendium on the Social Doctrine of the Church* reminds us that solidarity highlights in a particular way the intrinsic social nature of humans made in the image of the Trinity. Therefore, "the equality of all and the dignity and rights and the common path of individuals and peoples moves towards an ever more committed unity."[67]

4. Flourishing Social Spheres. Pope John Paul II explained in *Centesimus Annus* a vital principle called subsidiarity that weds human dignity with solidarity. When thinking about social justice, the principle of subsidiarity must be respected, namely, "a community of a higher order should not interfere in the internal life of a community of a lower order, depriving the latter of its functions, but rather should support it in case of need and help to coordinate its activity with the activities of the rest of society, always with a view to the common good."[68]

   Additionally, Kuyper developed an idea called "sphere sovereignty," which reminds us "that the family, the business, science, art and so forth are all social spheres, which do not owe their existence to the state, and which do not derive the law of their life from the superiority of the state, but obey a high authority within their own bosom; an authority which rules, by the grace of God, just as the sovereignty of the state does."[69] In other words, it is a violation of human solidarity and human dignity for higher orders of society to undermine and violate the functions of lower orders, as well as for spheres to extend beyond their expertise, competence, or design into other spheres.

67. "Compendium of the Social Doctrine of the Church," Pontifical Council for Justice and Peace, Sec. 192.

68. John Paul II, *Centesimus Annus*, Sec. 49.

69. Witte and Alexander, *Teachings of Modern Christianity*, 318.

5. Desert. Who or what determines what the truly disadvantaged deserve? This depends on how we care about those who are suffering, what we think about them as humans, and what we expect from people relationally. If we love people and seek their good, what people deserve are opportunities live out their vocations as human beings—having freedom to do the things that humans were created to do. This includes freedom from surrogate decision-makers for the development of moral virtue and also freedom to loose oneself in the good.

6. Reciprocity. David Schmidtz, a professor of philosophy and a joint professor of economics at the University of Arizona, coined a profound justice principle called "transitive reciprocity." Transitive reciprocity teaches that the response to help is to pass it on by helping someone else. Schmidtz said, "When people reciprocate, they teach people around them to cooperate. In the process, they not only respect justice, but also foster it. Specifically, they foster a form of justice that enables people to live together in mutually respectful peace."[70]

7. Equality. What does "equality" mean? Do we want a society that considers equality on the basis of treatment in accordance with human dignity? Or do we want a society that orients equality materialistically in terms of how much "stuff" some people have versus others? If justice is essentially material, then we will institutionalize injustice in the pursuit of "equality" of portions or shares between the "haves" and "have nots." We will regularly rob Peter to pay Paul.

8. Need. Unfortunately, "need" is culturally defined in a world where yesterday's luxuries have become today's necessities. Schmidtz argues that need-based distribution is not always what justice requires. Distributing according to need does not necessarily result in people being treated with dignity. "If we care about need—if we really care—then we want social structures to allow and encourage people to do what works," said Schmidtz. What the truly disadvantaged need is a context in which they are free to be truly human and virtuous in accordance with love, human dignity, solidarity, and our social and economic interdependence—that is, economic empowerment.

Because Christians tend to emote about justice instead of building sustainable frameworks that liberate and empower the poor to be fully human, well-intentioned people and organizations like T.D. Jakes, Cornel West, Jim Wallis, Shane Claiborne, most Christian "urban ministry" programs, the CCDA, and the Micah Challenge support wealth redistribution

70. Schmidtz, Elements of Justice, 79.

programs and policies that enslave people to permanent charity, dead aid, or government programs instead of initiatives that empower and liberate the poor to make their own virtuous contributions to helping the world become a better place without the patronization of surrogate decision-makers. Justice should lead to freedom.

When Conservative Denominations Decline

If your denomination is 25-years-old or older, it is has likely peaked and plateaued in terms of numbers and influence—unless you are from a Pentecostal or Charismatic tradition. The pace of social change is faster in our era than ever before and denominations cannot keep up. As denominations grow, they become slower, more bureaucratic, less creative, and less innovative. Denominations increasingly become centered on preserving their institutions while ignoring needed reforms to address social change. As such, the generation that initially grew the denomination becomes the primary target audience. As that population ages and become culturally leveraged, so follows the denomination they helped to grow.

Recent movements built on baby-boomers are plateauing and will experience future decline. Younger leaders with creative and innovative ideas in these denominations tend to be viewed as threats against the forms and methods of the past. This desire to conserve past forms and methods is often confused as orthodoxy. Are denominations, then, partly responsible for the decline in confessional Christianity in America?

Dr. John Frame, the J.D. Trimble Chair of Systematic Theology and Philosophy at Reformed Theological Seminary, writes about the trouble with denominationalism is his book *Evangelical Reunion*. Frame argues that the three major forms of church government—congregational, episcopal, Presbyterian—"require for their best implementation the organizational unity of the church and the elimination of denominations." This does not mean that non-denominational churches are preferred but that denominations don't have biblical support and tend to impair the ability of the church to affect society over time, Frame argues.

There is increasing concern about the shorter shelf-life that denominations have in our globalized and rapidly changing world. Listening to Mark Driscoll, founding pastor at Mars Hill Church in Seattle, deliver a 2009 presentation about the Acts 29 Network ("We Are a Movement") led me to ask new questions like "Has my own denomination peaked?" Driscoll speaks about the unfortunate cycle of Christian movements becoming museums. First, movements start with radical change and innovation. For example, a response to changes in culture or a desire for maintaining biblical orthodoxy can create a movement. Secondly, as a movement grows and gathers followers, there is a need to organize. Theology develops, leaders emerge, names are chosen, vision statements are created, and so on. Third, movements mature and become institutions. Institutions have structure, order, governance, and controls that emerge to reproduce desired behaviors to preserve a particular institutional culture. Fourth, movements become museums when their self-preservation distracts them from keeping up with addressing culture. They become irrelevant. Museums, says Driscoll, have pastors who are simply "curators" of the organization telling stories about people who did great things in the past.

In Driscoll's framework, your conservative denomination will become a museum if the following occurs: It fails to recontextualize the Gospel as needed according to shifts in culture; it becomes theologically focused on heresy hunting by making nonessential beliefs into the litmus test of orthodoxy; creates a "good ole boy" network so that younger leaders cannot have a respectable voice unless they know the right people; it makes an idol out of methods and preferences by attaching proof-texts to desires and calling those "orthodox"; it refuses to learn from and associate with Christians who are not in their tradition; it refuses to adopt ideas developed outside their tradition; or it abandons the Gospel and biblical orthodoxy altogether. For a tutorial on decline simply look at all of the denominations and movements that were birthed in Western Europe during the Reformation. They have no influence today. Will the same thing happen in America?

I'm not suggesting that denominations do not have a significant role to play in the Kingdom. Denominations can provide great resources for the church. I am wondering, however, if denominations may be a large factor in making Christianity culturally irrelevant when they do not radically reform methods while remaining faithful to the faith once delivered for every generation. Instead of changing for the better, many denominations simply split into new institutions that tend to influence one generation before the next group plateaus, becomes irrelevant, or splits again. The cycle continues and, in the meantime, the lost are not reached with the Gospel. Perhaps, then, progressive missional movements are needed outside of formal denominational structures for every generation so the church is reminded of her mission.

Farewell Emerging Church (1989-2010)

Reading a new book or going to a conference about the emerging church is a waste of time and money unless it's to understand the movement as a recent historical one. The emerging church movement has ended. Andrew Jones, a leader of the movement in the U.K., wrote about the demise at the end of 2009.[71] Rob Bell, the founding pastor of Mars Hill Bible Church in Grand Rapids, Mich., delivered an April 4, 2010 sermon on the Resurrection that marks, in my opinion, the end of an era. Bell recounted how Mars Hill started out to be a different kind of church without the baggage of watered-down "seeker" churches and the religious legalism of "traditional" churches. In a moment of wonderful honesty Bell admitted that Mars Hill had become a big institution that wounded people in similar ways as the churches many Gen-Xers swore they would not mimic. Jones affirms much of Bell's experience on his blog.

From Brian McLaren to Erwin McManus to Rob Bell to Tony Jones to Mark Driscoll and others, the theological lines have been drawn and are settled. We have all moved on. We know who fits into evangelicalism, post-liberalism, Anabaptism, Calvinism, and so on. If you are interested in the emerging movement as church history, pick up a copy of *Emerging Churches: Creating Christian Communities in Postmodern Cultures* by Eddie Gibbs and Ryan Bolger.

Gibbs and Bolger provide a good summary of the short-lived movement:

> Emerging churches are not young adult services, Gen-X church-es, churches-within-a-church, seeker churches, purpose-driven or new paradigm churches, fundamentalist churches, or even evangelical churches. They are a new expression of church. The three core practices are identifying with the life of Jesus, trans-forming secular space, and commitment to community as a way of life. These practices are expressed in or lead to the other six: welcoming the stranger, serving with generosity, participating as producers, creating as created beings, leading as a body, and taking part in spiritual activities.

There is a wonderful obituary for the emerging church for those still concerned that we need to spend time trying to understand it and protect people from it. Don't waste your time.

Bell's April 4 sermon recounts that Mars Hill entered a process of re-thinking everything about itself as it has grown and matured into an

71. Jones, "Emerging Church Movement (1989–2009)?"

institution over the past 11 years. Mars Hill and other churches born out of the emerging church era are no longer new, trendy, "cool," nor innovative. These formerly "cool" churches are full of singles, married couples, growing children, balding middle-age men, and so on, who are all trying to figure out how to live a redemptive life here and now while confronting daily struggles with sin, repentance, grace, loving the poor, marriage, raising children, the recession, ailing parents, etc. Bell is launching a new focus on the implications of the Resurrection. Resurrection signals victory over sin, death, and the devil. Bell's notes read:

> Resurrection announces that God has not given up on the world.
>
> Because this world matters.
>
> This world that we call home.
>
> Dirt and blood and sweat and skin and light and water.
>
> This world that God is redeeming and restoring and renewing.

Jesus is victory. God has a redeemed a people to be his intimate allies in the renewal of all things through the power of the resurrection of Jesus Christ. This is neither provocative nor cutting edge in the Kingdom. This is simply the teaching of the early church oriented around the Nicene Creed.

Because post-modernism as a movement is also dead,[72] as scientific realism[73] has emerged as a recent culture-shaping philosophical movement, the generation of Christians struggling to meet the challenges of post-modernism, instead of yelling at it hoping it would go away, are shifting as well to address a world asking different questions. While the effects of the emerging church movement will linger for some time we will begin to see books praising and attacking the movement go out of print.

"Calling" vs Choice

The abuse of the concept of "calling" creates serious injury to people in the church and can lead to poor or cowardly choices. There is no need to spiritualize good desires. I started thinking about this when a friend told me that he's staying in his current city because he felt "called" there? I thought, "How does he know that?" Does God "call" people to ZIP codes? What is wrong with just saying that you *want* to live somewhere because you like the place? Why spiritualize it?

72. For more see Kirby, "Death of Postmodernism and Beyond."
73. For more see "Scientific Realism" in the *Stanford Encyclopedia of Philosophy*.

For some perspective on this problem I asked a New Testament scholar to reflect on evangelical abuse of "calling." Dr. James A. Meek had this to say:

> Evangelicals have developed an unfortunate habit of seeking and claiming divine direction to a degree that Scripture does not appear to justify. We deceive ourselves by claiming that our wishes and hunches are divine instructions when we have no solid reason (biblical or otherwise) for believing them to be so. But once one person begins talking this way, it's hard not to want to sound as 'spiritual.'
>
> I think what we actually do is to baptize hunches and wishes in the mistaken belief that these represent divine guidance. It's a way of thinking (and talking) that has simply become accepted in many evangelical circles.[74]

Meek went on to say that reducing our hunches and desires to a "calling" saves us the trouble of thinking, drawing on Scriptural principles, and understanding the world; it absolves us of responsibility when things don't work out well. The false spirituality and false humility of "waiting on the Lord" to avoid wrestling over a wise course of action "in the flesh" often results in passively waiting for God to drop something into our laps. Not taking risks, moving forward, or taking decisive action could actually demonstrate cowardice or lack of faith. Dr. Meek said that he's been around long enough to have seen far too many things that "God directed" accomplish nothing. But you can't question failure because "God directed" the action in question.

Here's the bottom line: the Bible simply does not generally use "calling" to justify everyday choices or big-life decisions. There are a few notable exceptions for a few biblical characters. The Bible, however, does not generally use "calling" in terms of vocations, college attendance, numbering children, whom to marry, house purchases, which city or neighborhood to live in, and so on. In fact, the Greek word for "calling" is only used in the New Testament around 11 times, almost always in reference to divine callings related to salvation or callings to live a holy life. This is what it means to "live in God's will." God's "will" may have nothing to do with whether or not one should move to Seattle instead of Chicago but it does have something to do with what kind of person one will be in either Seattle or Chicago, working whatever job one might choose while living in whatever neighborhood one might desire.

Until Christians adopt better language we will continue to set people up for disappointment and theological crises when their "callings" don't

74. Personal correspondence, April 7, 2010.

work out. You do not have to be "called" in order to choose something good. If your choice turns out to be a disaster, it's okay; God is sovereign.

Beyond Racial Reconciliation

New Christian initiatives to reconcile whites and blacks are 50 years too late and outdated. Pioneers like John Perkins and J. Deotis Roberts should be applauded for their work during the 1970s in the area of racial reconciliation among whites and blacks in the aftermath of the civil rights movement. However, in light of today's differentiated multi-ethnic America, reconciliation initiatives focused primarily on past tensions between whites and blacks are as useful as new initiatives attempting to reconcile colonial tensions between Roman Catholics in Maryland and Anglicans in Virginia. Having conferences where the goal is to get whites and blacks to share stories and hug each other remain impotent to address new tensions in America along the axis of race and class.

Perhaps for those born prior to 1960, the same racial tensions they witnessed in childhood may still need space to work out those problems of the past. However, for most of us born after 1970, we simply do not have the same experiential racial history, so we need to be challenged in ways beyond black and white.

America's 2010 demographics—14.4 percent Hispanic/Latino, 12.8 percent black, 4.3 percent Asian[75]—call for ethnic initiatives that move the culture forward. For example, for a church to have a racial mix of whites and blacks nowadays is as impressive as having whites and blacks play football together at the University of Alabama. Big deal. In 1960, when white and black Christians should have been seen as leaders on race relations, a congregation of blacks and whites together would have been radical, but today it doesn't even raise an eyebrow except for those operating in a demographic past.

New tensions that the church has an opportunity to challenge in our culture require creativity and innovation. After moving into a mostly Dominican neighborhood in New York, I have learned about the massive tensions between Dominicans and blacks, Dominicans and Haitians, Puerto Ricans and Dominicans, and so on. Growing up in Atlanta in 1970s and '80s, the nasty and persistent tensions between African-Americans and immigrants from Africa, the Caribbean, and the West Indies are still not addressed. A church mixed with Mexicans and Puerto Ricans, or a church mix of Japanese, Chinese, and Koreans mixed with Vietnamese, and the like,

75. "Population of the United States," Infoplease.

would be impressive. A neighborhood and church with all of above cultures mixed together in various manifestations would be amazing. The only other place in our culture one would see this type of voluntary mixing is the audience at a popular hip-hop concert.

Black and white racial reconciliation efforts also distract us from tensions among classes within ethnic groups. A white middle-class church will "reach out" to blacks in the "inner city" or Mexican immigrants but will ignore white welfare recipients in trailer park communities. Will white middle-class Christians ever have huggy reconciliation conferences with the "white trash" people they often despise and ignore? The black middle-class' similar disdain for "ghetto" blacks is unconscionable and remains unaddressed. The animus that upper-class Dominicans have for "hick" Dominicans is simply inhumane.

In the end, if American Christians really want to show our culture what it means for the nations to come together (Galatians 3:28; Revelation 5:9) we must put the 1970s racial playbook on the shelf and speak to problems within and among races, ethnic groups, and classes however they manifest themselves in our communities, because group isolationism and conflict are not simply black and white.

No Tearless Spirituality

The way of Jesus is the way of tears. While many Christians in Western Europe and North America tend to present a Christianity that rescues and protects us from pain and suffering, Christians in the rest of the world are fully aware that, just as Christ learned obedience through tears and suffering, so will we. Suffering is the rule in the Christian life, not the exception (Hebrews 5:8).

Middle-class Western evangelicals, seduced by the idols of comfort and ease, often sacrifice being "salt and light" on the altar of easy living. The church has a responsibility to teach its children how to endure suffering instead of investing in suffering-avoidance techniques. When suffering comes, we act surprised as if tear-producing pain were absent in the lives of biblical characters like Adam, Abraham, Moses, Joshua, David, Jeremiah, John the Baptist, Jesus, Paul, Peter, John, and so on.

Could a life devoid of tears be a sign of spiritual immaturity or of being lukewarm (Revelation 3:15-16)? If Jesus learned obedience through suffering then so should all of us, including our children. As John Chryssavgis writes in his essay "The Spiritual Way":

> [T]ears are at once a foretaste of death and of resurrection. They are not, as unfortunately they are often perceived, a negative aspect of the spiritual life, a way of merely regretting past sins or ongoing weaknesses. As symbols of imperfection, tears are in fact the sole way of spiritual progress.[76]

Tears signify fragility and woundedness, Chryssavgis suggests, the broken window through which God enters the heart, bringing healing and wholeness to both body and soul. Human shortcomings and human failures should be embraced because they point us to the Triune God. Pain, suffering, and tears present the ultimate opportunity for receiving and appreciating the grace, mercy, and strength of God as are made perfect in weakness (2 Corinthians 12:9).

I'm not saying that we should live recklessly, unwisely, and sinfully in order to create suffering. I only stress the reality that suffering is a normal way of life in the Kingdom.

Theologian Louis Berkhof reminds us that Christ not only suffered on the cross but he also suffered during "his entire life." Perhaps one of the reasons young people walk away from the church is that when they begin to experience the reality of suffering, the Christianity of personal peace and affluence—as Francis Schaeffer once lamented—sterilized and coddled them from the truth that life is hard, and without the Triune God you will not make it. If Christianity has not been presented as the answer to suffering, then what good is it?

Is the Black Church Really Dead?

The black church in America may be lukewarm, but it is not "dead" as suggested in an article by Eddie S. Glaude Jr., the William S. Tod Professor of Religion and chair of the Center for African American Studies at Princeton University. While Glaude offers fantastic observations about the how the black church has lost her way, such analysis is troubling because it reduces what it means to be "alive" to socio-political and "prophetic" activities instead of focusing on moral formation.

Glaude rightly points out that the black church is in trouble, because for one thing, it is not homogenous. Historically, the black church has followed the theological trajectories of other major denominations and theological movements in broader Christianity. The idea that the black church began in a single theological tradition, for example, Reformed, and then

---

76. Chryssavgis, "Spiritual Way," 154.

became "liberal" is something that no black religious scholar would find evidence for. Secondly, black communities are socio-economically diverse, which broadens the need for differentiated applications of Biblical truths. And thirdly, much of the black church's historic prophetic voice to cultural immorality has been neutralized and often viewed only through the lens of history. Additionally, Glaude points out that the explosion of the prosperity megachurches has distracted and derailed many black Christians.

Again, Glaude raises vital matters but sadly dismisses black churches that are protesting genocidal abortion and supporting Judeo-Christian designs for marriage outlined in the biblical story. He wonders why those same protestors are not also speaking out on poverty or supporting a public option in our healthcare reform circus. Glaude does not emphasize enough that the claims of Christ and his Kingdom demand that Christians mediate between moral and social issues. The black church is dead if there is not a call for black people to follow Jesus with all their hearts, minds, souls, and strength. The black church would be doing a huge disservice to black people if she were not vigilant about the morals of human sexuality, the black genocide via abortion, building stable families, and the like, in addition to sociopolitical issues.

The black church, like all churches, must speak to society with a Truth-oriented "both/and." The moral questions are more easily discerned because of what is clear in the biblical text. The social questions, however, call for prudential judgment and may not be so easily defined and should never be reduced to a political party's narrow agenda. For example, maybe some black churches do not support a public option because they recognize that it likely will enslave blacks' healthcare choices, making them susceptible to another "Tuskegee experiment." Maybe some black pastors want blacks to have full and absolute authority over their own healthcare decisions, freeing them from dependence on government telling them what health services and procedures they can and cannot have. Maybe some black pastors are aware that a public "option" is a misnomer because having surrogate decision-makers for the physical bodies of black people will actually limit people's options. Again, these are prudential judgments and cannot be used as a litmus test for what an "alive" black church entails.

In the end, what is needed is for the black church to focus on her dual liberation emphasis: Liberating people from the power of the devil (Acts 10:38) and liberating people from the social structures that destroy human dignity (Proverbs 14:31) are both component parts of being "salt and light" (Matthew 5:13-16) so that God's will for how the world should be can be realized on earth as it is in heaven.

Doing Liturgical Justice to the Trinity

Do evangelical Christians do justice to the Holy Trinity, especially the Holy Spirit, with our "Jesus only" emphasis in worship? Non-evangelicals often criticize the "Jesus only" spirituality on Sundays, as many churches seem to offer little or no adoration to the work of all three persons of the Trinity from Genesis to Revelation. The story of redemption is the story of the work of all three persons of the Trinity. Salvation comes to individuals and the world through the work of the Triune God: Father, Son, and Holy Spirit.

For example, rarely do "Jesus only" Christians pray directly to the Holy Spirit. Rarely do we sing hymns and spiritual songs to the Holy Spirit. Rarely do we rightly assign the enabling work of the Christian life to the actual, real work of the Holy Spirit. Outside of charismatic and Pentecostal circles, there are many who are so "Jesus-centered" that the Holy Spirit may not even be specifically recognized on Sunday in any form. In some circles, it even seems that "grace" is the third person of the Trinity instead of the Holy Spirit.

Many evangelicals seem to forget in their liturgy (if they have one) that it is the Holy Spirit who unites us to Christ (1 Corinthians 12:13; Romans 8-9), regenerates us (John 3:5-8), converts us by bringing us to repentance (Acts 11:15, 18) and granting us faith (1 Corinthians 12:3), assures us of our adoption (Romans 8:16; Galatians 4:6), works to justify us (1 Corinthians 6:11), sanctifies us (2 Thessalonians 2:13;1 Peter 1:2), and perseveres us to glory (Ephesians 1:13-14; 4:30).

Irenaeus strongly emphasized the joint actions of all three persons of the Trinity. "The Father plans and gives commands, the Son performs and creates, while the Spirit nourishes and increases," writes Boris Bobrinsky, professor of Dogmatic Theology at the St. Sergius Institute of Orthodox Theology in Paris, in his essay "God in Trinity." Our liturgical and sacramental life and theology should lead us into understanding the work of the Holy Trinity. Bobrinsky brings a good reminder to evangelicals that Christian worship expresses "the gift of knowledge and of new life that comes from the Father, through Christ, in the Holy Spirit."

The mystery of Christ, the Word made flesh, seated at the right hand of the Father in the active work of the Holy Spirit allows us to define and clarify the specificity of Christian worship, Bobrinsky argues. As such, no worship experience should conclude without directed focus, worship, and glorification of God the Father, God the Son, and God the Holy Spirit. Doesn't the Holy Spirit deserve more than just an honorable mention on Sunday mornings?

A "Trinity Grace" Church

If I wanted to franchise a church name, it would definitely be "Trinity Grace." While theologically driven church names like "St. John," "St. Paul," "Christ the King," "Redeemer," "Covenant," "Trinity," "Grace," "Westminster," "Christ," "Calvary," "New Birth," "The Potter's House," and the like, all communicate fantastic dimensions of the redemptive story in the Bible, nothing seems to sum up the essence of the mission of the Kingdom like the juxtaposition of the Holy Trinity with the Old Testament and New Testament themes of God's grace.

The central actors in the drama of redemption are God the Father, God the Son, and God the Holy Spirit. Throughout the entire biblical story we are introduced to a Triune God who has not left the world in a state of chaos as a consequence of the Fall. God the Father has a plan, culminating in the person of Christ and His accomplished work, and applied to believers in time and space through the active work of the Holy Spirit, with cosmic implications for the world.

For example, we learn what it means to love God by looking at the relationships between the persons of the Trinity (John 16-17; 1 John 4:9-16). For example, we know what love is because God gave his only begotten Son so that sins are forgiven and true reconciliation with the Father through the work of Holy Spirit is possible.

Moreover, the redemptive story from Genesis to Revelation is a story of God's constant outpouring of his grace. By grace I do not mean holy "niceness," which has many confused about Christianity to the point of seeing it as a kind of holy passivity. By grace, I mean God showing mercy, affection, love, and liberation to people who do nothing to earn it (Ephesians 2:8-10). Grace is an active and ongoing work of the Triune God. A Triune God with a people engaged in the mission of pressing the claims of the Kingdom everywhere is the fuel of Christian social justice. Churches whose mission is to communicate the salvific and mighty acts of a Triune God in light of the victory of the Cross and implications for the Kingdom could ignite another Great Awakening.

There is actually a church in New York City named Trinity Grace. I've never attended the church and know little about it but I was pleased to find a church whose very name brings together the powerful and mysterious realities of redemption, the mission of God, and the roles of Christians in the Kingdom. Regardless of your church's name, in light of Jesus' longings for unity in John 17, I would hope that the life-changing dynamism of Holy Trinity, and the liberating mission of grace, changes people from the inside out as God renews and reconciles all things to Christ (Colossians 1:3-23) in the name of God the Father, Son, and Holy Spirit.

Adoption Together with the Black Church

Being a black male puts you in one of the least desired categories of Americans, because "dark skin" and "negro dialect"—as Sen. Harry Reid suggested—can keep you from being embraced by mainstream America. What is worse is being a black male orphan born in America. According to a 2010 study by the Centre for Economic Policy Research in Great Britain, African-American males are the least likely to be adopted. To reach that conclusion, economists analyzed specific data from an online adoption facilitator that assists child services agencies that deal with birth mothers and adoptive parents. The data, gathered from June 2004 to August 2009, cover more than 800 children who were available for adoption.

According to the report:

> We show that adoptive parents exhibit significant biases in favor of girls and against African-American babies. A non-African-American baby relinquished for adoption attracts the interest of potential adoptive parents with probability 11.5% if it is a girl and 7.9% if it is a boy. As for race, a non-African-American baby has a probability of attracting the interest of an adopting parent at least seven times as high as the corresponding probability for an African-American baby.[77]

This problem could easily be remedied if more evangelical adoption organizations partnered with black churches to increase the number of adoptions. In most black churches, adoption has not been popular because, historically, black orphans are usually rare, as family members, however distant, would take in the children of relatives. However, as the breakdown of the black family occurred in the 1970s, largely as a consequence of the social programming of the federal government, black orphans became more of a problem.

In 2008, the North American Council on Adoptable Children, the Child Welfare League of America, the Dave Thomas Foundation for Adoption, and the National Association of Black Social Workers sought to amend federal laws dealing with transracial adoption, arguing that black children in foster care are ill-served by a "colorblind" approach meant to encourage their adoption by white families. The colorblind approach may actually

---

77. Baccara, et al., "Gender and Racial Biases," x.

harm black kids if they are not consciously connected to black culture, as is inferred from a 2008 report by the Evan B. Donaldson Adoption Institute.[78]

Increasing the number of black adoptive parents will require more education, cooperation, and partnerships among the roughly 46,000 black congregations in America. Evangelicals are growing in their awareness of the implications of James 1:27 and are leading Christians nationally in this area. The next big step is to include more church leaders from minority communities in the Christian adoption movement.

According to the U.S. Department of Health and Human Services, there are only 36,913 black kids ready to be adopted in 2008 because they were truly without parents.[79] If one family in every black congregation would adopt one child, all the black children currently in the system would have a Christian home, including black males. It really is that simple.

Public Theology and Unity

One of the most exciting aspects of the unveiling of the Manhattan Declaration was to see Orthodox, Roman Catholic, and Protestant leaders in unity present their convictions about freedom and human life in the public square. In particular, the way in which the Orthodox communion expressed theology can teach both Catholics and Protestants how to communicate unity in other areas.

The Orthodox understanding of theology is that doctrine is "not an academic discipline or set of philosophical propositions, but an expression of the Christian life of prayer, both corporate and personal," write Mary B. Cunningham and Elizabeth Theokritoff, editors of *The Cambridge Companion to Orthodox Christian Theology*. As a Protestant submerged in a culture where spirituality is often confused with theological precision, the idea that theology is an expression of personal and communal prayer is foreign. If theology were to be oriented around greater personal and communal prayer it could serve as a healthy basis of greater unity among the Christian traditions.

While the Orthodox openly recognize that theology comes out of the experience of the church, conservative Protestants rhetorically speak of theology coming from the Bible, while using pastors and theologians in their tradition to justify theological correctness. What's the difference? Not much. It is the idea that my theology is "right" because the Bible and

78. For the full report see "Finding Families for African American Children," Evan B. Donaldson Adoption Institute.

79. "AFCARS Report." United States Department of Health and Human Services.

John Calvin, Martin Luther, John Owen, Jonathan Edwards, and others say so. Since most Christian communions function similarly in practice, I am beginning to wonder why there is not more unity.

The Orthodox "instinct," as Cunningham and Theokritoff explain, is to focus on synthesis rather than on individual strands of thought. Synthesis seems odd to me to because my own theological journey has been one of identifying myself with particular strains. Early on in my life it was John Wesley and later it became John Calvin. My own instincts are more divisive.

Additionally, the Byzantine doctrine of symphony sees the church and state as aspects of one organism because the incarnation of God has salvific implications to all that is human, including various spheres of culture. With the Roman Catholic understanding of subsidiarity and the Protestant understanding of sphere sovereignty, there seems to be great synergistic possibilities on the issues of culture and social justice. The possibilities for an increasing level of unity among Orthodox, Roman Catholic, and Protestant Christians as we face our culture together is encouraging in light of what Jesus prays in John 17.

Time for Change? Now What?

What happens when you wake up one day and realize you are not the kind of person you thought you would become? Or you realize that you have made a mess of things? Or you simply want to grow? What often follows is a pledge to find ways to change. A few simple changes, we believe, get life back on track. Here's the problem: we often try to change in ways that are only superficial.

In the book *How People Change*, Timothy Lane and Paul Tripp summarize the false ways in which people seek change that are incapable of delivering the internal heart-oriented change we really need. With my paraphrasing, Lane and Tripp offer this food for thought:

1. Formalism. The formalist is the one who changes by being a more dutiful Christian. "If I only get more involved in church life, that would grow my faith and make things right again." This is the person who is at church multiple times a week. For them the gospel is reduced to participation in the meetings and ministries of the church.

2. Legalism. The legalist is the person whose life is organized around a list of do's and don'ts. The children of this person suffer under the tyranny of performance-oriented conditional love. Being "good" is the goal of the legalist.

3. Mysticism. The mystic becomes a Christian conference junkie longing for the emotional high of an experience in getting closer to God. Following Christ becomes more about emotional experiences than being a different kind of person. The emotional quick-fix does not last.

4. Activism. The activists gets closer to God and makes sense of life by protesting against "liberals" and other non-conservatives. This is a person who falsely believes that religious consistency is demonstrated politically and confusing fighting the culture war with healthy spirituality.

5. Biblicism. The armchair theologian fills the change gap by learning more information about theology and the Bible. Quick to quote dead theologians, and making a sport of arguing theological minutia, the Biblicist believes that the gospel is reduced to a mastery of biblical content and theology.

6. Psychology-ism. There are some people who surround themselves with others who will comfort and pity them for the mess that is their life. The idea is this: "I'll get better if the right people support me and listen to my problems." The church is nothing more than a place to heal my brokenness. The right support network will change everything. The gospel is reduced to healing brokenness.

7. Social-ism. For some people the gospel is reduced to having a network of fulfilling social relationships. These are the people who may be in two or three different small groups or are constantly in need of being around other Christians. As Lane and Tripp explain, a person like this makes fellowship, acceptance, respect, and position in the body of Christ a replacement for communion with Christ.

What is most compelling about this list is that these things can both be good and disordered. Political activism, Bible knowledge, having good friends, and so on do not address the deep needs we have that can only be addressed by the work of the Holy Spirit to form and shape us according to the reality of the implications of the Jesus' death and resurrection. These easy balms may seem to fill the whole but they will never deliver what they promise. What really creates change is radical reorientation around the truth of redemption.

Young, Missional, but Not Emergent

I would like to apologize to all the missional pastors in America who are currently under attack and struggling to raise support because many religious traditionalists and conservatives do not know the difference between a missional church and an emergent church.[80] Many Protestants seem to easily equate missional church plants with emergent churches for reasons that might be generational. Increasingly I find myself defending missional church plants across the country from those who are so unfamiliar with what an emergent church is that many assume any young congregation organized to reach non-Christians by mixing historic forms in new ways and lacking propositional dogmatism must be an "emergent" church. This is what Protestants do: re-invent Christianity every generation or so.

Since we have not convened an ecumenical council to finalize the definitions of words like "emergent," "emerging," and "missional," they remain dynamic and unsettling for many. Tim Keller, pastor of Redeemer Presbyterian Church in New York City, defines missional churches as those "adapting and reformulating absolutely everything [the church] does in worship, discipleship, community, and service—so as to be engaged with the non-Christian society around [it]."[81] Now to some, this might sound like Brian McLaren. Is it, however, possible for a church with an unconventional church name that values innovative worship, informal dress, social justice, narrative and inductive forms of preaching, and less propositional theological dogmatism to still remain committed to a Bible inspired by God and the gospel message of hope, restoration, salvation, and the historic teachings of the church?

What if one of these so called, "emergent" churches posted something like this on a website regarding the Bible:

> It was in the Body of Christ, to 'the saints,' that our holy faith was delivered 'once and for all'; the one who does not belong to this Body cannot interpret correctly the holy Bible (2 Thessalonians. 3:6; 2 Peter 3:16; Jude 3-4). In this context, the Divine Tradition is the experience of the Church, the divine memory of the Church, which is kept like a priceless treasure (2 Tim. 1:13-14).
>
> The Holy Bible does not include the completeness of the divine revelation. The importance of the spoken tradition and the care taken for its spreading from generation to generation was already underlined from Old Testament times (Psalm. 43:2;

---

80. This video by Mark Driscoll makes a helpful distinction: http://www.youtube.com/watch?v=RcbnGXSYxuI

81. Keller, "Missional Church," 1.

44:1; and Joel 1:3). The New Testament notes that it does not contain the completeness of the words and works of Christ (John 21:25).

That very book, the Holy Bible, makes use of the tradition (Numbers 21:14-15; Matt.2:23; Acts 20: 35; 2 Tim. 3: 8; Jude 14). Christ did not motion his disciples to write books but to preach. . . .[82]

If this same hypothetical church then focused its congregation on experiencing community life together, especially in the liturgy, interpreting the Scriptures in community, opening parishioners to the idea that God is still revealing himself, and that the Bible, while sufficient for salvation, does not answer all of life's questions nor reveal how God thinks about everything. Plus, if the church is not interested in reading books about doctrine, and embraces mystery, it would likely raise eyebrows and suspicion of being postmodern and unbiblical. The fact is, however, that a church that would post such a statement is nothing but truly orthodox—that is, Eastern Orthodox.

Just because a young church planter adapts the practices of the church to engage unchurched people does not mean that the church is "emergent." It only means that the church is Protestant.

I'm Not Paul, but. . .

The grandiosity and confidence of some theologians and pastors in an age of democratic theology is something that the early church fathers would find puzzling. If you're attending a vibrant church, it seems easy to assume that your church must be "right." In evangelicalism, what qualifies as credible is often church size and pastoral charisma. If the church is big and the pastor is a good speaker, then the church must be preaching something right. God must be "in it." However, in an age where theological accuracy and fidelity to the historic teachings of the church and the Bible are authenticated by the size of parking lots, media appearances, profiles in Christian magazines, the pastor's "hipster" quotient, believing that Christianity began in the 16th century, and so on, I'm not so sure we should be as dogmatically confident as we profess.

Churches without pastoral leadership bound and accountable to higher ecclesial authority and oversight, outside of the local congregational setting, typically end up with pastors who surround themselves with "yes

82. I found this statement on an Eastern Orthodox website, but the domain is now defunct. November 27, 2013.

men." These men may be called "elders," but they were selected by the super-pastor and are not considered his theological equal.

For pastors driven by numbers (followers), influence, making the church catholic into their own image, and so on, it is also easy to fall prey to the group-selected narcissism that feeds the arrogant self-deception that "pastor X's" or "Dr. X's" theological preferences are best for the church universal. A congregation's "vision/mission statement" or "statement of faith" is treated as creedal and used as a basis for assessing the orthodoxy of the church down the street.

Perhaps this is why celebrities, in general, believe their own hype as suggested in Dr. Gad Saad's article, "I'm not a Doctor, But . . . ," in the November 2009 issue of *Psychology Today*.[83] Narcissism, grandiosity, fame, "yes, men," the post-modern democratization of opinion lead us to wrongly believe that well-known people must be right. I think issues may apply to well-known pastors, theologians, and Christian musicians, as well.

Honestly, I struggle with theological humility in my own writing and speaking. This is not a problem, then, exclusive to those who are well-known. There is also the opposite extreme of those who believe they are "right" because their church world is small and their pastors are not well-known.

What's different about a church world of democratized theology is that we no longer have the authority to declare something heretical or even just erroneous. We can't remove bad teaching from church communities. We can only blog about error or slander error on Facebook and Twitter. Sadly, numbers feed the self-deception that Paul the apostle would agree with whatever your church teaches and practices. Church history should remind us that it is entirely possible, because of sin and deception, for any of our churches to be large, or your favorite pastor or theologian to be famous, because God is, in fact, not "in it."

Dissolving Urban Youth Para-church Ministries

Do para-church urban youth ministries need to be dissolved and collapsed into neighborhood churches? Do we need urban ministry-minded Christians placing more efforts into teaching in inner-city public schools in order to truly serve the city? I think this may be the way forward. For those Christians with a calling to serve the needs of inner-city youth, teaching in the public schools may be the best way to have the greatest impact outside of the direct work of local churches. The para-church model is out of a 1950s

---

83. Saad, "Homo Consumericus," lines 1-27.

playbook and may not be best use of human and financial capital to meet emerging needs.

For example, in 2009, nearly 23 percent of all young American black men ages 16 to 24 who have dropped out of high school are in jail, prison, or a juvenile justice institution, according to a report from the same year titled "Consequences of Dropping Out of High School" from the Center for Labor Markets at Northeastern University.[84] There is no urban youth ministry that has the capacity to put much of a dent in this alarming trend. These students need academic discipleship in addition to spiritual formation.

The para-church model for helping black and Latino males has expired and does not have the full scope of influence that missionally minded teachers could have if they were to place themselves into a school setting while working directly with local churches. Teachers have the advantage of being with students most of the day for about nine months out of the year. No urban youth worker could come close to that many "contact" hours. If the minds of urban youth are not being cultivated, we aren't really helping them become makers of culture here and now.

As public school teachers, administrators, and coaches, urban-minded missional Christians wouldn't have to raise financial support, either. Moreover, until America begins to re-think our public school system disaster for black and Latino males, we will have to work with the current system. As such, the public schools need a cadre of missional Christian teachers, thousands of them, who understand that forming human dignity is spiritual, intellectual, physical, and emotional.

We must remember two things about the black male graduation crisis: (1) it is not reduced to the nation's largest cities—South Carolina, Nebraska, Michigan, Louisiana, and Georgia have among the lowest rates of black male graduates in country;[85] and (2) this has much to do with the breakdown of the family, which is the unique reparative work of the church. Urban para-church ministry is neither designed nor equipped to meet the holistic needs of families.

Having said that, I know that many people can offer countless lists of exceptions and personal stories about urban ministry "X" that helped kid and/or family "Y." Those are great. I'm not saying that current ministries do not help a few. We should celebrate and honor that good work. However, in 2007, 16 percent of persons between 16 and 24 years of age (nearly 6.2 million people) were high school dropouts. Among these dropouts, 60.1

84. Sum, "Consequences of Dropping out of High School," 10.

85. You can view the data at "State Graduation Data," Schott Foundation for Public Education.

percent were men, 18.8 percent were black, and 30.1 percent were Hispanic.[86] Only churches and teachers have access to this many students and their families.

Church Hoppin' to Rome

"Mom, I'm thinking about becoming Catholic." Protestant parents are hearing this statement more and more. As long as Protestants continue to devalue tradition, history, and social justice concerns, we should expect to hear more and more young evangelicals "going home to Rome." The combination of family church hoppin' to find the best children's and youth programs, combined with the mythology that Protestants embrace *sola Scriptura* in practice, creates the perfect conditions to usher young adults into Roman Catholicism.

I was recently in a room full of young adults raised in evangelical America. To my surprise, there was not a single person who had been raised in one congregation or denomination—they'd all changed churches at least two or three times. I'm not surprised, then, that we find among this generation a longing for tradition and consistency—especially in a culture of broken families and high levels of geographic mobility. People want to call something "home."

In the September 2002 edition of the *Journal of the Evangelical Theological Society*, Scot McKnight's article, "From Wheaton to Rome: Why Evangelicals Become Roman Catholic," offered good insight regarding the phenomenon of Protestants converting to Catholicism. The list included: (1) a desire for certainty, (2) a desire for history, (3) a desire for unity, and (4) a desire for authority.[87]

A desire for consistency exposes the fact that Protestant theology is wildly divergent on key issues like justification, salvation, grace, marriage, divorce, birth control, social justice, and so on. Moreover, the downplaying of history and distinctiveness among Protestants tends to undermine our connection to tradition. If you're Baptist, Anglican, Presbyterian, Methodist, and so on, your family should know why. Also, no church or denomination really practices *sola Scriptura* as the only, or final, rule of faith. If your church uses a statement of faith, recites creeds, uses confessions and catechisms, sings from hymnals, and so on, your church has dual authorities—Scripture and tradition. While Scripture has final authority for issues related to salvation and morality, tradition determines who gets ordained,

---

86. "Left Behind in America," Center for Labor Market Studies, 51-55.

87. McKnight, "From Wheaton to Rome," 451-72.

what is taught in Sunday school, what the sacraments mean, who holds what church office, and so on.

A desire for unity exposes grievous bifurcations among Protestants, of which there are over 33,000 different denominations in the world, a number hardly consistent with Jesus' desire for unity expressed in John 17. Of course, the "unity" of Catholic and Orthodox communions is often cosmetic. While Protestants put their disunity on display through church planting and denominations, others disagree off the record. The desire for authority is likely a reaction to being raised by a generation of anti-authoritarian baby boomers failing to distinguish between good and bad uses of authority. Trustworthy authority can be good for clarifying questions of theology and life as well as providing wisdom. Some forms of decentralization, however, may not be as helpful as we once believed.

To McKnight's list I would add a desire for intellectual leadership in public life. The Catholic Intellectual Tradition has a history of rigorous scholarship coupled with spirituality and ethical teaching toward forming people committed to piety and making the world a better place, especially for the poor.[88] There have been intellectual contributions by Protestants, but there is no comparable, consistent intellectual Protestant tradition that applies spiritual and moral formation to making the world a better place.

In the end, some young Protestants are exposing the weaknesses of their upbringing with their feet. Until Protestants recapture some sense of historic unity and mission to enter the world's cultures beyond evangelism, this trend will likely continue. McKnight's observations are cause for much reflection.

Jesus Goes to Boarding School

In 2009, I was introduced to a Jesus movement among New England's boarding and independent schools. It made me wish I was a billionaire philanthropist donor to Christian missions. In the 1960s, Peter Moore and others founded FOCUS (Fellowship of Christians and Universities and Schools) to organize gatherings for students attending New England boarding schools. For over 40 years Moore—an orthodox Episcopal priest and a graduate of St. Mark's, Yale, and Oxford—grew a ministry team with deep familiarity with the culture at leading independent boarding and day schools to nurture thousands in a life of following Jesus from the Northeast down the Atlantic seaboard.

88. "The Catholic Intellectual Tradition: A Conversation at Boston College," Boston College.

FOCUS seeks to "explore with independent school students a life of faith that is real, adventurous, intellectually sound, and eminently practical." Because boarding and independent schools are usually off the missions radar for many evangelicals, I was profoundly moved to hear about the activity there.

Rob Lofberg, the area director for the group's work at New England boarding schools, said he decided to work for FOCUS in part "because it is the ministry through which the Lord opened my eyes to the reality of his grace." While a junior at the Middlesex School in Concord, Mass., a FOCUS staff person came to a small student-led Bible study he attended. Shortly afterward, Rob became a follower of Jesus and now, with a strategic heart and passion for the "peculiarities of the boarding school culture," is uniquely placed.

Rob explained the honor of serving this population this way:

> FOCUS is an exciting ministry because so many of the students we work with are engaging with the gospel for the first time. Many are opening the Bible for the first time, and though they are the most competitive students in the world, there is so little religious predisposition. There is a freshness when they hear about Jesus and his claims, and many are excited to know more as they discover Him through the Bible.[89]

Rob said that he has one of the most exciting jobs in the world. I believe him. Bringing Jesus to that area of the country is sadly revolutionary to many who have given up praying and caring for students and families in New England's boarding school culture. "I enjoy being a witness to Jesus in New England," Rob said, "because every time I enter into a serious conversation about Christian claims I never know what I am going to get." The frankness and honestly of New Englanders when given the gospel fuels an exciting mission, especially among students who tend to be "very serious about intellectual honesty."

It is sadly rare that I meet Christians who desire a missional Christian presence in New England, in general. The work of FOCUS in the Northeast continues to confirm to me God's heart for all different kinds of people, that they would come to follow Jesus. FOCUS is one of the little known gems among Christianity's missional ministries. The revolution continues . . . .

---

89. Personal correspondence, October 6, 2009.

Celebrity Pastor Worship

Anyone aware of the alarming state of American evangelicalism's celebrity-driven church culture would not have to try hard to draw parallels with the church in Corinth. The "big name" pastors, as we sometimes call them, thanks to the Christian conference circuit, book publishing, the internet, and so on, tempt many evangelicals to cannibalize each other in the spirit of following "Paul" or "Apollos." In today's terms, these could be men like John Piper, Tim Keller, Mark Dever, C.J. Mahaney, Mark Driscoll, Rob Bell, R.C. Sproul, Tony Evans, or whomever people would rather download and listen to instead of their own pastor.

To be sure, these men are not the problem. The problem is with us, the people holding these great preachers and teachers of our time too highly and using them to attack other Christians who might not believe whatever we consider to be the "right" interpretation of what "the gospel" says the church should be doing in the world. I go through seasons of falling into this myself. It's embarrassing, but I do it.

Quarrels, dissension, and divisions are plastered all over the internet as Jesus followers poke passive insults at each other in the name of whatever peripheral minutiae we determine as "getting the gospel right." For example, not being Reformed enough, or not "traditional" enough, or too traditional, or too literal, or too involved in social issues, or not evangelistic enough, and so on. Paul challenges the Corinthian church saying:

> "You are still worldly. For since there is jealousy and quarrel-ing among you, are you not worldly? Are you not acting like mere men? For when one says, 'I follow Paul,' and another, 'I follow Apollos,' are you not mere men? What, after all, is Apollos? And what is Paul? Only servants, through whom you came to believe-as the Lord has assigned to each his task. I planted the seed, Apollos watered it, but God made it grow."
> (1 Corinthians 3:3-6)

Matthew Henry wrote wise words about this passage:

> Contentions and quarrels about religion are sad evidences of carnality [worldliness]. . . . Many professors, and preachers also, show themselves to be yet carnal, by vain-glorious strife, eagerness for dispute, and readiness to despise and speak evil of others.[90]

---

90. Henry, "1 Corinthians," lines 7-17.

Here's the rub: contentions and quarrels can make you famous among evangelicals. Evangelicals love strife. Marketing for Christian publishing, the speaker circuit, and the like, all feed into this pathetic trend. If you're a Paul or an Apollos you can easily get a book contract and draw large speaking fees, even if you're a dissension starter. If a preacher does not have a following like an Apollos, he will get no book contract and he will not be invited to speak at conferences. Have you noticed the various Apollos sections of the Christian bookstore? It's no wonder that many young preachers are busy trying to be like a famous Apollos instead of finding contentment with their own gift-mixes.

I've actually seen evangelical Pauls and Apolloses speak together at the same conference about "the gospel," and I have read blogs where their "followers" attack "followers" of the other guys. Again, it is not that admiration, respect, nor celebrating the gifts of any of today's great teachers is necessarily a problem. The problem is neither books nor conferences. The cancer in the church is the disunity created when "fans" of certain preachers create dissension over minutiae that we reinterpret as "the gospel." Maybe, then, it's not a good sign when large crowds gather to hear their favorite preachers speak together.

A short column like this is clearly insufficient to cover this topic, which is worthy of much discussion in book form at least. I'm not sure, however, who would be brave enough to write it and which publisher would be bold enough to publish it. However, I can't imagine that Jesus is smiling on a church in tension because of trifling Paul and Apollos followers. Something needs to be said soon. While Christians are busy fighting over which preacher is "right," evil in the world roams free without opposition.

From Youth Group to Agnosticism

Why do so many conservative evangelical kids walk away from Christianity altogether in their 20s? This is the question a friend and I discussed as we swapped stories of 20-somethings we now know who were "on fire for the Lord" as teens but now have an angry disposition toward the church and are agnostic. These are women and men who grew up in church-going, two-parent families in conservative, Republican-loving, Bible-teaching, evangelical churches with well-intended adults loving them the best way they could.

I once ran into a 29-year-old man who many expected to be an amazing youth pastor someday. I had been his counselor 15 years before at a leadership camp at Covenant College. He was one of those youth group kids who was "on fire" for the Lord. He wore Christian T-shirts and bracelets, was a fan of abstinence, didn't hang around non-Christians or drink or smoke or drive fast. I'm pretty sure he wore a purity ring too. He had great grades, led groups at church, had opportunities to teach, and so on. He actually rebuked me once for doing one of those youth group type icebreakers that wasn't godly. Today he's agnostic.

My friend and I have both been involved in youth ministry for years. I have spent 15 years as a youth worker at several churches around the country and three years as a Christian school teacher and administrator. My friend was a youth director in a very large conservative Reformed Presbyterian church for over seven years. Here are common "straws that break the camel's back" in young adulthood, as we follow up with these formally "on fire future leaders of the church" who have now walked away completely:

1. Being a victim of formulaic parenting: All of these young adults were victims of the evangelical idea that if you put your children in the right program "X" they will turn out to be like "Y." Strangely, adults seemed to be puzzled when their adult children walk away from Christianity because "they were so involved in youth group" and "went to Sunday school" every Sunday. Many evangelical parents will even "church hop" to find the perfect youth programs to plug their kids into as if church programs alone magically produce long-term followers of Christ. In fact, I'm not even sure "youth pastor" can be biblically defended.

2. Confusing doctrinal and biblical knowledge with true spirituality: As youth leaders, we all made the mistake of assuming that because these teens had good doctrine that they actually were developing a heart-driven affection for Jesus. Not surprisingly, most of these kids grew up in churches that elevate religious knowledge over religious experience and spirituality. Spirituality is assumed evident because they can recite Bible verses and answer theological questions while viewing religious experience and emotions as practices of the theologically unsophisticated.

3. Controlling friendships out of fear: These young adults were also in contexts where they were quarantined from two groups of peers: (1) non-Christians and (2) Christians not having the "right" theology. Friends are seen as potential threats and bad influences. What happens, then, when these kids leave high school and meet "non-Christians" and others who are actually more caring, socially concerned, and generous than many Christians they know? They start to develop anger and resentment toward the church. These young adults were

raised to believe that the only loving, caring, "nice" people on earth are Christians and the rest are demons just waiting to pounce. These young adults have no answer when confronted with the fact that you don't have to be a Christian to be faithful to your spouse, love your children, care for homeless people, be hospitable strangers, and the like. Maybe, then, Christianity is not as unique as many were led to believe.

This is only the beginning of what we have discovered. It really breaks my heart to see these young adults walk away and I am hopeful, because of the promises of God, that their departure is only temporary.

"Apologetics is not the silver bullet." I would love to shout this sentence from the rooftops of Christian communities believing that young adults walk away from the church because they're not able to defend the faith. This is another "spirituality as theological acumen" fallacy. I know many young adults who were grounded in Francis Schaeffer and Cornelius Van Til at a Christian school and still walked away in college. Here are a few more points of tension:

1. Christianity as a religion of "don'ts": Being more holy than Jesus seems to be a recipe for creating resentment against what Bible teaches by focusing on what Christians avoid. As Mark Driscoll points out, trying to be more holy than Jesus is sinful. Teaching a Christianity of avoidance rather than one of discernment becomes legalistic, pharisaical, and poisonous to the heart. The Bible naturally tells us to avoid things but some communities reduce Christianity to "good Christians don't do this or that."

2. Unrepentant arrogance: We have discovered that when kids grow up listening to adults constantly criticize others, focus on the problems in the church, point fingers at everyone else's lack of orthodoxy, and develop a posture of "we're right and everyone else is wrong," and so on, it sets the trap to misconstrue Christianity as a faith of self-righteous defensiveness instead of humility and grace.

3. Bible abuse: This happens when adults take Bible verses out of context to guilt manipulate kids into behavior modification. For example, misusing Bible verses to keep kids from wearing T-shirts promoting secular bands but saying nothing about shirts displaying "Ralph Lauren," or "American Eagle." The Bible becomes a twisted rulebook codifying cultural preferences. Or even worse, adults using the Bible to punish kids for disobedience. When a boy will not sit still in Sunday school,

is it really a good idea have him write Hebrews 13:17 50 times? What do we teach about God's word when it's used as a means of punishing?

4. Criticizing "culture" and not living differently from it: The confusing hypocrisy of constantly berating "culture" for its empty values while being just as materialistic, success-oriented, and safety-driven as many non-Christians. For example, it is particularly difficult to distinguish many Christians from their non-Christian neighbors in possessions, values, and lifestyle after 1 p.m. on Sundays.

5. Faith without struggle: We also discovered profound disillusionment when kids grow up around adults who never reveal their own struggles with sin and brokenness. If sin and brokenness are true, why does cowardice trump authenticity? For example, I know of boys who never hear about real struggles of being a man from their fathers or other men. As a result, Christianity is seen as contrived, fake, sugarcoated, and incapable of addressing the real challenges of life with the truth about the lives of adults exposed.

6. Political Christianity: There is not a single verse in the Bible that locks Christians into blanket support of a single secular political party. Christians can be in the Libertarian, Constitution, Democratic, Green, and so on, for various reasons. Hopefully, Christians are "salt and light" in all parties where possible.

There is much more to be said, but this brief unnuanced list is the beginning of a conversation that many of us are having regarding the consequences of adults digging spiritual wells for children instead of teaching kids how to dig deeply themselves. When the church's kids mature, those shallow, spoon-fed, moralistic, legalistic wells eventually run dry and young adults walk away. Roughly 3,500 churches die and close each year in America. We must act.

No Truth, No Love, No Justice

In 2009, Pope Benedict XVI released his first social encyclical, "Caritas in Veritate." Social encyclicals are fascinating documents that demonstrate excellent synthesis of theology, anthropology, economics, philosophy, and so on. This encyclical, translated "Love in Truth," addresses key issues of our time, ranging from moral relativism to globalization to caring for the environment.

The strongest and most compelling portion of the encyclical is the introduction, where a necessary connection is made between love and truth. Without truth, that is, *the* truth, love (referenced in the letter as "charity") cannot be fully realized:

> Without truth, charity degenerates into sentimentality. Love becomes an empty shell, to be filled in an arbitrary way. In a culture without truth, this is the fatal risk facing love. It falls prey to contingent subjective emotions and opinions, the word "love" is abused and distorted, to the point where it comes to mean the opposite. Truth frees charity from the constraints of an emotionalism that deprives it of relational and social content, and of a fideism that deprives it of human and universal breathing-space. In the truth, charity reflects the personal yet public dimension of faith in the God of the Bible, who is both *Agápe* and *Lógos*: Charity and Truth, Love and Word.[91]

Moreover, a Christianity without love is nothing but good sentiments, helpful for social mercy, but in the end, limited and temporal. Without full submission to the truth, love becomes distorted, confused, and misdirected. If we, as Christians, are committed to improving human society, we must be committed to giving people the truth that sets them free to be the people God created them to be.

Many questions could be raised about the unclear economics in the encyclical, with the language of wealth "redistribution," economic "inequalities," the support of labor unions, and so on. Pope Benedict strongly criticizes laissez-faire capitalism devoid of any moral direction or end. A healthy and free market seeks to create conditions where profit is a means to greater ends like social solidarity and the common good.

As would be expected, there is an excellent section describing the consequences of artificial contraception and abortion. Low birth rates in formerly prosperous nations are contributing to their decline, and when a nation's best social and economic resource, i.e. people, are kept from contributing to society because of pills, plastics, and other synthetics, the entire nation suffers. Here's how the encyclical addresses the life issue:

> *Openness to life is at the centre of true development.* When a society moves towards the denial or suppression of life, it ends up no longer finding the necessary motivation and energy to strive for man's true good. If personal and social sensitivity towards the acceptance of a new life is lost, then other forms of acceptance that are valuable for society also wither away. The acceptance of

91. Benedict XVI, *Caritas in Veritate*, section 3.

life strengthens moral fibre and makes people capable of mutual help.[92]

Pope Benedict is also careful to note that a right understanding of the environment as "God's gift"—to be used with responsibility, and as display of his wonderful "creative activity"—keeps us from the extremes of nature worship and abuse. The natural world is good and should be used for good ends.

On balance, the pastoral letter is a timely contribution to the international dialogue on the role of religion in public life in a world that is increasingly globalized. There is much more to do as we discern the most effective ways to stave off moral relativism while creating contexts, oriented by virtue, for sustainable wealth creation in the developing world so that things like clean drinking water and well-built homes are internationally normative.

No More Long Range Plans

Making detailed long-range plans is pretty pointless, my friends, as I have discovered. With great regularity I have come to see that I am always wrong about what I'll be doing "five years from now." One such realization occurred while I was sitting in a Manhattan restaurant with two friends of mine.

Sitting in an eatery near Sixth Avenue and 34th Street, we were all trying to figure out what happened. When I was 17, I had actually planned out my entire life. By now, I should be governor of the state of Georgia. I don't even live in Georgia. What happened? One of my dining companions was laid off a couple of weeks ago after moving to a city to take a new job with amazing "opportunities." The other pea in this lamenting pod has a very well-paying job but is disillusioned because the work is painfully boring and draining.

We were wondering why no one told us that life's direction is not in our hands. Life is mysteriously painful, and over-planning the details of my life to avoid potential future discomfort is a useless pursuit. Truthfully, I'm sure someone along the way told me that God's ways are not my ways, and that He has plans for my life that will take me places I may not expect at times that seem not to make sense. But no one told us to always expect that to happen.

It seems that the evangelical Christianity I've been swimming in the past few years has led me and my friends to believe that our lives work

92. Ibid., section 28.

linearly toward greater comfort and ease: Go to college, meet the girl, get a great job, buy a house, have a kid, find a church with a good youth program, live happily ever after, and conclude by going to Heaven.

Several of my friends and I are dealing with the profound disappointment of realizing that the suburban church narrative is actually a lie. Some guys get married and their wives cheat on them within a couple of years, or they lose a job, or they get diagnosed with cancer before turning 30 years old, or they have a child born severely handicapped, and the like. I wish someone had given us the real news instead of the sugarcoated fairy-tale of a life absent of the consequences of the Fall and the active work of the devil.

In the final analysis, the only long-range plan my friends and I agreed upon that night was to refrain from ever making long-range plans. For many of us, trusting Jesus for our salvation is the easy part. Trusting Jesus to lead us into what God has for us in the future is often more difficult than it appears.

In the uncertainty of what's next for my friends and me, these words from Jeremiah 29:11-13 provide a comforting echo: "For I know the plans I have for you, declares the LORD, plans to prosper you and not to harm you, plans to give you hope and a future. Then you will call upon me and come and pray to me, and I will listen to you. You will seek me and find me when you seek me with all your heart."

Calling vs. Desire

Many Christians consistently misuse the word "calling," which leads to a person who has a "desire" to do something being wrongly viewed as unspiritual or "fleshly." Is it accurate to say "I feel called to be pilot" or "We feel called to live in the city"? Not really. I guess God could "call" people to vocations and ZIP codes, but that's not the main emphasis of the concept in the Bible. Calling has more to do with becoming a member of the people of God and living a holy life rather than deciding which job to take or whom to marry. Those items are actually choices.

The Greek word that Paul uses to describe his "calling" to be an apostle is the same word he uses to express the divine calling to be in union with Christ (Romans 1:1, 1 Corinthians 1:1) and is only used 10 times in the New Testament. To say that you're called to missions or to parenting like Paul says he was called to the office of the apostle is to grossly misuse the term or concept.

As a matter of fact, the Bible primarily explains that when God "calls" people, he calls them to intimacy with Him and union with Christ, to join the Kingdom, to get saved, to live holy lives, and so on (Matthew 22:14; Romans 1:7, 8:28-30, 9:26; 1 Corinthians 1:9, 1:24, 1:26, 7:15-24; Galatians 1:6, 1:15, 5:13; Ephesians 1:18, 2:11, 4:4; Philippians 3:14; Colossians 3:15; 2 Thessalonians 2:14; Hebrews 9:15; 1 Peter 2:21; etc.).

We spiritualize our desires as if wanting to be a missionary, cop, pastor, seminary student, or mom, or wanting to live in Peru, Kenya, Spain, the city, the suburbs, and the like, for a season, were all unspiritual as personal preferences. If it's true that God gives us the desires of our hearts, and it's true that all good things come from God, why is not OK to say, "I want to be a missionary for a while"?

The Holy Spirit can equally compel preferences, desires, and choices, but this is different from "calling." The misuse of the word "calling" can lead to painful theological crises whenever situations don't turn out as expected. "But I thought I was called to this," we wonder. You weren't called. You freely chose what you did and it didn't work out. So what? Move on to something else. Your decision was not necessarily wrong, and God's not punishing you (unless it was clearly a sinful choice).

A Christian's calling is to live in righteous harmony with God, and this can be done regardless of vocation or geography. I'm cautious now when I write checks to people who say they are "called" to "this" or "that" ministry, vocation, region, because I would hate to send people off with a bad functional theology. The good news about freedom in Christ is that desires and preferences change, but callings do not.

No More Abstinence Pledges

A 2009 pledge study produced competing interpretations of pledge effectiveness. What the media seems to miss is that the study—conducted by Janet Elise Rosenbaum, published in the journal *Pediatrics* and titled "Patient Teenagers? A Comparison of the Sexual Behavior of Virginity Pledgers and Matched Nonpledgers," is about sexual behavior in young people *after* high school. The latest findings reveal that five years after abstinence pledges are made, pledgers and non-pledgers alike are equally promiscuous. The sexual behavior of young adults five years after taking abstinence pledges should not surprise us, regardless of their constrained sexual activity during their high school years.

The study also demonstrates that teens from supportive religious communities are much less likely to engage in premarital sex in high school. But is being less bad necessarily good? Here's an idea: Let's stop teens from making pledges altogether. The problem in our divorce culture is that marriage has been devalued to the point that abstinence until marriage makes less and less sense to many people.

I have never been a fan of abstinence pledge programs and generally see them as pharisaical and utilitarian when churches adopt them. In general, these programs are designed for teens to get through high school without losing their virginity, as if losing one's virginity at 16-years-old is morally inferior to losing it at 21-years-old outside of marriage. Deep spirituality, however, should not be confused with participation in extra-biblical church programs. Many parents seem more concerned about their children's sexuality than their children's love for Jesus and dependence on the Holy Spirit. If teens are not in love with Jesus, what's an abstinence program on a Sunday night, with pledge cards, purity rings, workbooks, and an annual conference going to accomplish in the long run?

True love pursues and seeks the Kingdom priorities of the Triune God no matter what those priorities are at any age. I would rather my teen publicly confess dependence on the Holy Spirit in all areas of life than make abstinence pledges with purity rings, bracelets, and car decals. Moreover, many well-intentioned parents believe that when their children make a public pledge to abstinence it is a cause for celebration. Would you like the blue pill or the red pill?

Over the past 15 years, I've worked in too many churches and in too many college ministries all over America to know that an adolescent abstinence pledge, outside of a passionate pursuit of the Triune God, is about as trustworthy in the long-run as pledges to call home every Sunday, to drive under the speed limit, to never abuse alcohol, to never lie, and so on.

If five years after their pledges, those who pledge and those who do not are no different in their rates of premarital sex, sexually transmitted infections, or participating in certain sexual acts, then what's the point of these programs? Why do churches use them? Outside of a commitment to Christ (John 14:15-31) these programs can be reduced to nothing more than rhetorical exercises.

Perhaps this why Jesus recommends that men and women seek first God's Kingdom and His righteousness (Matthew 6:33). What if teens were encouraged to devote their lives to the Kingdom in all areas of life, including their sexuality? Jesus-loving baptized teens, living out the implications of frequent partaking of the Lord's Supper, carried by the Holy Spirit, is the 2,000-year-old practice that never needed an extra-biblical religious ceremony.

It may be the case that the best way to settle the confusion over the effectiveness of abstinence pledges is to admit that they are well-intentioned but do not produce the intended long-term results and should be terminated.

Generation Vulnerable

Based on interviews with 16-to-25-year-olds conducted on behalf of The Prince's Trust,[93] younger generations in the United Kingdom are becoming "increasingly vulnerable."[94] Young people in the United Kingdom increasingly are describing life as meaningless and are struggling to understand why life matters. This type of confusion sets the stage for them to rely upon false systems-such as drug and alcohol abuse, gangs, and non-marital and risky sex behavior-to give life meaning.

Among the key findings from the survey that YouGov conducted for The Prince's Trust were:

- 12 percent of young people in Wales claim life is meaningless.

- 26 percent say they are often, or always, down or depressed.

- 39 percent say they are less happy now than they were as a child.

- 21 percent feel like crying often or always.

- 44 percent say they are regularly stressed.

- Those not in work, training, or education are twice as likely to feel their life has little or no purpose.

- Across the United Kingdom, young people feel relationships with family (56 percent) are key to overall happiness.

- Friends (52 percent), emotional health (29 percent), money (16 percent), and work (14 percent) are also important.

According to the survey, 9 percent of Scots believe that life is not worth living at all. If you are a person who believes that life is not worth living it will likely lead to severe depression. In response to the report, a London 32-year-old nicknamed "Yoof" wrote this in response the study:

> This is hardly surprising. . . . I'm 32 and have been clinically depressed for 7 years despite having a decent job and loving music. . . . [T]he problem I have and many like me is that we have no future. . . . [O]ur generation is the first one that has to deal with the proven knowledge that the world as we know it is coming to an end, and all that the generation above us (older) can do is attempt to nick as much money off us as possible before it all goes belly up.[95]

93. See the full report at "YouGov Youth Index," The Prince's Trust.
94. "Youngsters are More 'Vulnerable,'" BBC News.
95. "Life 'Meaningless' for Young." The Scotsman.

Yoof is correct that the findings are not surprising. But what seems obvious is that even family and work are not enough to give youngsters meaning in life. There must be something more—something transcendent to give even family and work deeper meaning other than the functionality of connection and productivity. Of course, what else can we expect from a region that has deliberately expunged Christianity from its culture? Without locating one's existence within the reality of a transcendent Triune God, all aspects of life will come to appear meaningless. Hmm, isn't this a familiar theme in the Bible somewhere?

As the reporting continues in the United Kingdom, there are more and more calls for government to come up with ways to find solutions to save the region's young people. Sadly, we know this will fail too because government is incapable of providing direction in this area.

Is America next? Possibly. As more and more Christians seem mostly interested in throwing rocks at the big bad "culture," focusing more on needs inside their local church by creating an alternative reality that's "safe for the family," and increasingly removing themselves from the public square (especially in the areas of education and entertainment), the general public is less likely to be in loving relationships with people who have answers to questions about meaning and existence.

As Christianity in America continues to follow religious trends in the United Kingdom, the church should be even more committed to sending Christians with the good news into as many public spaces as possible so that we will not find ourselves reading about such a report concerning our young people. Because the sad reality for youth in the United Kingdom is that without the active work of the church fulfilling her mission there, youngsters in that region will continue to be lost.

Race

Why do Black Lives Matter?

"Black lives matter." "All lives matter." These slogans may forever summarize the deep tensions in American life in 2014. Catalyzed by the deaths of Michael Brown, Eric Garner, and two New York Police officers who were murdered while sitting in a police car, Americans are in the midst of a crisis of human dignity. Are we still able to articulate why *anyone's* life matters? We can loudly protest that "Black lives matter" but it will mean nothing in the long run if we cannot explain *why* black lives matter.

Having desiccated our shared anthropology to the point that people are defined by the pursuit of individualistic and depersonalized rights, Americans can no longer ontologically justify the claim that anyone is worthy of dignity, love, and respect. In the current crisis, we are left to reduce some of our neighbors to depersonalized nouns: "suspect," "thug," "criminal," "felon," or "cop." This type of depersonalization is the gateway to dehumanization because it gives us permission to suspend the requirement to treat people with dignity, even if they have broken the law.

Black lives matter because black people are *persons*. One of the greatest tragedies in American history was the myth that America could flourish without blacks flourishing as persons. From the founding of this country, throughout slavery, Reconstruction, the Eugenics movement, and the Civil-Rights Movement, black Americans fought to establish themselves, first and foremost, as persons. At minimum we can define persons as centers of creativity, self-transcendence, communication, morality, self-direction, responsibility, choice, freedom, and spirituality, who come to know themselves in union and communion with the Triune God and other personal selves. Persons are simultaneously unrepeatable splendors with great capacity for good and also vulnerable to disordered loves that can lead to profound evil. Not only do they need moral formation; moral norms ought to shape how we structure the elements of justice in politics, jurisprudence, and the marketplace.

One of the greatest contributions that Christianity made to the world was to provide an ontological justification for human dignity and human rights. Black life matters because black people have been called to a vocation—to attain the end for which they were created in union and communion with others persons who have the same calling. Today, humans are reduced to depersonalized, abstract individuals possessing "rights" to be asserted and acquired for the purpose of self-actualization with little to no regard for the other. In a depersonalized, individualistic society people could not care less about the flourishing of their neighbors. What matters is the consumeristic flourishing of the self in a morally relativistic pursuit of desired passions. Too many Americans do not know how to distinguish between rights and passions.

In a culture that has done all it can to expunge moral virtue from the aspirations of human life, why are we surprised that we are shouting, "Black lives matter?" When human persons are not expected to be in communion with God and others, why are we surprised that the reverence due to the human person is lost? Black lives matter because persons are not autonomous, self-contained, individualistic creatures who do not need others for their flourishing. Black lives matter not simply because they are black but because blacks are persons—persons who are a necessary variable to the flourishing of others so that we all may attain the end for which we were created.

As we move forward, the fact remains that in order for there to be sustainable peace and justice following events such as those that happened in Ferguson and New York City in 2014—that is, if we truly want to heal the wounds that divide us—we must first understand what it means to be human. As Dr. Martin Luther King observed, "[E]very human life is a reflection of divinity, and . . . every act of injustice mars and defaces the image of God in man." Advocating for black life without a moral basis is throwing sand into the wind.

The LBJ Curse on the Black Vote

Gov. Mitt Romney's devastating loss to President Barack Obama in 2012 produced all sorts of interesting discussion. The analysis showed that, again, minorities had a clear preference for Obama. For example, according to exit polling data at Fox News, President Obama received 93 percent of the black vote. Over the years, the GOP has made honest attempts to attach racial weight to issues like abortion and gay marriage, but to no avail. These attempts have failed for an important reason: for black voters, entitlement programs trump moral-social issues every time. Even if African Americans are more socially conservative on many issues, black voters will choose the path of consequentialism at the ballot box. This is the belief that the morality of an action derives solely from its outcomes or consequences. The GOP seems blind to this tendency.

President Obama owes a debt of gratitude to former President Lyndon Johnson for the "War on Poverty" programs he proposed in his 1964 Great Society speech. Johnson was well aware that by federalizing his proposals he was cementing black allegiance to the Democratic Party for years to come. In fact, it is reported that Johnson, in an attempt to assuage the fears of southern governors, said that his plan was "to have them n*****s voting Democratic for the next two hundred years." Johnson's plan worked masterfully.

Even when there is evidence to the contrary—for example, that none of the entitlement programs introduced by the Johnson administration have improved the lives of blacks in the long-run anywhere in America—race-sensitive warfare rhetoric and the perception of genuine concern for the marginalized ensures that Democratic candidates prevail among minority voters. Even though Johnson's programs introduced perverse incentives against saving money, starting businesses, getting married, and they discouraged fathers from being physically and emotionally present for their children—resulting in generational welfare dependence—black voters are lured to choose dependence over liberation.

The Johnson administration successfully convinced generations of black voters to believe a two-part narrative. First, none of the challenges in your life are related to any decisions you or your family has ever made and all of your problems have been imposed on you, historically, by others. Second, you are, therefore, entitled to receive money and services through government that will remedy all of your problems. An additional sub-plot advances an evolving conflation of "government" with "society." Therefore, when the point is made that other institutions in society are better at caring for the differentiated needs of the poor in the long-run, progressives will always interpret that as "not caring for the poor," "ignoring the poor," "leaving the poor to fend for themselves," and so on. An anxious warning results: "If government doesn't provide for the poor, no one will."

What remains odd is how easily we have forgotten that the cultural production of evil that oppressed and marginalized blacks in the first place was the work of politics. The trans-Atlantic slave trade, American slavery, the Jim Crow era, the Eugenics movement, the Tuskegee Experiment, and the forced sterilization of black women were all made possible and perpetuated because of concentrated political power. Johnson brilliantly worked to whitewash the historical narrative with a speech and a few pen strokes to view government as the most effective means of remedying the kinds of problems that politics initiated in the first place—problems that are often more moral in nature rather than political. Years after the systemic oppression, politicians courted black voters to elect them to solve the problems catalyzed by previous eras' self-interested politicians just like them.

It seems plausible, then, that the only way to free black voters from the curse of LBJ is for some group to make the persuasive and factual case that black communities are better off when people in those communities are in full control of solving their own problems. This was the norm in the black community that led to higher black marriage rates and work force participation rates prior to the civil rights movement than after, for example. What should matter for black voters moving forward should not be allegiance to the unfulfilled promises of past proposals but a future that empowers and positions local communities to create the conditions for virtue formation, strong marriages, parental control in education, entrepreneurial freedom, and protection from the unchecked power of self-interested politicians lobbied by corporations, so that votes are cast to guarantee the actualizing of liberty rather than the promises of wished-for solutions.

Elephant Room Invite Undermines
Black Evangelicals

If I wanted to turn thousands of African-Americans and Hispanics away from churches committed to the Reformation doctrines of grace I would create a public event where a couple of white Calvinist pastors publicly argue against a well-known and respected black pastor in Pentecostal circles. This exact situation occurred in 2011, as James MacDonald, along with his co-moderator Mark Driscoll, hosted pastor T.D. Jakes for a public conversation in The Elephant Room.

According to the website, "The Elephant Room features blunt conversations between seven influential pastors who take differing approaches to ministry." MacDonald, a council member of The Gospel Coalition, organized the event as a way for people to hear from church leaders like Jakes. Conversation and dialogue are always good and can help bring about discernment, but that's not the problem here. There's more to this situation than theology. What baffles many evangelical leaders is why MacDonald chose, as his first African-American guest, a pastor that many consider to be a heretic because of his views of the Trinity.

Carl Trueman, who teaches church history at Westminster Theology Seminary, has raised questions about MacDonald's understanding and commitment to the doctrine of the Trinity and the Nicene Creed because of the way he seems OK with Jakes' view of the Trinity not as "persons" but as "manifestations"—a view often associated with a heresy called modalism.[96] Trueman also raised concerns about whether there's any accountability for MacDonald.[97]

What is even more devastating, some argue, is that MacDonald's invitation to Jakes undermines decades of work by black evangelical leaders and pastors to steer their congregations away from such theological beliefs. For example, an incensed Thabiti Anyabwile, senior pastor of First Baptist Church of Grand Cayman in the Grand Cayman Islands and a Gospel Coalition council member, wrote that the Jakes invitation is the equivalent to "Augustine inviting Muhammed." Anyabwile continued:

> The news of T.D. Jakes' invitation to The Elephant Room is widespread and rightly lamented by many. I'm just adding a perspective that hasn't yet been stated: This kind of invitation undermines that long, hard battle many of us have been waging in a community often neglected by many of our peers.

96. For more see Trueman, "Is Nicene Christianity that Important?"
97. For more see Trueman, "L'Orthodoxie? C'est Moi!"

And because we've often been attempting to introduce African-American Christians to the wider Evangelical and Reformed world as an alternative to the heresy and blasphemy so commonplace in some African-American churches and on popular television outlets, the invitation of Jakes to perform in 'our circles' simply feels like a swift tug of the rug from beneath our feet and our efforts to bring health to a sick church.[98]

Reddit Andrews III, senior pastor of Soaring Oaks Presbyterian (PCA) Church in Elk Grove, Calif., and a Gospel Coalition council member, lamented:

I must admit my heart sank a bit when I learned of the issue. I felt as though, in the context of the Coalition itself, to provide T.D. Jakes any significant evangelical (let alone Reformed) platform is a slap in the face of many African-American preachers who have made significant sacrifices to partner with Anglo ministers. We have often embraced issues that—if truth be told—have minimal import for our own communities in hopes that eventually we'll get significant engagement in our native communities. It feels like an unnecessary and uncalled for setback to we who passionately hope to see a return to orthodox views in the black community—along with every other community.[99]

Anthony Carter, pastor of East Point Church near Atlanta and a council member of The Gospel Coalition, added:

I agree with Thabiti, that the invitation to Jakes sends a mixed message and carries the potential of validating one the most pronounced purveyors of false teaching in the world. I would hope The Elephant Room (James MacDonald and Mark Driscoll, in particular) would reconsider this invitation.

The entire situation is such a punch in the stomach to blacks who have suffered to affiliate with gospel-centered evangelicalism that it now "raises association, separation, and accountability concerns for me that I did not have to the same degree before now," wrote Anyabwile. "It raises significant questions about how members of The Gospel Coalition associate and endorse beyond the Coalition meetings themselves."

MacDonald could have chosen from dozens of black pastors who have differing views but instead choose Jakes to display, before a mostly white audience, a *de facto* representative of the black church. Even worse,

98. Anyabwile, "Collateral Damage," lines 17-30.
99. Reddit Andrews III, comment on "Collateral Damage."

tens-of-thousands of Jakes' black and Hispanic followers could easily racial-ize the conversation if MacDonald or Driscoll seem to be attacking him in any way. One could say that this entire debacle undermines the racial unity and reconciliation sought by The Gospel Coalition and by men like John Piper through his book *Bloodlines*.

In solidarity with the men who have expressed their frustrations above, I chose not to pay to watch the event. Because of situations like this, black Gospel Coalition members and evangelicals might be justified in conclud-ing that mainstream leaders like MacDonald find their concerns irrelevant and not worthy of consideration.

Moving Toward Racial Solidarity

Two of my heroes who promoted racial reconciliation after the civil rights movement are J. Deotis Roberts and John M. Perkins. In different ways, these two men both wanted to see the church of Jesus Christ provide a post-civil-rights era image of racial unity and peace. While there has been much progress, many of their dreams have yet to come true.

But I am convinced that the church will only be able to lead society on race if it moves beyond reconciliation and pursues racial solidarity, which means embracing our common human dignity (Genesis 1:26-28) as a hu-man family in ways that celebrate and respect differences between ethnic communities for the common good. This is beyond the failed concept of "color-blindness" and recognizes the importance of racial, ethnic, and ideological differences as a catalyst for loving our neighbor's well (Matthew 22:36-40; John 17).

As such, I believe racial reconciliation has largely failed for four reasons:

1. Racial reconciliation fails to interrogate white privilege. There is no denying the dominant cultural group in America is Caucasians. Being a white person in America comes with many unarticulated advantages. In 1988, Peggy McIntosh launched a national discussion by suggesting a framework to engage this discussion—a topic that evangelicals have yet to explore. White privilege has been defined this way: "A right, ad-vantage, or immunity granted to or enjoyed by white persons beyond the common advantage of all others; an exemption in many particular cases from certain burdens or liabilities."[100]

---

100. Clark, "Defining 'White Privilege,'" lines 1-14.

2. Racial reconciliation advances according to the limitations of white social norms. Because there is little discussion of power in relation to white privilege, minorities are usually put in positions where they have to check their ethnicity at the door in order to engage.

3. Racial reconciliation does not advance nor advocate whites submitting to minorities in authority. Evangelicalism remains one of the few places in America where racial disparities in organizational structures seem no different than the era of *Mad Men*. But much of this is simply a consequence of scarcity.

4. Racial reconciliation misunderstands homogeneous ethnic churches as outmoded. This, in part, has much to do with many whites denying that they have cultural norms and the failure to recognize that ethnic minorities do need cultural centers for survival.

Moving forward, if Christianity is to put the difference the gospel makes in relationships on display, we need a racial solidarity movement that seeks to do at least the following:

1. Situate race discussions within an understanding of white privilege. It is what it is. Instead of denying it, we need to think creatively about how it can be used for the common good. I raised this issue recently at the Marketplace One Leadership Institute in Phoenix.

2. Advance racial solidarity in ways that do not require sub-dominant minorities to conform to white evangelical cultural norms. Evangelicals seem ignorant of Gordon Allport's 1954 "Contact Hypothesis" criteria.[101] As a result, many believe the myth that simply having multiple races share the same physical space changes racial attitudes. Allport's criteria demonstrate that racial attitudes change under certain conditions: when races have equal status, common goals, acquaintance potential, and support of authorities and customs.

3. Develop leaders who are not primarily white males. Christian conferences are great indicators of who evangelicals consider leaders. Great examples of progress would be racial diversity at the Coalition for Christian Outreach Jubilee Conference, while good groups like Together for the Gospel still lag slightly behind on displaying Asian-American, Latino, and black leaders as authorities worth following and those to whom others should submit.

---

101. For more see Allport, *Nature of Prejudice*.

4. Recognize the necessity and importance of homogeneous ethnic churches because of the reality of white privilege. So far, the Rev. Tim Keller, pastor of Redeemer Presbyterian Church in New York City, is the only white evangelical I know of who can accurately explain why ethnically homogenous churches are necessary in America.[102] Because of white hegemony, homogeneous ethnic churches provide a safe haven for minorities in a dominant culture that demands conformity to social customs and norms that are not their own. Also, as Keller highlights, ethnic churches serve as needed cultural centers for survival.

In the coming decades, there are great opportunities to put multi-ethnic implications of the gospel on display (Galatians 3:28) as we seek to love our neighbor in ways that Perkins and Roberts challenged us to do decades ago by incorporating new categories to an on-going problem.

Flash Mobbing King's Dream

Every black person apprehended for robbing stores in a flash mob robbery[103] should have his court hearing, not in front of a judge, but rather in front of the 30-foot statute of Dr. Martin Luther King, Jr. at his Washington memorial site. Each thief should be asked, "What do you think Dr. King would say to you right now?"

I was not angry when I initially saw the news footage of young blacks robbing convenience stores across America; I was brought to tears. In fact, as we approach the dedication of Dr. King's memorial we may all need to take a closer look at his chiseled stone face for the presence of tears. Tears like the one shed by Native American actor Chief Iron Eyes Cody in the 1970s public service announcement about pollution. The historic PSA shows the Native American shedding a tear after surveying the pollution in an America that had previously had none. It ended with the tagline, "People start pollution. People can stop it." If Dr. King were alive today he might proclaim, perhaps with tears in his eyes, that "people start flash mob robberies. People can stop them."

Dr. King's dream has been realized by many African Americans who have been able to take full advantage of the opportunities made available through his martyr's quest for justice. Would Dr. King ever have imagined that 40 years after his "I Have a Dream" speech that a black family would

---

102. He does so in this video: Keller, "Tim Keller on Churches and Race."

103. A "flash rob" is an event during which a large number of people suddenly enter and rob a store. The large number of people involved makes it hard to stop them from doing as they please.

be in the White House, not as maintenance or kitchen staff, but as the First Family? Yet, years after the civil-rights struggle affirmed black dignity, we have young black people ransacking stores in groups.

Every time a flash mob loots, it is robbing Dr. King of his dream. All over America, from Philadelphia to Chicago, from Washington to Detroit, young people who could be contributing to common good are trading in their dignity for the adrenaline rush of stealing from others. "We will not tolerate such reprehensible behavior here," said District of Columbia Mayor Vincent C. Gray in a statement responding to mob thefts there.[104] "Some news coverage of this incident has reported residents questioning whether the robbery could have been morally justified," he added, "Actually, both morality and the law are quite clear: It is wrong to steal from others. And if people do not obey the law, they will be apprehended, arrested and prosecuted." What Gray highlights is a troubling regression of public virtue and civil rights.

Dr. King's dream was one that harmonized morality and law. However, King's dream will never be realized in America as long as this country continues with the mythology that freedom does not require personal integrity and character. Proponents of dubious sociological and psychological theories allege that these flash mobs loot stores because minority young people feel disenfranchised and marginalized from mainstream society. What King taught us is that political and social frustration does not justify breaking the law. Perhaps if these disenfranchised youth where familiar at all with life under Jim Crow, or cared about the legacy of civil-rights heroes like Thurgood Marshall, Rosa Parks, Rep. John Lewis, Andrew Young, and others, they could tap into the imagination of an heroic generation, formed by the virtues of religion, who pursued public justice by pursuing public virtue.

An ailing American culture is responsible for this spectacle. In a society that does not value forming young people in the way of prudence, justice, courage, self-control, and the like, why should we be surprised that convenience stores are being robbed by youthful mobs? In a society that does not value private property and fosters a spirit of envy and class warfare through wealth redistribution, why should we be surprised that young people don't value someone else's property? Radical individualism and moral relativism define the ethics of our era and criminal flash mobs expose our progressive failure.

As we celebrate King's memorial, we must lament the fact that America's abandonment of virtue is destroying the lives of young black people and undermining the legal and economic catalysts that could end our recession

104. Landau. "Mayor Gray's Statement On Flashmob Shoplifting."

for good. In solidarity with Mayor Gray, I stand in front of the King statue, called "The Stone Of Hope," with a new dream: that a resurgence of virtue would give rise to a generation of moral and law-abiding citizens. In this way will young blacks truly experience the dreams of King and others who died for justice.

The Island of Black and Not "Progressive"

Independent black thinkers are expected to "groupthink" in ways that usually lead to rejection and isolation by multiple communities. I know this firsthand because it is where I have lived the past eight years of public life, loving both Thomas Sowell and Cornel West (for different reasons, of course). The new buzzword for "liberal" seems to be "progressive," and I'm neither. I also do not fit in with many conservatives because many of them want to go back to America's good old days, like the 1950s and prior when the country had family values, moral norms, and so on. But prior to the 1950s "conservatives" were more than content with white supremacy and Jim Crow. I don't want to conserve that culture. Moreover, when one thinks of the champions of the civil rights movement, what does not come to mind, especially in the South, are "conservatives." From 1776 to 1965 there was widespread social immorality in America because of the systematic dehumanization of non-whites and many immigrants. I have no romantic visions of America's past and likewise have no desire to return to a prior era, in which I would have to sit in the back of the bus and drink from "colored" water fountains.

In 2010, President Obama told a Hollywood fundraiser that he and congressional Democrats have passed the most progressive legislation in decades. "We have been able to deliver the most progressive legislative agenda—one that helps working families—not just in one generation, maybe two, maybe three," he said. "Progressive?" What does that mean? Big government? Socialistic? How is the government increasingly meddling in the private transactions of free people and free institutions considered progress? Is anyone who disagrees with Obama and other "progressives," then, regressive? Is anyone really against progress?

Of course, being black and not toeing the black party line by blindly supporting nearly everything President Obama says can get people like me in trouble too. I couldn't believe the number of blacks who sent me nasty emails and Facebook messages after I appeared on Glenn Beck's Fox News program to talk about my book for a combined on-air time of about 30 seconds. I had officially "sold-out," I guess.

To point out the unchallenged racism in some socially conservative circles renders the charge, "angry black man." Pointing out that big government has never really helped black communities in the long-term while promoting economic empowerment within the context of markets as a sustainable mechanism for socio-economic mobility, invites the charge of being "a sell-out." The intolerant fundamentalism of many "progressives" means that if one is passionate about justice issues one must adopt groupthink prescriptions for government solutions. The intolerant fundamentalism of many conservatives often carries with it cultural preferences that become necessary to accept to keep one's conservative credentials, like always voting for Republicans.

If I could resurrect one era, it would be one, if it ever existed, in which people were free to think as they pleased without pressure to adopt the tangential preferences of particular subcultures. But until that time, black independent thinkers will remain on the margins of everybody.

The Black Marriage Crisis

In the black community, the institution of marriage is essentially dead. While marriage in Western developed nations is declining in general, the black community and black women are being disproportionately affected. Unless marriage and family issues receive a higher priority, tackling other major problems, like declining high school graduation rates, will be like treading water in the Mississippi River 10 feet above a strong undercurrent.

ABC News released an article in 2010[105] citing a Yale University study, which reported that 42 percent of African-American women have yet to be married, compared to only 23 percent of white women. By their early 40s, 31 percent of black women have never been wives compared to 9 percent of white women. An alarming 70 percent of professional black women are single. ABC also reported, citing the *Journal of Blacks in Higher Education*, that at least 60 percent of black students who receive college degrees are women. Black women also make up 71 percent of black graduate students. According to the most recent data, only 43.3 percent of black adult men are married compared to around 60 percent for white males.

How the marriage and family crisis reached this current level is complicated. There is no one single culprit, because different social trends have affected different social classes within the black community separately. For example, while it is easy to point to the government welfare programs of the 1970s and '80s as nuclear bombs to marriage and family within the black

---

105. Johnson, "Nightline Face-Off."

underclass, this does not explain the declining marriage trend among the black middle class. The one institution that spans all social classes within the black community is the church. Since the end of the civil-rights movement, the black church has disappeared as the social, political, economic, and spiritual glue of the black community. The hip-hop generation—who Bakari Kitwana, a former editor at *The Source*, identifies as blacks born between 1965 and 1984[106]—is the first generation of blacks to be significantly un-churched since the 18th century. The cocktail of undermining government policies, political distractions with issues like affirmative action, challenges associated with black male incarceration rates, radical independence of black women introduced by black feminism, changing social norms, and eroded faith commitments have proven to be noxious. As such, the family, as the most important institution for forming and shaping character, spiri-tuality, morals, manners, etc., began to die (Deuteronomy 6).

By 2002 the black marriage rate was 35 percent compared to 63 per-cent in 1950. By 2007 only 25 percent of black children were born within the context of marriage compared to 80 percent in 1960. There is no govern-ment program that can reorient the black community toward those num-bers. There is no one-week summer VBS program by suburban teenagers that can come close to addressing the complexities of restoring families and promoting marriage. These problems are essentially moral and systemic, requiring more than government intervention or evangelistic programs dis-connected from local churches that can provide long-term spiritual nurture. Addressing this requires nothing less than long-term permanent spiritual care and discipleship. But this is costly because it demands more of our time than our money.

American Christians have been duped into accepting the insanity that short-term programs will solve multi-generational complex problems. The marriage and family crisis in the black community is a worldview crisis at its core. Until we are willing to follow Jesus' command and spend time lov-ing people and teaching them to obey everything Jesus taught, do not ex-pect much progress or change in the black community or anywhere else in America (Matthew 28:18-20). Quick-fix government programs and short-term church projects in this area are worse than attempts to plug holes in the Hoover Dam with superglue.

106. For more see Kitwana, *The Hip-Hop Generation*.

Why Black Liberation Theology Fails

I was thrilled to be a guest on Glenn Beck's show on the Fox News Channel in July 2010 discussing liberation theology and social justice and how they compare to orthodox Christian belief. I was reminded that others have highlighted flaws mentioned by Beck. In my book *Liberating Black Theology*, I also present the analysis of Alistair Kee, professor emeritus of theology at the University of Edinburgh. In his book *The Rise and Demise of Black Theology*, Dr. Kee concludes the following regarding the demise of black theology:

> There is the arrogance of Black Theology repeating year after year the same essentialisms and stereotypes which are frankly embarrassingly naïve in academic circles. There is a need for proper analysis of the worsening situation of Black poverty, a little more humility in view of the fact that 'we are more confused than ever about the reasons for it' . . . the forces of oppression and exploitation are increasingly taking control of the world through the processes of global capitalism. They cannot be successfully opposed simply by progressive Europeans. . . . Black Americans could play a vital part, if they read the new context and move their agenda forward.[107]

In fact, Kee views the plight of the black poor in terms of economic bifurcations, not racial variance. He writes, "In the present context the issue is the suffering of poor black people which no longer arises predominantly from race but from the inherent inequities of American capitalism."

According to Kee, in 2006, blacks are no longer victims of oppressive American life, "they are beneficiaries. The rising black middle class has done very well in recent years." Blacks in America are no longer victims because they now assume a commonality of interest with whites when U.S. companies strike deals with corrupt foreign regimes or decimate the environment of desperately poor communities. Kee goes on to argue that as American citizens, voters, and consumers, blacks should be able to have more influence in American policies toward Africa.

Again, one of Kee's primary critiques is that black theology fails to address the issues of class that are far more pervasive than race because of the new realities of this era. Racial discrimination and racial oppression are not the conditions that poor blacks find themselves in today. Poor blacks are not in their condition because of racism and racial discrimination.

---

107. Kee, *Rise and Demise of Black Theology*, 1.

Finally, Kee also notes that black liberation theology remains locked in the past. Now in many university posts, the second generation of black theologians employs a methodology that shackles black thought into historical sources, doing nothing more than regurgitating past formulas and critiques. You will find this often in the words of men like the Rev. Jesse Jackson and the Rev. Al Sharpton.

I discuss this more detail in my book on black theology,[108] but at the end of the day it is difficult to explain all of the problems in the black community today on race or the legacy of racism. While it is important to acknowledge that the past affects the present, Kee and others point out that black theology fails because it singles out race to explain many issues in communities that can only be remedied by the gospel, not the federal government.

No, Racism Does Not Explain Everything

One of the consequences of America's racial history is a tendency for some to read racism into all sorts of disparities that may be simply circumstantial. For example, maybe the reason organization "X" has no black or Latino senior staff is because the organization truly cannot find qualified minorities for certain positions. Is it at least possible? However, it would be dishonest not to acknowledge that in a world of sin some organizations continue to racially discriminate against certain people groups in hiring and promotions even when it's not in their economic or social interest to do so. Some organizations would rather discriminate than hire the best talent. In a free market, however, racial-discriminating organizations suffer the consequences of competing in a world that rewards the colorblindness of good performance.

To clarify my thesis, let's conjecture about what it takes for a conservative evangelical college to hire a black theologian to teach biblical theology. Let's say this college serves a very conservative set of churches in the German Reformed tradition primarily in the Midwest, and in 2010 the school still has no black faculty. If we think clearly about what this college must do to hire a black theologian we would be far less willing to assume that the reason the school has no black professors is because of "racism":

1. Blacks are only 13 percent of the U.S. population.

2. Less than 20 percent of blacks graduate from college in America (compared to about 25 percent for all Americans). Even less than that go on to graduate school.

108. For more see Bradley, *Liberating Black Theology.*

3. Blacks account for only 0.9 percent of all degrees awarded in theological studies.[109] The percentage of blacks earning Ph.Ds. in theology is so statistically insignificant that I couldn't even find the data.

4. The college requires all faculty members to sign a statement of faith and be a member of that college's denomination.

5. Less than 1 percent of the denomination's churches are in or near black communities and, of those churches, hardly any men go on to study at the seminary.

Any college with these types of constraints will have a real problem finding blacks (and whites for that matter) for teaching positions in theology. Given this reality, we should not be surprised by a lack of black faculty in this school. Among the small number of blacks graduating with a Ph.D. in theology, the school must find one from its own tradition who is actually qualified, and willing, to teach at that particular school. To assume that "there must be *someone* out there who's black and qualified" reveals a thought process void of knowledge and reason. It is hardly possible for a school from a very particular theological tradition that primarily serves churches traditionally in white communities to have a sufficiently sizable applicant pool to choose the best person for the position who also happens to be black.

Nothing is more irritating than a Christian school to be charged with "racism" because the school does not have any black or Latino faculty. Those accusing have no knowledge of the actual applicant pool available to make such a non-factual claim. Moreover, many fail to realize that blacks with a Ph.D. in theology have real options and may not want to teach at a particular school available to them. The bottom line is this: If the race conspirators want to see more minorities teaching theology at predominantly white institutions they should be a part of the solution by encouraging minorities to pursue a Ph.D. instead assuming that the only contribution blacks and Latinos can make in evangelicalism is in "urban ministry."

Whites: the Next Minority

A study from March 2010 suggests that today's white women are less interested in having children than previous generations.[110] According to the figures analyzed by the University of New Hampshire in a demographic

---

109. "Solid Progress," *The Journal of Blacks in Higher Education.*

110. See Johnson and Lichter. "Growing Diversity," 151–76.

study, white women increasingly are delaying having children and having smaller families, while growing numbers of Hispanic women are having large families at conventional childbearing ages. As these trends continue, America will likely have a white minority by 2050.

"Census projections suggest America may become a minority-majority country by the middle of the century," said Kenneth Johnson, a sociology professor at New Hampshire. According to the report, whites currently make up two-thirds of the total U.S. population, but the number of white women of prime childbearing age—20-39 years old—is in decline, dropping 19 percent from 1990.

"It looks like 'majority' births would drop below 50 percent around 2012," said Carl Haub, senior demographer for the Population Reference Bureau.

The researchers also discovered that fertility rates were higher among Hispanics, averaging three children per woman, compared to non-Hispanic white women, who average of just under two children each (1.87).

The research should serve as a "wake-up call" for denominations, churches, and Christian ministries serving predominantly white communities. If those institutions do not begin to reach Latinos and Hispanics successfully, they are headed for significant decline or extinction. On Sunday mornings or Wednesday nights or at your campus ministry, if you look out at the audience and it's predominantly white, then you are looking at an end of era should these demographic trends hold.

The study also indicates that birth rates among black women have declined as well. Black women are now averaging 2.13 children per woman. The sad truth is that black birth rates have been assaulted by an abortion genocide that the black church has been unaware of until recent years.

The interesting question is this: why do white women in America seem less and less interested in having children? Based on my anecdotal observations from my travels to Christian colleges and involvement with youth ministries, there does not seem to be any difference in how young Christian women think about children and family than non-Christians of the same age and class. Has the backlash against women's subjugation in the past created a new problem for the future?

Delaying having children and having small families for Christians seems to come into conflict with how many Christians have historically reflected on God's design for marriage as a sex-based institution between a man and woman for the purpose of uniting the couple as "one flesh" and procreation ("be fruitful and multiply"). This may seem like a stretch but the birth rate decline among white women has a simple marital solution if people are willing to make different lifestyle choices.

Atlanta's Lightening up, Demographically

On December 1, 2009, Atlanta's mayoral runoff election between city councilwoman Mary Norwood, who is white, and former state Sen. Kasim Reed, who is black, was still too close to call. In the general election the month before, Norwood won 46 percent of the vote, while Reed finished second with 36 percent, splitting the black vote among other African-American candidates. Since no candidate received a majority, a runoff between the top two became necessary. The real possibility of a white mayor in Atlanta corresponds to a steady transition in the city's demographics.

Atlanta residents have been proud of having decades of black leaders in government and business, and the city hasn't had a white mayor since Sam Massell was defeated in 1973. According to census data, the city is about 57 percent African-American (a decline from 61 percent in 2009) and 38 percent white. Why the proportional decline in the black population? Over the past 20 years, whites have been moving back into the very neighborhoods they fled when blacks moved in following the civil rights movement. Atlanta's "gentrification" has created quite a backlash of resentment and confusion among many blacks in the city.

When I fly into Atlanta, like I did for Thanksgiving several years ago, I remain amazed at the huge mural of a young African-American girl with outstretched arms facing the escalators and welcoming passengers to Atlanta as they head to the baggage claim area. As I grew up there, I was nurtured in a community of African-Americans, in which lifestyles of blacks like those presented on *The Cosby Show* were not fictitious. I even have a black doctor/lawyer couple in my family. Atlanta is a city where the black middle-class thrives and a place where blacks are key leaders in many sectors. To see a leadership change in the mayor's office would mean a new way of thinking about the city. I am not surprised, then, to find these demographic changes stirring real emotion.

In 2003, *Footnotes*, a newsletter of the American Sociological Association, published some of the angst that people felt back when the gentrification started: "The white folk moved out and are now paying anything to move back," said Frank Edwards, an Atlanta resident. "Regentrification, that's just a nice word for taking black folks' property," said Billy McKinney, a former Georgia State Representative.[111]

Kirkwood, East Lake, and East Atlanta are predominantly black neighborhoods in Atlanta that began to change nearly 20 years ago, as the newsletter noted:

111. Quoted in Reid and Adelman, "The Double-Edged Sword of Gentrification in Atlanta," lines 71-90.

Between 1990 and 2000 the white population in these neighborhoods doubled. The most dramatic racial change was in
Kirkwood, where white residents increased from 1% to 14% of
the population between 1990 and 2000. This area had not experienced such a shift since the 1960s. Between 1960 and 1970,
these neighborhoods changed from being almost 100% white to
almost 100% black. In Kirkwood, for example, 91% of residents
were white in 1960; by 1970, 97% of the population was black.[112]

For a white mayoral candidate to be elected over a black one might
just signal the end of an era of black middle-class dominance in Atlanta. As
whites move back into the city it will certainly continue to change the racial
makeup and priorities of city government. Demographic shifts are a normal
part of urban life, and Atlanta's residents, like many other minority residents
of large cities, are facing the reality that there are two-sides of the "change"
coin that President Obama emphasized during his presidential campaign.

No Racists in the Government?

I am growing more confused by many thought leaders in the black community who speak of how racist America is yet encourage more and more
blacks to put their lives into the hands of government officials who are white.
Is government bureaucracy immune from racism or classism? If American
society is categorically racist against blacks then black liberation would focus on divorcing blacks from dependence on the state—which is controlled
by "rich white people," as the Rev. Jeremiah Wright says.

In his book *Hope on a Tightrope*, Princeton University religion professor Cornel West makes the claim that in America "the very discovery that
black people are human beings is a new one." There was a time when blacks
were considered "three-fifths human—we were monkeys or rapists," writes
West. "Now we are projected as crack addicts or criminals." Moreover, he
adds, blacks have always been cornered into positions of "having to defend
our humanity."

West later explains that whites cannot avoid being shaped by white
supremacy:

White brothers and sisters have been shaped by 244 years of
supremacist slavery, 87 years of white supremacist Jim and Jane
Crow, and then another 40 years in which significant progress
has been made. The stereotypes still cut deep. Any white brother

112. Ibid.

or sister who deeply revels in the humanity of black, brown, yellow, and red brothers and sisters must undergo a kind of conver-
sion, metamorphosis, and transformation.

According to the government data from 2006, about 60 percent of
non-postal federal employees are white.[113] If whites have a white supremacy
problem and will not change without "metamorphosis," then blacks should
wish to avoid reliance on the federal government. Right? Isn't injustice inevitable for blacks if the majority of government employees recently learned
that blacks are human?

Why, then, is there such blind trust that government officials will serve
the interest of blacks and other minorities? Or is it the case that the assumption of racism only applies to those white people with whom black elites do
not agree on policy issues?

I agree with West that white racism toward blacks, sanctioned and
promoted by many Bible-believing Christians, describes most of America's
history. It would seem, however, that black leaders employing racial reasoning would promote initiatives to free blacks from the risk of coercion and
injustice at the hands of whites in government by doing all that is necessary
to position blacks to be free from the surrogate decisions of white government bureaucrats. Or, maybe "racism" is simply a convenient charge to distract us from having principled arguments about what is best. Sadly, until
many black leaders can justify trusting whites in government, the race card
remains on the table to be used against whites and others who disagree with
socialistic public policy.

The Americas' Legacy of Slavery

I once had to fight back tears while having lunch at a prestigious tennis club
in Ecuador after noticing that nearly all of ball boys were black. The club
didn't seem to have blacks even touching the food like you would find in
the United States. Food service seemed to be reserved for the lower class,
mixed-raced Native Americans.

Like many countries in North, Central, and South America, there is a
mixed population of folks who are of Spanish (i.e. from Spain), European,
Native American, and African descent. Native Americans are descendants
of those oppressed by Spanish and other Europeans, and we all know about
the "cruise ships" on which the black's African ancestors arrived. Centuries

---

113. "Executive Branch (non-Postal) Employment," United States Office of Personnel Management, 1.

later, however, not much has changed for the masses. Those of European descent tend to sit at the top of American societies while those of Native American and African descent remain at the bottom.

As I told my father about my experiences, he recalled the "whites-only" public golf courses where all the caddies were black throughout most of his life. I am still processing the looks I got from these black Ecuadorian kids, the look of shock on their faces to see someone who is dark like them having lunch at the club instead chasing behind the yellow balls of someone of European descent.

When several of the black ball boys stared at me with confusion and curiosity, they seemed to be asking, "Who is this?" It reminded me of the looks I received recently during dinner at a very prestigious tennis club in Philadelphia where the members were all white and the servers were, as usual, all black. And the wedding reception I attended last year at an all-white country club in South Carolina where I experienced the same thing. It was as if it were 1930. It's strange to be the only black person not serving food or busing tables in a room of hundreds of white people.

As our lunch in Ecuador ended, I was overwhelmed at what had happened. When we were leaving the tennis club, one of the black Ecuadorian boys ran to me to shake my hand. This black kid had an explosive smile on his face. I didn't know what to do. I regret not engaging him in short conversation to encourage him that it is possible for him to rise above being the perpetual servant of Europeans.

Later that day, while waiting on my flight to Quito, I lost the fight to hold back the tears, as I reflected on my encounter with this black kid. The black Ecuadorian ball boys reconfirm a pattern I see throughout the Americas when I travel: Wherever African slave trading ships docked or crashed, there you will find African descendants at the bottom of society and European descendants at the top. Hundreds of years later, this legacy of slavery and conquest is emotionally taxing to witness repeatedly and leaves me wondering if change is possible for the masses of African slave descendants and Native Americans who remain, in general, stuck in low socio-economic classes.

White Cops, Black Suspicion

In his nationally televised press conference in July 2009, President Obama said that the white cop who arrested Harvard professor Henry Louis Gates Jr. acted "stupidly." The cop, Sgt. James Crowley, rejected President Obama's comments, saying he was "way off base" for the accusation of stupidity. The day after Crowley's response, Obama said that he regretted his choice of words and called Crowley to talk it over. Despite this smoothing over, this entire situation resurrected another conversation in the race debate and burst the myth of our "post-racial" Obamanation. The officer arrested Gates, in part, because of the statements the scholar made out of anger and frustration, which, candidly, I understand.

Crowley, an 11-year veteran of the Cambridge Police Department, responded to a reported break-in at the professor's home. A neighbor reported seeing two men break into the home. The neighbor was unaware the man forcing his way inside was Gates, who had locked himself out.

When Crowley arrived, he told Gates he was investigating a report of a break-in and asked for his identification. "Why, because I'm a black man in America?" Gates responded according to the police report.[114] Gates initially refused to hand over identification, instead charging the officer of being racist.

If Professor Gates had been white would he have been arrested? Would the call from the neighbor have been made at all? Probably not, many would say. Is a bearded 58-year-old black man at a home in Cambridge suspicious in early in the afternoon? Obviously. The saddest part of the story is that the neighbor called in the afternoon and had no idea who Gates was either. When neighbors don't know each other, unfortunate situations like this happen.

My guess is that Gates will make at least $500,000 from this incident: a book deal, speaking engagements, interviews, etc. I am actually jealous. When I was pulled over in Creve Coeur, Mo., a wealthy white suburb in St. Louis, for a "rolling stop" at a stop sign, the president of the United States never accused the officer acting stupidly when I had to defend how it was that "a guy like [me] could afford a car like this."

Granted, I didn't come to a complete stop at the stop sign (like everyone else) but for the life of me I could not understand why the officer did a walk-around to check the inside of my vehicle and begin to question how a person like myself could afford a brand new Jeep Cherokee. Was it maybe because I was in graduate school and the vehicle was given to me as a graduation present? I'll never forget telling my seminary friends about the line of questioning about my ability to afford the vehicle and many responded, "Well, the Bible does say that Christians will be persecuted."

Since that day, whenever I'm in a neighborhood where I'm not supposed to be—in a white, middle-class suburb, for example—I get uneasy

---

114. You can find the report at http://www.samefacts.com/archives/Police%20 report%20on%20Gates%20arrest.PDF.

whenever I see a white cop driving near me. I wonder if I will once again have to explain how I can afford my car. Then again, I'm no Henry Louis Gates Jr., with his M.A. and a Ph.D. in English literature from Clare College at the University of Cambridge, a B.A. summa cum laude in history from Yale University, and his positions as the Alphonse Fletcher University professor and director of the W.E.B. Du Bois Institute for African and African American Research at Harvard University.

Three Cheers for the Supreme Court

In June 2009, the U.S. Supreme Court handed down justice on behalf of a few white firefighters. Awesome. According to the court's decision, several white firefighters were mistreated by the city of New Haven, Conn., when it refused to promote them despite their high scores on a promotional exam. In a 5-4 decision, the high court ruled that the city should not have trashed the exams because black firefighters performed poorly. Is this not what Martin Luther King Jr. wanted—that one day blacks would be judged according to their character, not their skin color? So why would four judges encourage racial preferences?

The court's decision actually moved the country in the right direction toward achieving true fair treatment under the law. Why not celebrate the fact that we even have black firefighters, or the fact that promotion is equally open to firefighters of all races? In the 1940s it probably would not have been so. This is a classic example of the conflict we have in our country with those who understand equality in terms of manufactured, cosmetic social results versus those who understand equality and justice in terms of fair processes that do not discriminate.

What would have represented real injustice would have been a scenario in which the black firefighters scored higher than all the whites on the exam and still were not promoted because they were black. The idea that a fair and equal process is ignored because we want to achieve cosmetic racial results to remedy discrimination against previous generations creates a new form of injustice.

In dissent, Justice Ruth Bader Ginsburg said the white firefighters "understandably attract this court's sympathy. But they had no vested right to promotion. Nor have other persons received promotions in preference to them." What? Actually, they do have a right to promotion because they scored higher on the exam. Questioning the utility of the exam in evaluating promotion candidates is one thing, but it is not the role of judges to misuse the law for the sake of social "remedies" to historical events.

New Haven, seeking to fill senior fire department vacancies, administered the test to 77 candidates for lieutenant and 41 candidates for captain. Fifty-six firefighters passed the exams: 41 whites, nine blacks, and six Hispanics. Of those, however, only 17 whites and two Hispanics could expect promotion. If the exam was racially biased in favor of whites, would it not have also excluded the Hispanics? Did the exam discriminate against the other whites that performed poorly as well? Maybe they weren't the right kind of white people.

Racial preferences that override the rules do nothing but create more injustice and do not represent equality and fair treatment at all. If the black firefighters really believed in equality they would have been thankful that they were free to take the exam in the first place and congratulate the Hispanics and whites who performed better than them like everybody else who did not make the cut.

The Supreme Court Tackles Race (Again)

Remember when Attorney General Eric Holder inaccurately described America as "essentially a nation of cowards," saying that people "simply do not talk enough with each other about race"? In 2009, we talked about race for months as the Supreme Court heard several racially charged cases. The cases, as reported by USA Today, involved four main categories: voting rights, employment, housing, and education.[115]

Holder's jab is not entirely accurate because Americans talk about race, it seems, without ceasing. We're obsessed with the topic. We love to constantly bring it up, love to balk at those who constantly bring it up, or love to balk at those we assume have no concern about the issue. We even see it in the church with this constant talk about "racial reconciliation" and the misapplication of Revelation 7:9 as the goal of every local congregation in America.

Rulings from Supreme Court sessions that deal with race issues will reveal whether or not there truly is injustice, but will also ignite emotional reasoning and irrationality. One thing that contributes to racial hysteria is the continued belief that any racial disparity is the result of premeditated racial discrimination. Thus, the solution to racial disparity becomes government coercion. I realize that there are real cases in which discrimination occurs and that institutions act unjustly at times, but that does not mean that racism is always the cause of apparent racial disparity.

115. Biskupic, "The Supreme Court Tackles Race," original online link now defunct.

The cases before the court in 2009 primarily addressed a conflict between two visions of understanding racial demarcations in institutions and political society. One vision says we ought to use merit to equalize the process for all, while the other says that we ought to let surrogate decision-makers use race to create cosmetic outcomes even when injustice is not proven. For example, a group of white and Latino firefighters sued their city because exams used for assessment of promotions were discarded because black firefighters had low scores. If advancement was determined on the basis of performance, the black firefighters would not have benefited. As such, all the exams were thrown out.

It seems that if we want a society that moves forward, not judging people on the basis of race, then we should let everyone compete freely and fairly. Racial discrimination occurs in its most aggressive form when individuals are not given a chance to prove their own merit freely and fairly.

The outcome of one's performance tells us nothing about "racism" in the process. If my company has no black male managers why assume that racism is the cause? Perhaps I cannot find many blacks who are qualified for the position. Instead of assuming "racism" it may be good to notice that black males are approaching a 50 percent high school dropout rate. Maybe the perceived lack of racial progress institutionally and culturally in America is actually an indicator that major sabotaging forces other than race are at work keeping the whole nation from progress.

Sadly, the rulings of any judicial body cannot solve our race issues. In any case, I will most likely be left saying, "Oh well, here we go again."

So, What is Race?

As I reflected on the "race question" that Ann Compton asked at President Obama's press conference in March 2009, I was left pondering what "race" even means. We use the term as if there is one clear definition, but I'm not sure if this is the case.

Christianity, of course, has a complex history of both embracing and rejecting cultural norms for demarcating between groups of people according to race. While the Scriptures plainly teach that all human persons are of one human race as image-bearers of God (Genesis 1:26-27, Acts 17:26), Christians, have not always held this position consistently.

Race, however, is a sociological construct. For centuries human societies have created arbitrary divisions based on physical differences that the church has not been immune from adopting. Biologically, human beings have the same genetic constitution. What distinguish human characteristics are various combinations of genes expressing themselves on particular chromosomes—hardly enough to justify physical differences as a basis for distinguishing people groups.

While it is true that genetic differentiation has occurred in human history, there is no justifiable basis, biblical or scientific, to categorize human beings according to physical characteristics. Although there is no valid typology of human races, Christians have embraced the arbitrary categorizations and at times perverted the Scriptures in the process.

The Gospel brings individuals from all people groups together for a common mission. The effects of the Fall that turn people against each other and segregate on the basis of physical characteristics will remain—in violation of God's shalom—without the work of the Church as she spreads the Gospel.

In the end, I'm still left with the question of what will define race in the future and what role it plays in making any good distinctions between people.

A Race Question?

Did she really ask a race question?

This is exactly what I thought after seasoned ABC News correspondent Ann Compton asked President Obama about his use of race in decision-making during a press conference in March 2009. The economy was tanking, the government was growing like kudzu near Interstate 285 in Atlanta, China was talking about a world currency, and she asked the president if race has played a role in decisions he's made as president. What? Seriously? Who cares?

Here's how the dialogue proceeded:

"Ann Compton—hey, Ann," Obama called out.

"You sound surprised," he added with laughter at her reaction.

"I am surprised!" Compton replied. "Could I ask you about race?"

"You may," he said.

"Yours is a rather historic presidency, and I'm just wondering whether, in any of the policy debates that you've had within the White House, the issue of race has come up, or whether it has in the way you feel you've been perceived by other leaders or by the American people," Compton said. "Or have the last 64 days been a relatively color-blind time?"

President Obama's response was appropriate. After mentioning that the inauguration displayed a "justifiable pride on the part of our country" because of what we have accomplished racially, he said that all the hoopla about race "only lasted about a day" because of the other pressing issues before us. The president ought to be judged according to his effectiveness at addressing the big issues of our time, he pointed out.

At the time, Ann Compton was the national correspondent for ABC News Radio in Washington, D.C., as well as president of the White House Correspondents' Association, coordinating coverage and access issues with the White House staff.

It is possible that Compton was not expecting to ask a question that night, as President Obama even noted that she seemed surprised when called upon. Perhaps Compton had no question in mind so the best she could think of, on the spot, was a race-related question. After all, she was looking at a black man who must obviously think only along racial lines when thinking of new ways to grow the government. Other than race-related questions, what else would one ask America's first black president?

At least Compton did not ask about the president's dogs or where his wife buys her shoes. Given the pressure of possibly being taken off guard, I imagine that I could have offered a series of strange questions as well, such as "Mr. President, have you read F.A. Hayek's book *The Road to Serfdom?*" Or "Mr. President, do you think you'll make a Clemson football game in the fall? They have a new head coach. Go Tigers!" Or "Mr. President, what is your favorite snack food during meetings?" These are the kinds of questions Americans want to know the answers to during an economic crisis, right? Actually, reading Hayek now would be very helpful in Washington these days.

When people in the media ask questions like Compton's, I feel sorry for them because of the ridicule I expect them to face. A few folks almost immediately posted complaints about her question at ABC News.com. "Tonight's question by Ann Compton to the president of the United States was the lamest, worst conceived I could have imagined," one critic posted. In the end, here's the moral of the story: If you're at a White House press conference, always have a good question ready to ask even if you do not believe you'll be called on to speak. Always.

When Racists Repent

I had hoped that 2010 would be the year during which I would not be referred to as a "negro theologian." 2009 certainly wasn't that year. Some blacks I know would find it hard to believe that it is possible for a white racist to change his or her views, like former Ku Klux Klansman Elwin Wilson did when he flew to Washington, D.C., to apologize to Rep. John Lewis for beating him in Rock Hill, S.C., 48 years ago.

ABC news reported the following:

> Wilson, a young, white, Southern man, attacked Lewis, a freedom rider for Martin Luther King, in the "white" waiting room of a South Carolina bus station.
>
> The men had not seen each other again until Tuesday when, with "Good Morning America's" help, Wilson approached Lewis again — this time offering an apology and a chance to relieve a burden he'd carried for more than four decades.
>
> "I'm so sorry about what happened back then," Wilson said breathlessly.
>
> "It's OK. I forgive you," Lewis responded before a long-awaited hug.[116]

While watching the video clip of this story, I was struck by the powerful account of what changed Wilson's views on race and what prompted his desire for reconciliation. Everything changed for him when a friend asked, "If you died right now do you know where you would go?" Wilson responded, "To hell." After being changed by the reality of grace of God, he began to publicly apologize his previous racial views and actions. Wilson even has the Christian maturity to pray for President Obama even though he says, "I didn't vote for him."

Wilson recounts past actions with some regret: "I had a black baby doll in this house, and I had a little rope, and I tied it to a limb and let it hang here." However, in the spirit of Matthew 18, he met Lewis to ask for forgiveness and pursue reconciliation.

Wilson has been harassed and attacked for publicly repenting of his racism. In a CNN interview, he told of a telephone call he received from a college student: "He said, 'You are [a] slummy black n dog.' And he just kept on talking. He told me, he said, 'Here you are with KKK, took an oath, and here you are going back on your word and against the white people.'"

Rep. Lewis said what Wilson did in coming to him shows "the power of love and the power of grace, and the power of people to be able to say, 'I'm sorry.'" The gospel is indeed powerful (Romans 1:16-17), and, as see in the book of Galatians, the gospel transforms race-hatred into racial solidarity. We all long to see the gospel change people so that the racial slurs of the past are no longer a part of public discourse.

---

116. "An Emotional Reunion with the Klan?" ABC News, 3:49.

Politics and Economics

On Wages, McDonald's Gets it Right

IN TODAY'S CULTURE OF entitlement, people believe that they deserve certain rewards simply because they exist—not because of hard work, perseverance and wise choices. Entitlement is the only way to explain the lunacy behind demands that fast food chains like McDonald's pay workers at a rate as arbitrarily high as $15 per hour. Unlike many politicians, business leaders do not make decisions according to public opinion, because they have fiduciary responsibilities to their boards and shareholders. As a result, McDonald's Corp. Chief Executive Officer Don Thompson is doing the right thing by not cowing to ridiculous wage demands. In short, McDonald's has become a scapegoat for a series of failed economic and public policies.

The protest narrative recorded in the news media goes something like this: "McDonald's should pay more because life is hard for employees." For example, in the *New York Daily News* a McDonald's worker, Shaniqua Davis, said, "I'm not going to stay quiet . . . I'm going to continue to fight. . . I've got a daughter to take care of. I struggle to make ends meet."[1] The *St. Louis Post-Dispatch* tells of LaShunda Moore, a 36-year-old mother of five children who, after 14 months at McDonald's, earns $7.85 an hour. "I start work at 5 a.m., and by 5:05 a.m., I'm sweating," she said. "I work in the grill area, and people don't see all the work we do." Moore's children live with their father. "I don't get paid enough to support everyone," she said. "He's a telemarketer and sits down all day but gets paid better than I do."

These stories raise important questions. For example, why it is that McDonald's workers cannot make ends meet? Do we expect McDonald's to

---

1. Sandoval et al., "Fast-food Workers Strike," lines 5-7.

make up the difference between challenging circumstances and poor personal choices? Is it McDonald's fault that you are in your mid-30s, unmarried with several children, and have not acquired the requisite skill set to improve your employment opportunities? Is it McDonald's fault that politicians have over-regulated the market, inadvertently encouraging businesses to move out of low-income neighborhoods? Are we blaming McDonald's for the fact that technological innovation and automation continue to eliminate low-skilled, entry-level jobs? It is beyond outrageous to think that fast food restaurants are going to reconcile these tensions.

Don Thompson is even being accused of being greedy and out of touch. Are the protestors aware that Thompson himself came out of poverty to become McDonald's first black CEO? Thompson grew up just three blocks north of the Cabrini-Green housing project in Chicago before moving to Indianapolis in the sixth grade to be raised by his grandmother. He understands struggling to make ends meet. Thompson, however, protested the crime-ridden and low-wage earning future to which he seemed consigned by his circumstances by working hard in high-school, graduating from college, getting married, becoming active in his church and, after 22 years at McDonald's, eventually rising to become CEO. Thompson's advance is a clear illustration of the strong correlation between morally responsible decision-making and personal financial stability.

There was a time in America during which taking responsibility for your long-term goals was neither the government's job nor your company's. It was yours and yours alone. You protested by improving your situation. If your current job was not sufficient to make ends meet, then you did not simply demand a 100 percent raise; rather, you sought a better job by doing things like moving to a different city or learning a new trade. You saw the wage ceiling and moved on.

Today's fast food protests are misplaced. Perhaps these protestors should protest in front of Congress for the following: the failed 70-year attempt by government to manage the economy, the failure of social welfare programs to get people out of poverty, creating policies that destroyed the urban family and undermined Judeo-Christian morals, the introduction of regulatory disincentives that pushed businesses out of low-income areas, and the subsidizing of substandard public education that leaves students incapable of competing with innovation in a global marketplace. Perhaps the protestors should also protest themselves for making poor decisions that placed them in difficult circumstances.

In the end, McDonald's is already doing its fair share by employing and paying a market wage to hundreds of thousands of workers with minimal training and education. What is needed in the future is for employees to take advantage of their fast food entry point, work hard, make wise life choices, and for politicians to get out of the way of small businesses so that people can take responsibility for their futures—and perhaps someday, like Don Thompson, become the head of one of the world's largest companies.

Mass Incarceration: the New Eugenics?

In May 2014, the United States had over 2.3 million prisoners incarcerated in federal, state, and local jails around the country. According to an April 2014 report from the same year by the Sentencing Project, that number represents a 500 percent increase in incarcerations over the past 40 years. This increase produces "prison overcrowding and fiscal burdens on states to accommodate a rapidly expanding penal system" despite the evidence that incarceration is not working. How did this happen? The culprit is usually identified as the failed policies associated with the War on Drugs. Because blacks are disproportionately swept up in the campaign against drugs, some scholars refer to the results of mass incarceration as the new "The New Jim Crow." While the original intentions may have been well-meaning, the long-term consequences may be worse: the War on Drugs may actually be class-based eugenics by another name.

In her groundbreaking book, *The New Jim Crow*, Michelle Alexander hypothesizes that, given the similarity between the "law and order" appeals between the creation of Jim Crow Laws and similar appeals in the War on Drugs, as well as the resultant economic marginalization of felons after release from prison, today's mass incarceration is "The New Jim Crow." The drug war is simply a new way to control the futures of African Americans. As hip hop artist Sho Baraka says, "The war on drugs is the war on us." Does the racialized narrative work?

Based on the most recent government data from the Bureau of Justice Statistics, it is true that drug offenses account for 51 percent of prison inmate presence and that black males constitute a higher percentage, per capita, of drug prosecutions than any other group. What is even more important, however, is that 37 percent of the entire federal prison population is black, 32 percent is Hispanic, and 28 percent is white. If mass incarceration were the New Jim Crow, we would expect a greater racial disparity between whites and blacks in prison overall. Moreover, in 1964, at the height of the Jim Crow era, only 34 percent of US prisoners were black while 65 percent were white. Alexander's race narrative is misguided and misses the fact that mass incarceration might be just another historic example of elites using government power to control the country's "degenerates"—namely, the lower classes—and to create and control social outcomes that benefit the interests of those in power.

In 1877, a prison reformer by the name of Richard Dugdale noticed that prisons were increasingly populated by a particular group of people—poor whites—and that the offspring of the same group were likely to be criminals as well. After the Civil War, social progressives, relying on scientific inquiry into human nature, raised a class of social science intellectuals who concluded that America needed to deal with her degenerate populations. Matt Wray, in *Not Quite White*, explains how Dugdale's research and findings launched the eugenics movement in America.[2] The backward citizens who were impeding America's progress were "lazy, lustful, and cunning," writes Wray, and were particularly sexually immoral. The reference was to lower class whites exclusively. Progressive eugenicists, taking action to control "white trash" and the like, launched a campaign to use government coercion to forcibly sterilize lower class whites (and later blacks). Eugenics was considered good for America's social welfare and economic progress. According to Wray, progressives sought "legislative reform campaigns aimed at restricting foreign immigration, mandating state institutionalization of the biologically unfit, and legalizing eugenical involuntary sterilization." Eugenics was a way to protect society from social traits like "pauperism, laziness, promiscuity and licentiousness, inbreeding, nomadism [idleness], and delinquency." Does this sound familiar?

Today's prison population is largely comprised of "lazy, lustful, and cunning" lower class whites, blacks, and Hispanics, whom elites and progressives institutionalize in "correctional" facilities and then nearly permanently control them and their families in a closed ecosystem of government programs, including "reproductive services," while never addressing the core moral issues that sabotage freedom and success. Sentencing someone to prison for one year on a marijuana possession charge, or in the 2011 case of Patrick Carney in Louisiana, sentencing someone to 30 years for selling $25 worth of marijuana is a waste, both of financial and human capital. Represented by public defenders and often unaware of their legal rights, many of these offenders are manipulated into pleading guilty to charges that high-powered attorneys would get dismissed altogether.

The scandal of today's mass incarceration associated with the War on Drugs is the failed attempt to use the police, lawyers, judges, corrections officers, and social workers to address issues that are profoundly moral in nature. People should be sent to prison because they are dangerous to

2. Wray, *Not Quite White*, 1.

society, not because we are mad at them and want to reform them. Prisons are not churches. Without this preventative moral formation, we set the lower classes up for a lifetime—sometimes, generations—of government control. This softer form of eugenics is worse than Jim Crow.

When Freedom, Creativity, and Opportunity Meet

Thomas L. Jennings (1791–1856) was the first African-American to be granted a patent, for his discovery of a process called "dry-scouring"—what we now know as "dry cleaning." Jennings' life is a model of what happens when people of virtue have the freedom to use their skills to meet needs in the marketplace and contribute to the common good. What the United States and the rest of the world need are social, political, and economic contexts where people can flourish in the same way that Jennings did.

Jennings was born a free man soon after the state of New York banned the slave trade in 1788. In the following years, New York slowly began to expand the sphere of freedom for blacks, creating more opportunities for them to participate in all levels of society. As a young man, Jennings dug trenches on Long Island during the War of 1812. After bouncing around from job to job, he finally landed an apprenticeship with a clothier, which set the stage for him to become an expert tailor. In fact, Jennings was so remarkably skilled that people from all over the New York City area would come to him for alterations or custom-tailored items. The demand for his services was so great that, in his early 20s, he was able to open his own store on Church Street, which soon grew into one of the largest clothing stores in New York City during that era.

In the course of operating his business, Jennings became increasingly aware that many of his customers had few options for cleaning their clothes without damaging them. Conventional cleaning methods of the time would normally ruin the fabric, leaving owners with the unattractive options of wearing dirty clothes or disposing of the clothes after a few washes. After experimenting with different solutions and cleaning agents, Jennings found the right combination to effectively treat and clean clothes without destroying the fabric. Jennings called this new method "dry-scouring."

In 1820, Jennings applied for a patent. His application created substantial controversy, because a 1793 U.S. patent law prohibited slaves from receiving patents for their own inventions and thus no patent had ever been awarded to a black person. Since Jennings was born as a free man, however, the patent courts had no legal reason to prevent Jennings from receiving his patent, making him the first black to acquire one (March 3, 1821, U.S. patent 3306x).

Jennings' contributions to society, however, do not end there. He used his earnings not only to improve his business but also to promote good social causes. For example, he spent much of his profit to purchase his family from slavery and to support the abolitionist movement. In 1831, Jennings became assistant secretary to the First Annual Convention of the People of Color in Philadelphia, Pennsylvania, and he spent many years fighting for the liberation of blacks. Jennings was neither coerced nor pressured by the rhetoric of "corporate social responsibility" nor "paying his fair share"; he simply did what was good for his customers and right for society because he was free to do so.

Do we not want new stories like this in the United States and around the world? Do we not want people to be free to use their creativity to meet marketplace needs in their communities and freely use their wealth creation to contribute to civil society as they see fit? Ironically, if Jennings were alive today he would have had a much more difficult time succeeding because of the obstacles to innovation and philanthropy erected by ever-increasing federal regulations and ever-expanding government bureaucracy. As such, many burgeoning entrepreneurs are currently barred from capitalizing on opportunities to address market needs and to solve real problems in society because politicians believe they know how to meet the needs of society better than the rest of us.

Jennings is a wonderful example of what happens when political and economic liberty meet in virtue. Now if we could only get our politicians and regulators to get out of the way of the yet-to-be-discovered innovators like Jennings, we could all enjoy the benefits.

Crisis and Constitution: Hitler's Rise to Power

On Jan. 30, 1933, Adolf Hitler became Chancellor of Germany. While he was being sworn in he said, "I will employ my strength for the welfare of the German people, protect the Constitution and laws of the German people, conscientiously discharge the duties imposed on me and conduct my affairs of office impartially and with justice to everyone." Neither the German people, nor the rest of world, had any idea that this day was the beginning of an incremental concentration of power that would later lead to the death of millions of people and catalyze World War II. The lesson the world learned from Hitler concerning the dangers of unchecked power should never be forgotten.

In the week following his oath of office, Chancellor Hitler convinced German president Paul von Hindenburg to do two things: dissolve parliament and authorize the Minister of the Interior and the police to prohibit public meetings and publications that might be considered a danger to public safety. The conditions that made this kind of anti-democratic move possible were economic depression, political instability (including the threat of revolution), and a widespread desire to regain national dignity following the shame of defeat in World War I.

The Nazis played on these fears and desires. On the night of Feb. 27, 1933, the Reichstag building, where parliament met, was set on fire. Whether the action was undertaken at the behest of the Nazi Party or was an independent act remains debatable, but that Hitler capitalized on the panic that ensued is certain. The next day Hitler urged Hindenburg to respond by issuing a new law that suspended sections of the German Constitution that protected individual liberties. In this "Decree of the Reich President for the Protection of the People and the State," the German people were informed that "Restrictions on personal liberty, on the right of free expression of opinion, including freedom of the press; on the rights of assembly and association; and violations of the privacy of postal, telegraphic and telephonic communications and warrants for house searches, orders for confiscations as well as restrictions on property, are also permissible beyond the legal limits otherwise prescribed." In a later section of the decree, Hitler laid the foundation for abolishing the country's federalist system and centralizing power in Berlin: "If in a state [regional government] the measures necessary for the restoration of public security and order are not taken, the Reich Government may temporarily take over the powers of the highest state authority."

In March 1933, through various political maneuvers, Hitler successfully suppressed Communist, Socialist, and Catholic opposition to a proposed "Enabling Act," which allowed the Cabinet to introduce legislation without first going through parliament, thus by-passing Constitutional review. The act would give the executive branch unprecedented power. Hitler's regime designed the act as a temporary measure requiring reauthorization by the Reichstag every four years. Once the Nazis were the majority, reauthorization became perpetual. On March 23, 1933, the day votes were cast for the act, all of the Communist deputies and 26 Socialist deputies were missing because they had either been arrested or had fled the country, according to Lucy S. Dawidowicz in *The War Against the Jews: 1933–1945*. When the vote was taken, 441 deputies voted in favor of the Act and all 94 of the Social Democrats present voted against it. Hitler now had legal authority for dictatorship. Five days later, with the announcement of a plan to silence complaints about Germany by Jews abroad, Hitler began his long-term campaign against the Jews, which began with the boycott of German businesses and later escalated to the murder of an estimated six million Jews.

Hitler's rise to power is a sobering story of how a crisis and calls for quick solutions can tempt citizens and leaders to subvert the rule of law and ignore a country's constitutional safeguards. Adolf Hitler swore to protect Germany's constitution, yet he pursued expanded "temporary" executive power that circumvented due process for the sake of the "safety" and "protection" of the people. Germany's descent into totalitarianism is yet another example of how calls to concentrate decision-making in the executive branches, as we now see all over the world, too easily set the stage for political, social, and moral evil. It would serve us well to remember that among the best protections citizens have against tyranny and oppression is insistence that all, including politicians, be held accountable to the same laws and that due process is always honored. These guarantees should be part of a system where decision-making is dispersed, not concentrated, because, as Lord Acton reminds us, "Power tends to corrupt, and absolutely power corrupts absolutely."

Ten States Further Crippling Workers in 2013

In December 2012, the Pew Center on the States reported that ten states voted to raise the minimum wage for workers in 2013.[3] Teens and low-skilled workers should be protesting in response. According to the report,

> Nine states will adjust the wages to accommodate the rising costs of living, as required by state laws, while Rhode Island will implement a law signed by the governor in June that raises its minimum wage to $7.75 per hour. The wage hikes range between 10 cents and 35 cents per hour, adding between $190 and $510 to the average affected worker's annual pay.

In Washington State the rate rose to $9.19 per hour, the highest in the nation at the time.[4] While this may sound like good public policy, these wage increases actually hurt the very same people they are supposed to help. Whenever lawmakers decide to arbitrarily determine the price of labor (wages) we need to stop and ask this simple question, "Where are employers

3. For the full report see Malewitz, "New Year Will Bring Higher Minimum Wages in 10 States."

4. As of August 2015, the highest minimum wage rate in the country is $10.50/hr in the District of Columbia.

going to find the money to cover the wage increase?" It has to come from somewhere. Why is that not a natural "next question?"

As I have said in my earlier book, *Black and Tired*, minimum wage increases hurt teens and low-skilled minorities the most because minimum wage jobs are usually entry-level positions filled by employees with limited work experience and few job skills. When the government forces employers to pay their workers more than a job's productivity demands, employers, in order to stay in business, generally respond by hiring fewer hours of low-skill labor. Low-skill workers become too expensive to employ, creating a new army of permanent part-timers.

Washington State, for example, with its 2011 $8.67 minimum wage also had one of the nation's highest teen unemployment rates at 34.5% in that same year.[5] The tragedy is that lawmakers seem incapable of seeing the connection between artificially high wages and increased unemployment. In the meantime, teen and low-skilled workers continue to suffer the consequences of politicians meddling in the market place while business gets blamed for being greedy.

Unemployment and Despair in the UK

In January 2013, BBC News reported that 1 out of 10 young people between the ages of 16 and 25 are struggling to cope with life.[6] The main culprit: despair related to unemployment. The survey of 2,000 teens and young adults was conducted by The Prince's Trust Youth Index.

The survey commentators seemed surprised that education and training opportunities alone are not enough to provide hope for unemployed young people. Young people rightly want to know why they are training for jobs that do not exist. This has been particularly difficult in Northern Ireland where 20% of 18 to 24-year-olds cannot find employment. From the BBC:

> Ian Jeffers, regional director of The Prince's Trust in Northern Ireland, said: "A frightening number of unemployed young people in Northern Ireland feel unable to cope—and it is particularly tough for those who don't have a support network in place. . . .
> "Life can become a demoralising downward spiral—from a challenging childhood into life as a jobless adult. But, with the

5. "Washington State Teen Unemployment Rate," *Puget Sound Business Journal.*
6. "One in Ten Young in Northern Ireland 'Cannot Cope with Life,'" BBC News.

right support, we can help get these lives on track across the region."

Add to the unemployment data a dominant cultural secularism, the dehumanization and trappings of long-term government social welfare assistance, broken families, and self-sabotaging social pathologies, and one can easily understand why young people in Northern Ireland and the United Kingdom feel hopeless and unable to cope with life.

The BBC story reminds me of a section on Pope John Paul II's encyclical Laborem excercens describing the moral and economic importance of work:

> [Work] is not only good in the sense that it is useful or something to enjoy; it is also good as being something worthy, that is to say, something that corresponds to man's dignity, that expresses this dignity and increases it. If one wishes to define more clearly the ethical meaning of work, it is this truth that one must particularly keep in mind. Work is a good thing for man-a good thing for his humanity-because through work man not only transforms nature, adapting it to his own needs, but he also achieves fulfilment as a human being and indeed, in a sense, becomes "more a human being."[7]

Without this consideration it is impossible to understand the meaning of the virtue of industriousness, and more particularly it is impossible to understand why industriousness should be a virtue: for virtue, as a moral habit, is something whereby man becomes good as man.

Without a clearly defined moral compass, strong families that provide love and a sense of meaning, and economic opportunities that give young people a vocational imagination for the role they might come to play in making the world a better place, the inability to cope with life among young adults is only going to get worse. If Americans think that cultural secularization, increasing dependence on social welfare assistance, and undermining wealth creation in the business sector will "make America great," then I would suggest that they look across the pond.

Government Subsidies Not So Sweet For Health

It's yet another example of the unintended consequences of government meddling in the economy, a study released late in 2012 showed that large amounts of high fructose corn syrup (HFCS) found in national food supplies

7. John Paul II, *Laborem Exercens*, section 9.

across the world may be one explanation for the rising global epidemic of type 2 diabetes and resulting higher health care costs.

The study, "High Fructose Corn Syrup and Diabetes Prevalence: A Global Perspective," conducted by a group of scholars led by Michael Goran and published in *Global Public Health*, reports that countries that use HFCS in their food supply had a 20 percent higher prevalence of diabetes than countries that did not use the additive. Thanks to government subsidies of the corn refining industry, HFCS is unbelievably cheap compared to sugar, and has made its way into foods and beverages all over the world. The current administration has an opportunity to show international leadership by ending corn subsidies in the United States and encouraging other nations to follow as a good first step in lowering health care costs and promoting good nutrition.

According to a California Public Interest Research Group and the U.S. PIRG Education Fund 2010 report, federal farm subsidies contribute significantly to the nation's obesity epidemic. The report shows that, from 1995 to 2010, $16.9 billion in federal subsidies went to companies and organizations in the business of producing and distributing corn syrup, high fructose corn syrup, corn starch and soy oils. Using California as a model, the report explains the math in this way: taxpayers in the San Francisco area spend $2.8 million each year in junk food subsidies and Los Angeles taxpayers spend $13 million. The bottom line is that, while advocates of corn subsidies focus on the benefit to farmers and food suppliers, the possibility of long term negative effects on public health is ignored.

From an international perspective, the Goran study reports that out of 42 countries examined, the United States has the highest per-capita consumption of HFCS at a rate of 55 pounds per year. The second highest is Hungary, with an annual rate of 47 pounds. Canada, Slovakia, Bulgaria, Belgium, Argentina, Korea, Japan and Mexico are also relatively high HFCS consumers. Germany, Poland, Greece, Portugal, Egypt, Finland and Serbia are among the lowest HFCS consumers. Countries with per-capita consumption of less than 1.1 pounds per year include Australia, China, Denmark, France, India, Ireland, Italy, Sweden, the United Kingdom and Uruguay.

These correlations are particularly troubling in light of the fact that HFCS's association with the "significantly increased prevalence of diabetes" occurred independent of total sugar intake and obesity levels, according to Goran. The production of HFCS is simply aggravating poor health around the world. According to recent estimates, 6.4 percent of the world population is currently diabetic, and that number will rise to 7.7 percent by the year 2030. Another study cited by Goran showed that across the globe, the number of people with diabetes rose from 153 million in 1980 to 347 million in 2008. These increases are projected to affect developing countries disproportionately, with an estimated 69 percent increase in the number of diabetic adults as compared to a 20 percent increase in developed countries.

Dr. Amy Kristina Herbert, an assistant professor of pediatric dentistry at the University of Texas at Houston, explains the relationship this way: "it is the subsidizing that keeps the foods that contain [HFCS] low cost [to consumers] and more attractive to low income populations. It is a major additive in fast food, as is corn in general which, since subsidized, keeps fast food cheap as well. Anything processed tends to have corn/HFCS in it which is a major cause of the overconsumption of high energy, low nutrition foods, or empty calories, which leads to weight gain and diabetes."

In our national debate over health care reform, most Americans have accepted the fact that we have a moral obligation to ensure that our fellow citizens have access to basic health care, and that government may play a role in that task. But what if the same government that purports to be aiding our quest for a healthful life with one hand is with the other hand dumping money into the production of foods that undermine that quest? With the mountains of research from scholars and advocacy groups building, it seems that a prudent first step in reducing diet-related diabetes is for the U.S. government to withdraw from the corn production industry altogether and stop making bad nutrition artificially inexpensive. As the main global producer of HFCS, the United States has a moral obligation to lead the world by letting prices provide the information we need to encourage healthier choices here and around the world.

Can a President Really Fix America?

Both conservative and progressive (liberal) churches seemed to be anxious about the 2012 presidential election. The anxiety was so great that many pastors were willing to bind the consciences of other Christians by telling them how to vote. Over at *The Daily Beast*, David Sessions highlighted the much complained about annual "Pulpit Freedom Sunday" during which "copies of hundreds of illegal sermons [were] being mailed to the IRS to challenge its restriction on tax-exempt organizations endorsing political candidates." On the other hand, black pastors, like the Rev. Ottis Moss, pastor of President Obama's former church in Chicago for example, are directing Christians in black churches in the same way. Should pastors be doing this?

According to SpeakUpMovement.org the current restriction on pastors talking politics from the pulpit began in 1954, when, then senator,

Lyndon B. Johnson proposed the restriction as an amendment to the 501(c)(3) tax exemption for charitable organizations "to keep two nonprofit organizations in Texas from supporting his political opponent, but the amendment has also had the effect of restricting the right of pastors to speak freely from the pulpit." In other words, the law represents the abuse of law as a political maneuver instead of the use of law for the common good. During the 2008 presidential campaign, many Americans were alarmed how politicized Rev. Jeremiah Wright, President Obama's former pastor, was from the pulpit. Sessions worries that "on the ground in evangelical churches, explicit political talk carries the risk of being divisive and alienating, two things that are deadly to most churches' goal of getting as many people as possible into the fold." I wonder, however, why this is not also true for all pastors regardless of tradition.

Rev. Otis Moss II and Rev. Charles Jenkins explicitly state that all black Christians in black churches "must" vote to reelect president Obama.

> As African-American clergy deeply committed to the welfare of our communities and the future of our country, we are writing to offer our strong and enthusiastic endorsement of President Barack Obama. In the face of laws designed to limit democracy, and voices seeking to depress the participation of our community rather than to empower it, we will not be silent. Too much blood was shed for us to remain on the sidelines. We must stand up once more, and we must keep marching on this November. We must reelect this President.[8]

I am beginning to wonder what Barack Obama can do to support human flourishing in black communities when the prevailing pathologies destroying those neighborhoods, and the rest of America, are primarily moral in nature. The culture of death that sees an unborn child as a non-human, women birthing children out of the context of marriage, the black-on-black violence sending young black men to graves, the breakdown of the family, and so on, are all moral problems that politics cannot fix.

I'm no passivist by any means but it seems that Christians, progressive and conservative alike, may be expecting more from politics than politics can deliver. Our politicians and laws reflect the morality of America's citizenry. Does it not, then, seem more effective for social change for pastors to admonish Christians to focus on pointing their neighbors to Christ? The social change that Christians truly want in America will come when we, the people, desire to live according to our Creator's design.

---

8. Moss and Jenkins, "Black Church Must Stand Up," lines 1-12.

Black Scholars Give Obama an "F"

At a July 2012 NAACP convention in Houston, one prominent black leader did not address the historic group: the nation's first black president. President Obama's absence from major NAACP events could be called a pattern, as he has not addressed the group since 2009, during the honeymoon phase of his presidency. His absence is turning out to be wise because he can avoid answering this question, "Are blacks better off since he took office?" If the president were to give an account of his administration's advancement of African Americans he would be hard pressed to describe anything significant beyond funneling redistributed wealth into government bureaucracies, a traditional path to the middle class for blacks. His policies have done nothing to improve the economic standing of people of color on the margins.

Here are the facts: In November 2008, the black unemployment rate was 11.1 percent. By June 2012, the number had risen to 14.4 percent. In the same period the overall unemployment rate increased from 6.5 percent to 7.4 percent. As such, under the policies and leadership of the Obama administration, the economic lives of struggling blacks are now worse, not better, than they were three years ago.

Even with the economic failure, the "African Americans for Obama" section of the President's campaign website lists his "accomplishments" in the black community noting increased government-backed bank "lending for low-income Americans," the passing of Obamacare, and increased government-funded education programs. Also, through government welfare programs Obama "doubled" funding for Pell Grants, secured $2.55 billion in tax payer funding for Historically Black Colleges and Universities, "awarded nearly $300 billion in federal contracts to small businesses," and so on. In other words, the President has helped blacks by redistributing the taxes collected from American workers and using government to provide race-based preferential treatment opportunities. But he has not created conditions favorable for broadly increasing black wealth through market-based economic growth.

Perhaps the economic lapses explain why prominent black scholars, like Dr. Cornel West of Princeton University and Dr. Boyce Watkins of Syracuse University, are so openly critical of Obama. Sustained unemployment is not the change many black Americans expected back in 2008. When asked about the 2012 presidential race, Cornel West, a self-proclaimed Marxist, said, "Mitt Romney is a catastrophic response to a catastrophe, whereas Obama is a disastrous response to a catastrophe." West has accused Obama of pandering to the lobbying special interests of large corporations calling the president "another black mascot" of "Wall Street oligarchs" who is not doing enough for black people.

Joining West in highlighting Obama's economic inadequacy, Boyce Watkins finds that "black American enthusiasm for President Obama is dead." Watkins explains, "Obama was not skilled enough, nor strong enough to meet the high expectations in front of him" when he took office. As a frustrated former supporter, Watkins laments, "defending President Obama is like demanding a better grade for your child when you know that your baby has been lazy in class." The Obama administration seems only interested in "the black community around election time (when they need us to show up to the polls)." In the end, Watkins centers his criticisms on his belief that "white folks are experiencing an economic recovery, while black unemployment remains at levels that would never be acceptable to the rest of America."

The critiques of West and Watkins are important, but they do not fully articulate the damage done by stratospheric unemployment levels. What is so unconscionable about black unemployment rates, which were as high as 16.7 percent in 2011, is that unemployment has moral as well as financial implications. In *Laborem excercens,* Pope John Paul II stressed that work allows us to realize our humanity, "to fulfill the calling to be a person." The high black unemployment rate is robbing thousands of blacks of their dignity.

A successful administration must go beyond even what many of Obama's black critics envision by radically removing regulatory and legislative barriers that interfere with entrepreneurs doing what they do best— namely, creating jobs. This would decrease the unemployment rate for blacks and anyone else, and who wouldn't want to reelect someone whose policies are actually effective?

The Power of Market-Driven Diversity

The story of Chicago-based Supreme Life Insurance Company of America, one of the most venerable black-owned businesses in American history, challenges the prevailing fiction that minority customers need the government to guarantee services for them and is a dynamic reminder of the power of markets as a basis for economic freedom.

Supreme was originally incorporated as the Liberty Life Insurance Company in 1919. An amazing 1969 study of this company by Dr. Robert C. Puth in Harvard's *Business History Review* inadvertently dispels all sorts of myths about black businesses and black life during the era of legalized racial discrimination. The article, "Supreme Life: The History of a Negro Life Insurance Company, 1919-1962" details, for example, the existence of thriving black-owned businesses during that era, a fact of which many are unaware. By 1960 the forty-six firms of the National Insurance Association—a coalition of all black owned, managed, and operated firms—had $1.7 billion of insurance in force and held $300 million in assets. In today's terms, that is approximately $17 billion and $2.3 billion, respectively. In 1965, Supreme Life had assets over $33,000,000 ($251 million inflation adjusted for 2012). Even though black incomes were very low and blacks worked mostly in unskilled labor, black-owned businesses prospered.

These black-owned firms were successful for several reasons. First, legal segregation created a concentrated market free from competition. As such, there was a surge in the 1920s in black entrepreneurship. Second, especially in the North, blacks gained access to manufacturing jobs through the cessation of immigration during World War I. Third, black families epitomized a culture of saving, even more so than white families, making them desired customers. Lastly, it was normal for leaders at Supreme Life and other black firms to maintain relationships with and gain experience working with white business, civic, and religious leaders.

After surviving the Great Depression, the black insurance industry faced new challenges during and after WWII. Blacks' incomes began rising more rapidly than those of whites, and black mortality rates, which had been high, continued to fall relative to the national average. This change not only benefited insurance firms owned and operated by black people but also made their predominantly black customers attractive to white firms. White firms increasingly broke from racial discrimination norms to serve black customers, including hiring blacks from the black-owned firms to reach an emerging black customer base. While companies were free to discriminate against blacks it was not in their economic interests to do so because, at the end of the day, every company's favorite color is green.

By the 1950s, five large white firms had increased their black customer based by three times the amount of increases by all black-owned firms combined nationwide. This "invasion" by white firms, as Puth puts it, siphoned off the type of black customer and employee that would have raised the performance of black firms. Blacks firms began to lose their competitive edge because they could not in turn cross the racial divide and draw white clients. Black consumers, meanwhile, benefited because they had wider access to insurance markets at lower prices.

What is most intriguing about this set of developments—growth of black incomes from WWI through the 1950s, decreases in black mortality rates, the moral culture of saving and investing among black families, greater access to markets, the increased hiring of black employees by white firms, and lower-priced insurance products for black customers—is that they occurred as a result of competition rather than race-based government policies. Market forces, operating on their own principles, provided greater access for blacks before the Civil Rights Act of 1965 or the race-based preferential business policies of the Johnson and Nixon administrations.

In the end, racial discrimination is no match for the power of competition. The only way companies are protected from the economic consequences of racism is through government policy, like Jim Crow—otherwise companies cannot survive. Oddly, this process of market forces eroding the accumulated prejudice of American culture was thwarted by government supported race-based policies in the 1970s that did not let racists lose their businesses but propped them up through corporate welfare diversity incentives. We can only wonder how much more diverse corporate America would be if those who racially discriminated were given two choices: respect the dignity of blacks as customers and employees or fall behind while watching others advance by doing so—because in a virtuous society no unethical business is too important to fail.

Indian Country's American Nightmare

Anyone who believes that the federal government knows what is best for local communities should visit an American Indian Reservation. Native Americans are currently immersed in a health care and economic deprivation nightmare that is the consequence of government interference, inefficiency, and inhumane policies. The Native American narrative is one of government creating problems and then, in the name of offering solutions, making matters worse by depriving local communities of their autonomy.

According to research led by Jeffrey E. Holm, professor of psychology at the University of North Dakota School of Medicine, national data show that American Indians (AIs) have a lower life expectancy than other Americans. In fact, Holm reports, AIs die at higher rates than white Americans and most other ethnic minorities from cardiovascular disease, tuberculosis, alcoholism-related diseases, motor vehicle crashes, diabetes, unintentional injuries, homicide, and suicide. [9] National data show that AIs have a higher prevalence of many risk behaviors including cigarette smoking, obesity, absence of leisure-time physical activity, and binge alcohol use.

Many of the obesity and diabetes related pathologies share the same root cause: poor diet resulting from government programs. In the

9. Holm, "Assessing Health Status," 68–78.

mid-19th century, under the Indian Removal Act, Native American tribes turned their lands over to the U.S. Government and relocated to Indian Reservations. This relocation disconnected AIs from their usual diet of lean meats, fruits, and vegetables as well as from an active lifestyle of hunting and gathering. By 1890, the government had banned Native Americans from leaving allocated lands to acquire food. In exchange, the government offered rations of commodities such as flour, lard, and sugar. Today, thanks to corn subsidies, these rations consist of highly processed foods rich in carbohydrates and high-fructose corn syrup. These do not meet the requirements for a healthy diet.

Thanks to government regulations, AIs also suffer from the type of economic deprivation that leaves Reservations with virtually no small businesses, including, for example, grocery stores. Communities lacking flourishing businesses are communities that become trapped in cycles of poverty and dysfunction. In fact, the economic malaise in and around reservations stems from a lack of property rights. Terry Anderson, executive director of the Political Economy Research Center, says that AI property rights were also affected by those 19th century treaties which put millions of acres of tribal and individual Indian land under the trusteeship of the Interior department's Bureau of Indian Affairs. [10] As a result these lands cannot be developed, used as collateral for taking out loans to start businesses, easily inherited, or managed productively. Anderson argues that what AIs need is freedom to develop their own property, borrow against it, and make it productive or order to start businesses that lead to wealth creation. The result of a continuation of current policy, says Anderson, is that "Indian economies are likely to remain enclaves of poverty in a sea of prosperity."[11]

Because welfare and government programs removed the need for institutions such as banks in the areas where AIs live, those institutions left. Drew Tulchin and Jessica Shortall, of Social Enterprise Associates, reported in 2008 that 86 percent of tribal lands had no bank in the community and that 15 percent of Native Americans are 100 miles or more from a bank.[12] And even for reservations with a bank nearby, only one in three financial institutions on or near reservations offer start-up loans or small business loans, while only one in four offer micro-business loans. Assertive AIs who might be inclined to better their situation have few entrepreneurial models

---

10. See Anderson, *Property Rights and Indian Economies.*

11. Anderson, "Self-determination," 5.

12. Tulchin and Shortall, "Small Business Incubation and its Prospects in Indian Country," 1.

to emulate: only 13 percent of Native American entrepreneurs had entrepreneur parents, versus 75 percent in the general population.

The social and moral breakdown among AIs that we all lament is situated within a context of economic nihilism, and without economic hope we should expect many self-sabotaging behaviors to continue. When a country takes a group of people, restricts their liberties, undermines their economic development, and keeps them dependent on welfare programs that provide unhealthy foods, we cannot expect anything more than what we see today among AIs.

In the end, what Native Americans need—like all Americans—is an economic future that allows local communities to develop their property to meet their own needs in local ways, that frees people from government dependency, and that encourages an entrepreneurial spirit that brings innovation and hope rather than limitation and nihilism. Our Washington leadership, whoever is in the White House, should make Native American flourishing a priority because, for them and for all those shackled to government dependency, the American Dream continues to be a nightmare.

Corn Subsidies at the Root of U.S.-Mexico Immigration Problem

America's immigration debate will never be adequately addressed until we think clearly about the economic incentives that encourage Mexican citizens to risk their lives to cross the border. In fact, if we care about human dignity we must think comprehensively about the conditions for human flourishing so that our policies effectively promote the common good. Sadly, U.S. government farm subsidies create the conditions for the oppression and poor health care of Mexican migrant workers in ways that make those subsidies nothing less than immoral.

Dr. Seth M. Holmes, a professor of Health and Social Behavior at the University of California, Berkeley, identified the source of the problem in his watershed 2006 paper, "An Ethnographic Study of the Social Context of Migrant Health in the United States." In the study we learn that 95 percent of agricultural workers in the United States were born in Mexico and 52 percent are undocumented.[13] Most researchers agree that inequalities in the global market make up the primary driving force of labor migration patterns. Mexico's current minimum wage is US$4.60 per day. In contrast, the US federal minimum wage is $7.25 per hour, while it is $7.65 in Arizona, $8 in California, $7.50 in New Mexico, and $7.25 in Texas.

13. Holmes, "Ethnographic Study of the Social Contexts," 1777.

The 2003 North American Free Trade Agreement (NAFTA) deregulated all agricultural trade, except for corn and dairy products. The Mexican government complains that since NAFTA's initial implementation in 1994, the United States has raised farm subsidies by 300 percent. As a result, Mexican corn farmers, who comprise the majority of the country's agricultural sector, experienced drastic declines in the domestic price of their product. It should come as no surprise, then, that the United States began to experience an influx of Mexicans looking for employment in the latter half of the 1990s. Mexican farmers are now rightly protesting because they cannot compete against prices that are artificially deflated for the sake of protecting Americans from necessary market corrections.

Holmes explains that migrant and seasonal farm workers suffer the poorest health status within the agriculture industry. For example, migrant workers have increased rates of many chronic conditions, such as HIV infection, malnutrition, anemia, hypertension, diabetes, anxiety, sterility, blood disorders, and abnormalities in liver and kidney function. This population has an increased incidence of acute sicknesses such as urinary tract and kidney infections, lung infections, heat stroke, anthrax, encephalitis, rabies, and tetanus. Tuberculosis prevalence is six times greater in this population than in the general United States population. Finally, Holmes reports, children of migrant farm workers show high rates of malnutrition, vision problems, dental problems, anemia, and excess blood lead levels.[14]

Economically speaking, according to Mexico's central bank, the $22.7 billion in remittances that Mexican migrant workers sent home from the United States in 2011 represents an increase of 6.86 percent over the previous year. Remittances are Mexico's second-largest source of foreign income following oil exports. Nearly all of that the money comes from the United States, with a Mexican citizen population of 12 million.

Can you imagine what would happen if the United States had no farm subsidies, Mexican farms were flourishing, and $22.7 billion was generated within Mexico's economy to catalyze more wealth creating opportunities? We can only dream at present, but one thing is for certain: Mexican migrant workers would be far better off. As such, through federal corn farm subsidies, America's government is morally culpable for the oppression, dehumanization, and poor health of Mexican migrant workers.

Mexican migrant workers are sick and dying because politicians create perverse and immoral incentives by interfering with the market. Ignoring the dignity of Mexican workers and the common good, they instead pander to a powerful special interest group, the corn lobby. What Mexico needs

14. Ibid., 1778.

from U.S. political leaders is the fortitude to let market mechanisms foster human flourishing in Mexico so that families do not have to the suffer the hazards of migrancy. In sum, it would be better for both countries if the Mexican economy were not sabotaged by the politics of protectionism.

Despite Economic and Social Ills, Blacks Give Obama a Pass

With the approach of Black History Month we are reminded of the historic presidency of Barack Obama, the nation's first African-American president. Some black leaders, however, believe that Mr. Obama has let the black community down. For example, prominent voices like Dr. Cornell West and PBS's Tavis Smiley, former supporters of Obama, believe that having a black president has not led to significant progress for blacks. The truth is not just that Obama's presidency has made blacks worse of, but that blacks are grappling with deep-seated economic and social issues that the President himself has little or no expertise in solving.

In spite of these realities, some leaders asked the black community to support Obama in the 2012 election just because of his race. For example, Tom Joyner, host of one of the highest rated morning shows in America, said in an October 2011 column, "Let's not even deal with facts right now. Let's deal with our blackness and pride—and loyalty. We have a chance to reelect the first African American president . . . And I'm not afraid or ashamed to say that as black people, we should do it because he's a black man." The historic enthusiasm is understandable but we must deal with facts that tell us race-based voting is futile.

Take unemployment, for example. According to a January 2011 report by the University of California, Berkeley's Center for Labor Research and Education, black worker unemployment steadied around 15-16 percent in 2011, while unemployment for the rest of the workforce dropped below 9 percent. That is, in 2011 the unemployment rate for African-Americans stayed almost exactly the same and declined for everyone else.

Second, with respect to family issues, it is well known that blacks continue to lead the nation in single motherhood. According to 2008 figures, 72 percent of black children were born to unwed mothers compared to 17 percent of Asians, 29 percent of whites, 53 percent of Hispanics, and 66 percent of Native Americans. By extension, then, fatherlessness continues to undermine black progress in America. According to FathersUnite.org, 90 percent of runaway children, 85 percent of all children who exhibit behavioral disorders, 70 percent of all high school dropouts, and 85 percent of all youths sitting in prisons are from fatherless homes.

How would voting again for Barack Obama—simply because he is black—fix these problems? Barack Obama is not an entrepreneur, nor can he be a father to the fatherless. The best thing that President Obama could do would be to remove all the barriers in the way of entrepreneurs so that they can do the things that they do well, such as provide the sustainable employment opportunities that allow adults to take care of their families and permit the marketplace to meet the needs of all of us. Government is neither designed nor equipped to create and sustain jobs. Thousands of years of experience show this clearly: only entrepreneurs have the gifts and expertise to create jobs. We need to encourage them because sustainable employment is the only long-term solution to poverty and unemployment.

With respect to family, one important thing President Obama can do is to continue to provide an encouraging example. Even if you do not agree with Obama's politics, the president is certainly a model of a man who is committed to his wife and children. In fact, if more black men were committed to their children and their mothers in the way that President Obama is through the institution of marriage, many of the statistics listed above would plummet. However, there is no political solution that President Obama can promote because fatherlessness is fundamentally a moral problem. If we want to make a better black history—and leave a better legacy for our youth—we have to morally form black men so that they remain committed to loving women and children within the context of marriage.

If blacks want to chart a new course reversing these statistics, we should look not to politicians for answers but ask them to get regulatory barriers out of the way of entrepreneurs and moral institutions so that they can do what they have proven the best at for centuries—creating the conditions for virtuous human flourishing.

Taxing America into Destruction

I never thought I would say this, but I am beginning to believe that the general American electorate will never have any economic common sense. The idea of increasing taxes on millionaires, who already pay more taxes than others, because they need to "pay their fair share" should automatically raise red flags for anyone thinking clearly about a plan to get our economy back on track. In fact, I would submit that the American romantic love affair with all things Europe is going to destroy this country. It seems that Americans have forgotten that this country was founded on political ideas that were categorically different than our friends across the pond.

The United States of America is a nation that has grown in her understanding of what it means for religious, political, and economic liberty to create the conditions necessary for human flourishing. No doubt this nation has imperfectly put these ideas into practice, but the commitment to do so has made this country the only place in the world where an "average Joe" can go from poverty to wealth in one or two generations. Political and economic liberty, as principles for prosperity, are now on death row, and there is little, I believe, that will stop the inevitable: America is on a pathway to bankruptcy because we believe the European illusion that raising taxes and coercing wealth redistribution creates wealth.

I do not blame President Obama for the ignorance that leads people to believe the myth that millionaires are not paying their "fair share." President Obama only represents the ignorance of many Americans who have no idea how our convoluted tax code actually works. For example, Stephen Ohlemacher wrote an article that sets things straight, exposing the lie that most Americans believe about who pays what in taxes:

> On average, the wealthiest people in America pay a lot more taxes than the middle class or the poor, according to private and government data. They pay at a higher rate, and as a group, they contribute a much larger share of the overall taxes collected by the federal government. . . . The 10% of households with the highest incomes pay more than half of all federal taxes. They pay more than 70% of federal income taxes, according to the Congressional Budget Office.[15]

Using government data, Ohlemacher reports the following:

> In 2009, 1,470 households filed tax returns with incomes above $1 million yet paid no federal income tax, according to the Internal Revenue Service. . . . This year, households making more than $1 million will pay an average 29.1% of their income in federal taxes, including income taxes, payroll taxes and other taxes. . . . Households making between $50,000 and $75,000 will pay an average of 15% of their income in federal taxes. Lower-income households will pay less. For example, households making between $40,000 and $50,000 will pay an average of 12.5% of their income in federal taxes. Households making between $20,000 and $30,000 will pay 5.7%.[16]

15. Ohlemacher, "Fact Check," original link now defunct.
16. Ibid.

If the economic facts demonstrate that the wealthy already pay more taxes than everyone else why are Americans in support of raising taxes on this small population *again*? Class warfare could be the culprit, but I think the real reason is much worse. At least in class warfare you know you're harming the other, but what we have today is pure multi-generational economic ignorance and the absence of fiscal common sense. Americans increasingly think like Europeans.

It is important to remember that Otto von Bismarck, the Prussian prime minister/German chancellor from 1862 to 1890, is the father of the welfare state. He advanced the vision that government should serve as a social services institution by taking earned wealth from the rich and from businesses to deliver services to those who are not as advantaged. European governments fully implemented Bismarck's economic ideology and now the entire region is on the verge of bankruptcy. This will be our destiny as well unless the sound political thinking that created this nation's prosperity in the first place is released from the prison of America's Bismarckian economic ignorance.

Losing Hope in Obama

The Barack Obama fan club dwindled in 2011. For example, Princeton University religion professor Cornel West and journalist Tavis Smiley's nationwide "Poverty Tour" offered a serious critique of the administration's policies with regard to the poor. In a devastating article, Bard College foreign affairs and humanities professor Walter Russell Mead concluded that as far as employment goes, "the Obama administration has been a total bust for blacks."[17]

Mead highlights issues in urban America that would justify President Obama receiving an "F" grade for his administration's inability to effectively address the following:

> [T]he devastating impact of what for most blacks is a still-deepening recession; the unfolding effects of the fiscal crisis meshed with the decline of the blue social model;[18] competition for jobs, resources, and power between African-Americans and mostly Spanish-speaking immigrants; the increased fragmentation and disintegration of black political leadership; and the contrast

17. Mead, "Obamageddon Coming to a City Near You?" 7ff.
18. Mead, "American Challenges," 8ff.

between the high hopes of 2008 and the grim realities that have come clear since.[19]

The lack of progress on these issues may explain, in part, why West, Smiley, and other progressives are now some of Obama's most vocal critics. Is the jig up? For those blacks who were expecting their situations to improve with the swearing in of the nation's first African-American president, many are now standing around today sucking wind like a Hoover vacuum cleaner.

Back in 2011, blacks had an unemployment rate just above 16 percent, compared to 8.7 percent for whites. Mead reports that the states with the lowest black unemployment rates are generally the more conservative, low-tax states, while the ones with the worst black jobless rates are among the bluest states in the nation: Wisconsin (25 percent), Michigan (23.9 percent), Minnesota (22 percent), Maine (21.4 percent), and Washington (21.4 percent).

One the reasons blacks are affected more significantly by the current recession is because of the high percentage of African-Americans working in government and the public sector. To date, approximately 20 percent of working blacks are employed by government compared to 15 percent for whites and 11 percent for Hispanics. The public sector, according to Mead, is the single largest employer of black men in America and the second largest employer of black women. During a recession, when government cuts spending and cuts jobs, those measures tend to affect African-Americans far more than any other racial group.

More and more blacks are now questioning Obama's vision of expanding government to bring about economic liberation for those who are struggling. While many progressives and liberals seem content to blame Republicans in Congress for blacks being worse off under President Obama's tenure, leading African-American and Democratic thinkers-like West, Smiley, and Mead-are pointing their fingers solely at the administration of the man who promised "change." Maybe progressives (liberals) and conservatives alike can share in looking forward to the end of Obama's presidency.

Wealth Creation Helps the Poor

"As the rich get richer, the poor get richer."

That may sound like a ridiculous overstatement, but it's true in the sense that nations that create wealth redefine what it means to be poor. Being poor

19. Mead, "Obamageddon," 7ff.

in a wealthy nation is radically different than being poor in a developing one. The above statement also challenges the zero-sum myth—"As the rich get richer, the poor get poorer"—which has so tainted the understanding of economic imaginations of those in the West.

In a study titled "Air Conditioning, Cable TV, and an Xbox: What Is Poverty in the United States Today?," Robert Rector and Rachel Sheffield of The Heritage Foundation demonstrate that the federal government's definition of "poor" differs from what most Americans imagine it to be in reality.

For example, according to the data from 2005, the authors point out:

> [T]he typical poor household, as defined by the government, had air conditioning and a car. For entertainment, the household had two color televisions, cable or satellite TV, a DVD player, and a VCR. In the kitchen, it had a refrigerator, an oven and stove, and a microwave. Other household conveniences included a clothes washer, clothes dryer, ceiling fans, a cordless phone, and a coffee maker. The family was able to obtain medical care when needed. Their home was not overcrowded and was in good repair. By its own report, the family was not hungry and had sufficient funds during the past year to meet all essential needs.

In fact, to be more specific, 99.6 percent of individuals the federal government defines as "poor" have refrigerators, 97.7 percent have televisions, 78.3 percent live in homes with air-conditioning, and 62 percent live in homes with washing machines. These percentages are only possible in a nation as wealthy as the United States; it certainly is not the case in Sudan.

It is important to keep in mind that "the poor" does not represent a static population of individuals over time. In the real world, individuals cycle in and out of poverty in the same way they move in and out of social classes. One of the great tragedies of our current recession is that many people are worse off than they were five years ago regardless of class. Many lower-middle-class, working-class, and poor individuals have experienced the recession in worse ways than others because they lacked the economic cushion to weather the storm. But when the economy recovers, many of the individuals currently defined as poor by government standards will likely move out of poverty and regain their standing as middle-class.

Interestingly Rector and Sheffield also point out how liberal and progressive Christians like Ron Sider are misleading the church because of insufficient economic distinctions and rhetoric detached from real facts:

> Sider begins his book [*Just Generosity: A New Vision for Overcoming Poverty in America*] with a chapter entitled 'What Does

Poverty Look Like?' in which he informs his readers, 'In 2005, in the United States, 37 million people lived in poverty in the richest society in human history.' He asks, 'Who are the poor? Where do they live?' and proceeds to answer these questions with a lengthy description of the home of Mrs. Onita Skyles, a 68-year-old widow.

The widow in Sider's example is experiencing abject poverty, and he proceeds to use her to define what poverty means in America. "Sider is seriously misleading when he implies that such living conditions are representative of 37 million poor people," note Rector and Sheffield. "In fact, the situations he presents are not at all representative of the poor in America. The described conditions are very unusual and probably found in no more than one in 500 households."

Political liberals and progressive Christians are vulnerable to accepting zero-sum ideology without taking the time to test those theories against real data and facts. The argument here is not that American poverty is "OK"; the point is to highlight the fact that making public policy decisions about "helping the poor" and "ending poverty" in America needs to take into account how "the poor" actually live in reality. Otherwise we will continue to miss the mark and not help the truly disadvantaged. Our public policy needs to be directed toward people who are truly suffering and stuck in cycles of poverty so that we create the conditions that allow for the possibility of sustainable economic mobility.

Treating Africans as Friends, Not Dependents

Many African countries lag behind the rest of the world economically in ways that perpetuate cycles of poverty and dysfunction. These cycles can give the wrong impression that more developed countries are superior to these African nations.

In *Dead Aid*, Dambisa Moyo argues that Western nations have undermined African economies by giving cash to countries that are often corrupt and by providing aid to some nations trying to get off the ground. This is the result of unintended paternalism. The West needs a new way of thinking. What would it look like for Western nations to treat struggling African countries as friends instead of just recipients of their help?

This may seem like mere semantics, but for many African leaders it's important. For example, on a trip to Cameroon, journalist John Allen asked

Bishop John Onaiyekan of Abuja, Nigeria, how the West could help Africa. Here's what Allen reported about that exchange:

> 'The problem is the way you phrased the question,' [Onaiyekan] said. 'You asked how the West can "help" Africa. We're not interested in "help" in that sense, meaning that we are exclusively the receivers of your generosity. We're interested in a new kind of relationship, in which all of us, as equals, work out the right way forward.'
>
> The most important thing the West can do, Onaiyekan stressed, is not giving increased development aid or more trade, but what he called a 'change of mentality'—including, he said, a change of mentality within the church.

What really struck me about this conversation was Onaiyekan's challenging the perspective that many African nations are simply standing around with downtrodden faces and outstretches hands waiting on the West to help. Perhaps part of the blame for this mentality on my part has been the years and years of seeing images of Africans depicted as helpless in TV commercials for relief organizations. In the past I may have thought of Africans as needing our "help" rather than thinking about what it means to partner with them as friends so that they can help themselves and find solutions to their own problems.

It seems that the East may view Africa differently than the West. In fact, the Chinese are sending strong signals that they do not see Africans as inferior dependents. For example, Chinese businessmen are marrying African women and are seeking out new business opportunities on the continent.[20] Jennifer Brea explains:

> While Americans are pestering their leaders to Save Darfur—an unlikely prospect absent full-scale military intervention—the Chinese are busy building roads and hydroelectric power dams. China believes Africa is a huge economic opportunity and deals with Africa like a business partner. The Chinese see Africans the way many would like to see themselves.[21]

Building infrastructure instead of sending over things like clothes is the type of initiative that helps Africans help themselves in the long run.

Not seeing Africans as equals has become such a tense issue that some Africans are even telling U2's Bono to change his mentality. After he delivered a standard development speech about the need to give Africa more

20. Ma, "Chinese Workers in Africa."
21. Brea, "Africans to Bono."

cash, an African man in the audience asked Bono, "Where do you place the African person as a thinker, a creator of wealth?"

Maybe we've been going about this all wrong. Maybe the best way to help Africans is not to see them as recipients of our "help" but potential thinkers and wealth creators who need friends to provide the support that moves countries off the path of dependency and onto the path of freedom and prosperity.

Should College Athletes be Paid?

In light of scandals at Ohio State, Southern California, Auburn, and other schools, answering that question with a "yes" seems increasingly to make sense as a way to end much of the corruption found in the top-tier of collegiate sports.

On Aug. 9, 2011, NCAA President Mark Emmert convened a meeting of college presidents to discuss the future of college athletics. In addition to the pay-for-play question, the meeting addressed the issues of how to hold athletes to higher academic standards and higher standards of behavior while keeping the college athletics economy sustainable. And what an economy it has become: In 2010, the richest college football programs generated more than $1 billion in profits. And those profits have been earned on the backs of student-athletes.

But paying college athletes doesn't sit well with most because it would destroy the amateur nature of the college game. But if college sports are so "amateur," why do college coaches make as much as or more than their "professional" counterparts? According to USA Today top college basketball coaches are paid exceptionally well for their skills: Louisville's Rick Pitino, $7,531,378; Duke's Mike Krzyzewski, $4,195,519; Kentucky's John Calipari, $3,917,000; Kansas' Bill Self, $3,615,656; Florida's Billy Donovan, $3,575,400; and Michigan State's Tom Izzo, $3,565,000.[22] The average salary for an NBA head coach is $3,400,000.[23] Top college football coaches earn more than comfortable salaries as well: Alabama's Nick Saban, $5,997,349; Texas' Mack Brown, $5,161,500; Oklahoma's Bob Stoops, $4,375,000; and Louisiana State's Les Miles, $3,905,000.[24] Yes, top NFL head coaches tend to earn more, but only slightly. For example, Bill Belichick, head coach of the New England Patriots, earns $7,500,000 a year.

22. Dougherty and Thomassie, "Analysis of Salaries for College Basketball Coaches."
23. "NBA Salaries," InsideHoops.com.
24. Dougherty, "Salary Analysis of 2010 Football Bowl Subdivision Coaches."

If college coaches are being paid what the market demands, should not their players be paid something too? What would happen if college athletes were simply considered employees of the university working for the athletic program? Some students earn money working for the school library or the cafeteria; athletes could receive paychecks for their contributions on the basketball court or the football field.

If a worker is worth his wages (1 Timothy 5:18), why can't that principle be applied to college athletes? Perhaps in the future, college presidents will consider taking steps to compensate student athletes for the value they add to their schools.

Prosecuting Drug-Addicted Pregnant Women

Should pregnant women struggling with addiction to illegal drugs be criminally prosecuted for child neglect and endangerment? Since the 1992 sentencing of Cornelia Whitner to eight years in jail—when her son Tevin, although born healthy, tested positive for cocaine at the time of his birth—there has been heated debate among legal scholars and women's rights activists regarding such incarceration. In the Whitner case, the South Carolina Supreme Court held that a viable unborn child is a "person" and that pregnant women who abuse drugs are endangering their babies in the womb. It may seem obvious that women are morally responsible for endangering their unborn child by abusing illegal drugs, but is it criminal?

Scholars who say that drug-addicted pregnant women should not be prosecuted for child endangerment and neglect argue some combination of the following points:

First, they argue that in America there is no legal consensus that an unborn baby is a person and therefore does not have legal standing as a "child." If an unborn child is not a person, a drug using or addicted pregnant woman cannot be legally charged with child endangerment. Denying the personhood of an unborn baby has been the most effective way of protecting these women from prosecution. But many states are inconsistent with their laws because an unborn child *does* have legal standing with respect to fetal homicide—for example, in the case of a drunk driver being charged for manslaughter in a car accident in which a pregnant woman's unborn child dies.[25]

Second, scholars argue that having a drug addiction is not illegal, so to penalize women for something they have no control over criminalizes

25. You can find more information on fetal homicide laws here: http://www.ncsl.org/research/health/fetal-homicide-state-laws.aspx.

women who are suffering from painful struggles. Even if drug-abusing women are putting the viability of their unborn baby at risk, her addiction is not necessarily *criminal*. What other addictions do we prosecute?

Third, they argue that these laws tend to be racist because black women are 10 times more likely to be reported for using drugs while pregnant than white women.[26] Even though the difference between the drug use rates among white women compared to those of black women is negligible, black women are more likely to be criminally prosecuted. Such laws, then, they say, unfairly target women of color.

Fourth, scholars point out that it has not been proven that putting women in jail and separating them from their children is necessarily *better* than other options such as government-funded, mandatory drug rehabilitation. Even worse, some argue, the knowledge of potential prosecution could introduce incentives for women to abort their babies to avoid going to jail.

Fifth, they ask if we should prosecute pregnant women for other types of negligence. That is, should we prosecute pregnant women for smoking, drinking alcohol, eating poorly, reckless driving, etc.? Why isolate the use of illegal drugs and not prosecute women who smoke cigarettes when smoking tobacco is far more potentially dangerous to unborn children than cocaine? To complicate the issue further, we do not actually know how these drugs affect fetal development; the data is inconclusive at best. In fact, maternal drug use tends to make no difference in the health of a child after birth.

In the end, women who abuse drugs during pregnancy may violate moral norms but said violations need not be criminal. If you were elected to your state legislature, how would you argue for or against a law proposing criminal penalties for drug-abusing pregnant women? Could there be better alternatives than jail? Is this even a good use of the law?

No Evangelical Vote for 2012?

What would happen if we had disbanded evangelicalism for presidential elections in 2012? That is, what if evangelicals suspended affiliations with each other through any organizations or networks and simply embedded themselves as voters among non-religious constituencies? This would mean no voter guides published by any Christian non-profit or para-church organizations; no indirect endorsements of candidates on Christian talk radio, or on television, or by pastors; and no giving political candidates, or their

26. Filipovic, "Prosecuting Pregnant Drug-Addicted Mothers," original link now defunct.

emissaries, access to any churches, Christian colleges, or any group of gathered believers for any reason. What would happen?

I was prompted to think about this after watching a documentary produced in England titled *God Bless America*, which reveals how evangelical
Christians, and their organizations, were nothing more than mere pawns in
a political game of chess during the 2008 presidential race. I don't get nause-
ated often, but the ways in which this film shows how easily manipulated
evangelicals were by candidates who would opportunistically say whatever
itching church-going ears wanted to hear literally turned my stomach.

For example, "progressive" Christians on the left played right into the
hands of the Obama team. The emergence of a "new kind of evangelical,"
one that doesn't care about so much about the politics of abortion or same-
sex marriage, was nothing less than high-octane gasoline for the Barack
Obama machine. These "social justice" evangelicals threw out the window
economic thinking and facts about human nature in order to do all they
could to disassociate themselves with "conservatives" and the "religious
right"—the kind of evangelicals who would rather "end poverty" than create conditions for economic empowerment and liberation for poor. I nearly
jumped out of my chair watching the Obama team parade Donald Miller
around like a puppet to Christian colleges as its poster boy for this new kind
of Obama-loving evangelical—that is, one who holds on to evangelical convictions while embracing the mantra "You can love Jesus and not to be like
your old crusty abortion-as-politics-obsessed parents and grandparents."

I later reached for a bottle of Rolaids when the film pieced together how
the McCain campaign reconstructed its platform to appear more evangelical in its rhetoric to garner the "evangelical vote." John McCain's reticence
to speak publicly about his faith left evangelical pawns unmoved on the
chessboard. The Republicans were stomped because there was a Democratic
candidate in Obama who was extremely comfortable talking about Jesus.
McCain's religious awkwardness was a problem. Then, surprisingly, McCain
chose Sarah Palin as a running mate and evangelicals were back in! Locked
and loaded. In fact, I was caught up in the drama of it all and wrote about
the difference Palin would make for evangelicals. She spoke to issues that
the old kind of evangelicals needed to hear in every election: Jesus, abortion,
traditional marriage, and family values. The film presents members of the
McCain team courting the gatekeepers of evangelical groupthink in cities
like Colorado Springs, Colo., and Washington, D.C. The whole thing made
my blood pressure rise.

I wonder, then, what would happen if evangelicals, on the traditional
right or the progressive left, decided not to be pawns or puppets for any political party. What if attempting to court the "evangelical vote" would be as

nebulous as trying to court the "left-handed vote?" Wouldn't it be exciting to have a presidential campaign that was more about what the candidates actually believe than voters having to decipher the planned duplicity of much of today's political rhetoric? I can only dream.

Too Missional for Abortion

The number one social justice issue for African-Americans in New York City is abortion. Period. The city's abortion rate is twice the nation average, with 41 percent of all pregnancies ending in abortion. And the rate for blacks is even higher: 59.8 percent. For Hispanics it's 41.3 percent, Asians 22.7 percent, and whites 20.4 percent. In 2009, unmarried women accounted for 84 percent of the abortions in the city.[27]

To make matters worse, in 2011 the city passed a piece of legislation which heavily regulated New York's pro-life Crisis Pregnancy Centers, effectively shutting them down as most centers do not have the capacity to comply.

Around the same time, a billboard saying that, "The most dangerous place for an African American is in the womb" caused significant controversy. The billboard was only around for a few days.

All of this has me wondering why the missional, center-city evangelicals, who are all about "justice," "loving the city," "renewing the city," "serving the city," etc., do not seem to consider abortion one those flagship "justice" issues.

I've been browsing the mercy and justice websites of several of New York's well-known churches and Christian non-profit groups for discussion of New York's abortion crisis. Outside of the crisis pregnancy centers themselves, I have not found much of anything. What one will find are very good discussions on subjects like fighting homelessness, improving inner-city education, opening women's shelters, and dealing with sex trafficking and juvenile delinquency. I raise this issue because I am concerned that perhaps the missional pendulum has swung too far in one direction.

There are groups of 30-something-and-under Christians in cities who are trying to present a different kind of evangelical Christianity—one that's not so political and not so much about "culture wars," protesting abortion, or escaping "the culture" to the safety of the suburbs. These groups have made a conscious decision to not live out Christianity politically.

But Christian withdrawal from politics can inadvertently undermine the justice work of the church by not having a voting presence to maintain

27. Ghosh, "New York City's Abortion Rate," lines 1-20.

religious liberties for Christians to do what they are called to do. I fully recognize how an organization's non-profit status constrains certain types of activities and speech, but if New York's Christians are not encouraged to get involved in the politics of religious liberty, people are going to die, literally.

Had there been pro-life Christians on New York's City Council, Bill 371 would have failed and the crisis pregnancy centers would be fine. Bill 371 is a reminder that if your center city church is too missional for the politics of abortion and religious liberty, Christianity eventually will be limited to serving and renewing the city in rhetoric only.

Let the Hustlers Hustle

If necessity is the mother of invention, then there is nothing worse than imposing arbitrary constraints on the entrepreneurial spirit of people who are seeking to improve their situation. America's unemployment problems linger because hustlers cannot hustle.

For many, "hustling" connotes business activity that is shady, or even illegal. But in the black community it is common to use the term to describe the entrepreneurial spirit that drives people to take risks to meet their needs and to provide legitimate services through creative enterprise in the marketplace. This is the view taken by indie Hip-Hop mogul Hotep, who founded Hustle University as an effort to redeem hustling as a way to create space for economic empowerment. Clients include the NAACP, the Urban League, Clemson University, the National Education Association, Illinois Public Schools, and Morehouse College.

Hotep defines a "hustler" as "an enterprising person determined to succeed, [a] go-getter."[28] Participants in Hustle University are exposed to the idea that human beings were made to be innovative and creative and "to manifest our dreams into creation," says Hotep. Among the Hustler's 10 Commandments that Hotep aims to teach today's entrepreneur are the aphorisms "your network is your networth," "the early bird gets the worm," and success is "where opportunity meets preparation."

Hotep offers helpful direction, but for independent-minded hustlers to succeed and thereby benefit both themselves and their communities, they need an environment that provides them with opportunities to work freely. While factors such as laziness, the absence of mentors, and deficiency in skill can keep entrepreneurial spirit dormant, one of the greatest obstacles is the mass of regulations generated by federal, state, and local governments.

28. Hustle University, "About."

In 2011, the Institute for Justice released a report describing how government regulations prevent entrepreneurs from taking off. [29] In Houston, for example, starting a mobile food truck business is nearly impossible. A would-be mobile food entrepreneur must first obtain a license from the City of Houston Department of Health and Human Services. Potential hustlers must submit, in-person, two sets of plans that satisfy a 28-point checklist. During the government truck inspection, the vendor must provide extensive documentation including an itinerary and route list. He is required to pay $560 in fees, which includes $200 for the installation of an electronic tracking device. Operators must also disclose their menus, including every ingredient used as well as its origin, and how each dish is prepared. Even worse, a form must be filled out for each ingredient. This is just a sampling of the regulations in one city. Similarly daunting tangles of red tape exist in every jurisdiction in America, preventing entrepreneurs from starting and maintaining small businesses.

It's clear that this regulatory regime disproportionately harms small businesses, the primary source of new jobs. In September 2010, a study by Mark Crain, the William E. Simon Professor of Political Economy at Lafayette College, was released that described the burden that federal regulations impose on small businesses. Crain found that firms with fewer than 20 employees spend 45 percent more per employee in order to comply with federal regulations than do larger firms. Small firms spend 67 percent more per employee on tax compliance than larger firms do, and, compared to the largest companies, more than 4 times as much ($3200 for small firms vs. $700 for large firms) per employee to comply with environmental regulations.

The black unemployment rate in January 2011 stood at 15.7 percent. The rate for Hispanics was a little better at 11.9, but both lagged the rate for whites (8 percent). The last thing we need are burdensome government regulations preventing hustlers from hustling. Regardless of their intentions, these types of government regulations dampen the entrepreneurial spirit of people who are trying to improve their situation and make contributions to the civic good by providing services that people need. Based on employment figures, these regulations arguably affect blacks and Hispanics disproportionately.

If America is really serious about addressing abysmal unemployment rates, then federal, state, and local governments would do well to take the handcuffs off of hustlers and free them from the regulations that keep them from creating wealth. In other words, get government out of the way and let the hustlers hustle!

29. "El Paso Vending," Institute for Justice.

Walmart and the Common Good

There is nothing better for ending poverty in the long-term than creating sustainable employment opportunities. Walmart is one of the world's best at creating jobs. In 2009, the world's second largest corporation reported nearly $400 billion in sales worldwide, according to its 2009 Sustainability Report. The company employs more than 2.1 million people worldwide, including more than 1.4 million in the United States. In its international operations, Walmart creates employment opportunities in situations where there are not very good employment alternatives. In 2008 alone, the retailer created approximately 63,000 jobs around the world including more than 33,000 stateside. Despite the social good of job creation, Walmart finds itself the object of attack for not doing more.

But creating jobs is one of the most significant ways companies can contribute to the common good, because employment is the platform for wealth creation and allows people to meet their needs. Companies like Walmart are not morally obligated to do anything philanthropic outside of normal business operations, like give money to charities, because the company *already* meets the demands of justice by creating sustainable employment opportunities, and Walmart does so for more than 2 million people.

Walmart says it is primarily beholden to its customers, shareholders, and employees, and it does so by focusing on sustainability instead of random "social responsibility" activities. Sustainability allows the company to keep profitability as its primary objective while recognizing that in doing so the company provides customers what they need at a low price. Walmart's sustainability goals include using 100 percent renewable energy, creating zero waste, and selling products that sustain natural resources. These measures are not out of some moral duty. On the contrary, they make Walmart more profitable. Walmart CEO Mike Duke explains:

> The fact is sustainability at Walmart isn't a stand-alone issue that's separate from or unrelated to our business. It's not an abstract or philanthropic program. We don't even see it as corporate social responsibility. Sustainability is built into our business. It's completely aligned with our model, our mission and our culture. Simply put, sustainability is built into our business because it's so good for our business. Sustainability helps us deliver on our Every Day Low Price business model. Using more renewable energy, reducing waste and selling sustainable products helps us take costs out of the system.[30]

30. "What Does It Mean to Be a Sustainable Business?"

Walmart is so serious about sustainability that it is now being criticized for being too sustainable and green. In the end, most Walmart customers don't care about Walmart's contribution to the common good through job creation and sustainability but simply enjoy purchasing products at low prices, especially at Christmas!

Socially Responsible Businesses

In 2010 the National Standards Authority of Ireland (NSAI) launched the world's first standards on social responsibility for businesses. I had hoped that Ireland's actions would not spread around the world, but it's too late. In November 2010, the American National Standards Institute (ANSI) announced that "Guidance on Social Responsibility" is now available for dissemination to businesses.[31] Expecting business to morally form socially responsible executives, boards of directors, and employees is a direct consequence of secularization. In a secular state, citizens tend to turn to business or government to perform tasks properly. Formerly, virtuous men and women lived this out by pursuing the common good while being formed and shaped by the applied teachings of the Christian church.

ANSI oversees the creation, promulgation, and use of thousands of norms and guidelines that directly impact businesses in nearly every sector of the market. The guidance document originated from the work of the International Organization for Standardization (ISO), which convened an international team to outline "the issues organizations need to address to operate in a socially responsible manner, and what the best practices are for implementing social responsibility effectively and efficiently."[32] The problem, of course, is that social responsibility is a moral category and is the responsibility of a community's citizens. Business is a theater where morals are lived out, not formed. Europeans and Americans want socially responsible citizens but they do not want Christianity, which specializes in forming individual and social virtues.

In the working draft of the guidance document there are standards outlining the core subjects for businesses to concern themselves with, including "social well-being," "citizenship awareness," "promotion of peace," "promotion of culture," "promotion of universal education," and "promotion of democracy." In terms of action steps, businesses are told to consider "investment in basic infrastructure—schools, hospitals, roads, housing,

31. "ANSI Announces Availability of International Social Responsibility Standard, ISO 26000," American National Standards Institute.

32. No longer available online.

education," "social services," "community cohesion, stability, social and spiritual well-being," and more. These social responsibility expectations confuse the nature of business with other institutions in society like the church and the state.

It seems that secularist Europeans and North Americans would do well to read again Milton Friedman's 1970 essay "The Social Responsibility of Business Is to Increase Its Profits." Friedman reminds us that business leaders have a responsibility to keep companies owned by shareholders profitable:

> In a free-enterprise, private-property system, a corporate execu-
> tive is an employee of the owners of the business. He has direct
> responsibility to his employers. That responsibility is to conduct
> the business in accordance with their desires, which generally
> will be to make as much money as possible while conforming to
> their basic rules of the society, both those embodied in law and
> those embodied in ethical custom.[33]

Profit provides the jobs and capital that enable individuals to meet their basic needs and make contributions to the common good by participating in churches, schools, charities, educational institutions, and other civil society institutions. You can't get more socially responsible than by providing the primary means through which society is advanced: ennobling and dignifying work. Conducting virtuous business practices is the socially responsible way of empowering people to care for their communities. Instead of turning to business for moral guidance, Europeans and North Americans would do well to return to the teachings of the Christian church, which specializes in the human virtues that render the "Guidance on Social Responsibility" unnecessary.

Profit Helps the Jobless

If Congress is concerned about America's economic recovery, one would hope that lawmakers would want to create the best possible environment for businesses to make profits. Profitable companies provide jobs. Unprofitable companies cut jobs. If lawmakers and the Obama administration continue the Bismarckian approach of taxing businesses and wealthy citizens to pay for government-created projects and services it will interfere with entrepreneurs' ability to create jobs. When people are able to meet their needs in solidarity with others through employment there is less need for

33. Friedman, "Social Responsibility of Business."

government to confuse itself as a beneficent institution and properly view itself as an institution providing a just context, established by the rule of law and property rights, to support the flourishing of economic, social, and moral spheres.

Both Protestants and Roman Catholics understand the social good that profit plays in helping the social needs of the people. In the book *Business for the Glory of God*, Wayne Grudem explains that profit is "fundamentally good and provides many opportunities for glorifying God." Profit is an indication of good stewardship. "Profit," wrote Grudem, is "an indication that I have something useful for others, and in that way it can show that I am doing good for others in the goods and services that I sell." Pope John Paul II, in the encyclical *Centesimus Annus*, reminded us that "the Church acknowledges the legitimate role of profit as an indication that a business is functioning well. When a firm makes a profit, this means that productive factors have been properly employed and corresponding human needs have been duly satisfied."[34] In other words, profit demonstrates that needs are being met.

But acknowledging the potential of profit does not mean that all profit is good. Although Christianity teaches that there is nothing necessarily nefarious about making a profit or wanting to make a profit, the presence of sin, Grudem cautioned, can introduce a number of temptations like cheating, taking advantage of people, and attempting to create monopolies. Pope John Paul II also warned us that "profitability is not the only indicator of a firm's condition. It is possible for the financial accounts to be in order, and yet for the people-who make up the firm's most valuable asset-to be humiliated and their dignity offended."[35] Market activity can tempt greed in such a way that it can undermine the virtuous possibilities of the market as well as undermine human dignity through poor work conditions or by bringing immoral products and services into the marketplace to meet the demands of people with disordered passions. Profit is best used, then, when directed by virtue.

Profit can give companies the correct incentives to take risks and provide sustainable employment so that men and women can obtain what is needed to survive in life, which comes only by earning a paycheck. Changing those incentives through Bismarckian taxation schemes discourages risk and decreases profitability. The most long-term, sustainable way to help those who are jobless is not by redistributing other people's earnings but by

---

34. John Paul II, *Centesimus Annus*, section 35.
35. Ibid.

distributing the freedom for entrepreneurs to virtuously make a profit with products that serve the common good and create jobs.

Competing Visions Frustrate Progress

When Americans ponder what is good for society, because of our competing visions and definitions of what is best, it is difficult to arrive at a consensus. Many Christian theologians naturally rely on the Bible and often argue that what God commands therein is best for America. But other Christian theologians believe that what's good is revealed in the Bible *and* in the moral order embedded in creation. They look to evaluate the common good on the basis of whether or not it leads to flourishing according to the God-given nature, purpose, and design of human life. In a pluralistic society, presuppositions in conflict are even more complicated. What follows are three key categories that explain, in part, why well-meaning people find it difficult to agree on what is best for us.

First is the teleological approach, which desires that society care about larger principles, goals, and consequences. This approach asks, "How are morally worthy goals or purposes to be advanced in society?" and, "What is best insofar as it furthers a morally good purpose, goal, or consequence?" Those thinking in terms of creation norms are concerned that what we do furthers human flourishing/well-being, objectively defined. Consequentialists in this framework are chiefly concerned that we do what produces the best outcomes and tend not to care much about the justice of achieving those ends.

Second is the deontological approach, which wants to make sure that members of a society have rightly understood principles, duties, and standards as prerequisites for arriving at social prescriptions. The principled approached asks: What is the duty or law that is to be followed? What is best for society is good to the extent that it reflects, protects, or obeys the relevant moral law or principle. Consequences or outcomes are secondary, and may even be irrelevant in some cases.

Third is the virtue approach, which wants society to have certain kinds of people, because a good society is one that promotes certain virtue, habits, and dispositions that lead to a genuine human flourishing/wholeness of society. The specific outcomes are not all that important and neither are specific shared duties and principles.

Put these three approaches to work in Congress and you would have a legislative mess. In terms of addressing poverty, for example, the teleological camp would attempt to legislate an end to poverty by any means necessary, including coercion. The deontological camp would try to legislate us into a worldview that leads to us all caring about poverty in the same way. The virtue camp would believe that poverty could not be rightly dealt with by society until we had a country made up of a certain kind of people who would be resistant to the approaches of others. All three approaches have periods of influence but all three keep the rest of us mighty frustrated because progress is impeded in such ideological theaters.

The Bismarcking of America

Otto von Bismarck, the Prussian prime minister/German chancellor from 1862 to 1890, is the modern father of the prevailing worldview that government should serve as a social services institution by taking money from the wealthy and from business to give to those who are not as advantaged. On the Social Security Administration website, Bismarck is heralded as a visionary who introduced social insurance to "promote the well-being of workers in order to keep the German economy operating at maxim efficiency, and to stave-off calls for more radical socialistic alternatives."[36] He initiated the concept of big and ever-expanding government as a primary means of social services, which was imported to the United States by President Roosevelt's "New Deal," expanded further with Lyndon Johnson's "War on Poverty," and picked up again, many argue, in the Obama administration's mantra of "Change." While calling the Obama administration a band of socialists sounds extreme, calling the administration Bismarckian seems unquestionable.

Bismarck's approach remains popular because political responses to economic crises tend toward higher taxation of the wealthy and increased centralization. Nineteenth-century Europe found itself in transition from agrarianism and feudalism to industrialization—a transition that created new economic pressures demanding fresh perspectives on political economy. A radical and often violent form of Marxist socialism began to rise all over Europe that threatened the stability and unity of many young nations like Germany, Italy, and the Netherlands. To fight off socialism, Bismarck proposed a system where government provides an economic safety net using high taxes on business and the wealthy to meet the needs of the poor.

In 1891, William Dawson, in *Bismarck and State Socialism*, explains that Bismarck believed that it was the positive duty of the State to promote the welfare of all its members, especially the poor. This led to a national system of insurance that provided funds for people when they were sick

36. "Otto von Bismarck." Social Security.

and could not work, when they suffered work-related accidents, and they became senior citizens and were unable to work. Bismarck believed that working was a human right, and if people were unable to work, government should take money from businesses and the wealthy to give to them. If this sounds familiar, it should. Bismarck's experiment led to our own Medicaid, Medicare, disability insurance, workers' compensation, welfare, and the conceptual framework for universal healthcare.

The United States has undergone Bismarckian restructuring since the 1940s, and it is now unquestioned dogma in the West that the wealthy should bear the financial cost of meeting the needs of the poor by force instead of by virtue, love, choice, or charity. Bismarck did not value a role for civil-society institutions, like the church, in meeting the needs of the poor.

Is the Obama administration a band of 19th-century Marxists and socialists? No. Is the Obama administration attempting to deal with economic crisis in a Bismarckian fashion? Absolutely. Even though Germany abandoned Bismarck's vision by the 1890s, because they were ideas that did not work in practice in the long run, the hope that these measures bring prosperity still linger. Welcome to Bismarck-nation.

A New Generation, A Constitutional Conservatism

There is a new generation of articulate conservatives on the rise in America. These new conservatives will not be charged with religious syncretism, the throwing of random Bible verses at political issues, or using the Bible to legislate morality. Instead, they employ clear and simple reflections on the implications of the United States Constitution and the Bill of Rights for American life and public policy. Robert Wheeler and John Amble have assembled a provocative new generation of thinkers in their new book, *Reinventing the Right: Conservative Voices for the New Millennium*, which introduces to liberals, conservatives and moderates new ways of thinking about the foundations of liberty. The conservatives in this volume seem to want to expand the reader's imagination of an America that is committed to the rule of law and a robust constitutionalism.

The book's contributors are among the brightest women and men from multiple disciplines ranging from law and business to education and ecology. The contributors' academic credentials, including degrees from Harvard, Princeton, Dartmouth, Emory, and Berkeley, just to name a few, are sure to impress readers. With political savvy, these women and men apply the Constitution to the hottest political issues facing America's future, including the roles of the First and Second Amendments, a defense of religious liberty, as well as multiculturalism, abortion, energy conservation, healthcare reform, public education, crime, immigration, American foreign policy, national security, globalization, taxes, and more. Needless to say, if you love *WORLD Magazine*, you will enjoy this book immensely.

For example, conservative readers will be encouraged by Wheeler's chapter on abortion, where he writes that many people forget the damage abortion does to the dignity of women and the innocent in light of liberty and the Constitution:

> We offer a society in which human beings are respected and given the dignity they deserve, particularly women. . . . It is a society where people are treated with enough dignity and respect to *expect* of them the ability to make decisions and to require that they take responsibility for the results. In such a society, women are truly empowered.
>
> The right to on-demand abortion does not empower but rather dehumanizes women. It treats them as children, unable to make complex decisions, and gives them as reprieve against poor decisions the ability to infringe upon the rights of others without consequence. Infringing upon the rights of others without consequence is not empowerment. It is enablement. In a better society, women are empowered enough to make decisions about their bodies without violating the rights of the innocent.[37]

Abortion is a constitutional issue in addition to a religious one. For those familiar with the Constitution Party's position on the sanctity of life, they will be reminded of a similar defense of the pre-born "whose life begins at fertilization." The Constitution Party says, "[T]he first duty of the law is to prevent the shedding of innocent blood. It is, therefore, the duty of all civil governments to secure and to safeguard the lives of the pre-born." It could be argued that in the past many conservatives have not applied the United States Constitution enough to issues they care about. Wheeler and Amble intend to not let that happen again.

On the whole, for those who consider themselves conservatives, what Wheeler and Amble have put together will be a great encouragement to representatives of an emerging generation who intend to move forward to invite Americans to embrace the implications of the documents that shape and form the liberty given to U.S. citizens.

---

37. Wheeler, "Voices of the Damned," 97.

Barack von Bismarck

The November 2010 congressional elections were not so much a referendum on the Obama administration as they were a check on whether President Barack Obama's implementation of a Bismarckian vision of government would continue.

Otto von Bismarck, the Prussian prime minister/German chancellor from 1862 to 1890, is the father of the welfare state. He advanced the vision that government should serve as a social services institution by taking earned wealth from the rich and from businesses to deliver services to those who are not as advantaged. Bismarck's *Kulturkampf* campaign intended both to keep radical socialists at bay and undermine the church's role in meeting the needs of local citizens by positioning government to be the primary source of social services. He initiated the ideal of an ever-expanding, beneficent government, which was subsequently imported to the United States in Franklin Roosevelt's New Deal, expanded further with Lyndon Johnson's War on Poverty, and currently drives the policies of the Obama administration. Barack Obama is not a 19th-century socialist, but his agenda is unquestionably Bismarckian.

In 1891, William Dawson, in *Bismarck and State Socialism*, explained that Bismarck believed it was the duty of the state to promote the welfare of all its members.[38] On November 22, 1888, in response to Germany's 1873 economic crisis, Bismarck proclaimed, "I regard it as the duty of the State to endeavor to ameliorate existing economic evils." In Bismarck-like fashion, commenting on America's economic crisis, President Obama declared in January 2009 that, "It is true that we cannot depend on government alone to create jobs or long-term growth, but at this particular moment, only government can provide the short-term boost necessary to lift us from a recession this deep and severe. Only government can break the cycle that are crippling our economy—where a lack of spending leads to lost jobs which leads to even less spending; where inability to lend and borrow stops growth and leads to even less credit." In a Bismarckian world, "only" government can set the national economy right.

Regarding universal health insurance, on March 15th, 1884, Bismarck asked, "Is it the duty of the State, or is it not, to provide for its helpless citizens?" He answered, "I maintain that it is its duty." It is the duty of the state to "the seek the cheapest form of insurance, and, not aiming at profit for itself, must keep primarily in view the benefit for the poor and needy." Similarly, under the federal healthcare reform law, Congress forbids health

---

38. For more see Dawson, *Bismarck and State Socialism*.

insurance companies from raising insurance premiums until insurers submit to Obamacare officials "a justification for an unreasonable premium increase prior to the implementation of the increase." In effect, government determines health insurance premiums.

On unemployment, Bismarck believed that government is ultimately responsible for finding jobs for those unemployed through no fault of their own, those lacking opportunity to work and thus prohibited from properly sustaining themselves. On March 15, 1884 Bismarck exclaimed, "If an establishment employing twenty thousand or more workpeople were to be ruined . . . we could not allow these men to hunger"—even if it means creating government jobs for national infrastructure improvements. "In such cases we build railways," says Bismarck. "We carry out improvements which otherwise would be left to private initiative." Likewise, in July, President Obama proclaimed, "I believe it's critical we extend unemployment insurance for several more months, so that Americans who've been laid off through no fault of their own get the support they need to provide for their families and can maintain their health insurance until they're rehired." Then, in September, President Obama announced a six-year, $50 billion infrastructure proposal "to rebuild 150,000 miles of our roads," "maintain 4,000 miles of our railways," and "restore 150 miles of runways." To keep America working, Obama is channeling Bismarck's vision of government as creator of jobs.

By the 1890s, for several reasons, Germany was forced to abandon many of Bismarck's specific reforms. However, Bismarck's method of using of government as the ultimate provider of social services paid for by the earned wealth of others is the modus operandi of the Obama administration. The outcome of contests for congressional seats will determine whether the nation continues down the path chosen by Barack Obama, but blazed long ago by the visionary of the omnicompetent state, Otto von Bismarck.

Government Intervention Hypocrisy

Is it not odd that many people who complain about government involvement in the housing market are the very ones who encourage zoning laws for their preferences? While there are good critiques on the short-sightedness of the Obama administration's plans to increase the government's role in helping the poor acquire access to better housing, the problem is that government intervention is one of the largest variables in the housing crisis in the first place. And this includes zoning laws.

The major government players in the housing market include the Federal Reserve, the government-created and privately owned Federal National

Mortgage Association (Fannie Mae) and the Federal Home Loan Mortgage Corporation (Freddie Mac), the U.S. Department of Housing and Urban Development (HUD), and multiple state and local agencies. These agencies tend to serve as guarantors of risky lending practices that, when left to market forces, would have saved thousands from taking on debt they could not manage.

One of the unnoticed villains in the 2008 financial crisis were local zoning laws. Zoning laws are generally ways in which the elite use government intervention to keep "riffraff" out their communities as well as to thwart local land development that does not fit with the social preferences of the elite, explains Thomas Sowell in the book *The Housing Boom and Bust*. Restricting the use of land for the sake of "preserving open space," "saving farmland," "protecting the environment," "historical preservation," and other political mantras actually work to drive up property values in ways in which the market would reduce. Having minimum lot-size restrictions, for example, is a sinister way in which the elite, according to Sowell, "watch the values of their homes shoot up after the restrictions, so that they gain financially as well as by keeping out less affluent people and thereby preserving the character of the community as they like it."

Local planning commissions often introduce so many regulatory impediments for housing developments that it is no longer cost-effective to build new housing in the first place. Land use restrictions, used by both liberals and conservatives, over the past 50 years had a role to play in distorting the supply and demand matrix in the housing market. The market was not free to meet real needs because the elite used the government to prevent development. The elite doesn't want low-income people living near them, either. Why aren't those against government intervention fighting against zoning laws that prevent low-income housing developments?

Because of property inflation due to zoning restrictions, there are more and more calls to "make housing affordable." This is happening in some areas because lower-priced options like trailer parks, apartments, homes on smaller lots, and so on are similarly not available nor allowed in certain areas. If conservatives are truly against government intervention in low-income housing, they should also be against government intervention used to codify social preferences of the elite.

Conservative vs Liberal

There are times when I do not know whether to call myself a liberal or a conservative. By liberal, I mean "classical" liberal, which is connected to a tradition of individual liberty and small government instead of today's popular construction with its socialistic worldview. I generally have to ask people, "What do you mean?" when I'm asked about my political ideology. David Koyzis offers helpful distinctions in his book *Political Visions & Illusions: A Survey & Christian Critique of Contemporary Ideologies*, which is well-worth reading.

Koyzis rightly points out that we all tend to waffle between idolatry and gnosticism when it comes to our political alignment. We are idolatrous when we believe that our political preference is the remedy for the world's problems, and we are gnostic when we believe that competing ideologies are inherently evil. In an honest moment, I would confess that I do believe that my political ideology is right and all others are wrong because, at the end of the day, I think I'm always right. This is why I struggle with whether I am liberal or conservative.

To conserve something, says Koyzis, means to keep it, maintain it, in the face of forces that might tend to eliminate it over time. A conservative fears that something is being lost with change that cannot be replaced. Conservatives tend also to regret nothing more than the loss of their own power and privilege. What makes someone a conservative is not so much one's views on government but one's attitudes toward tradition and change. Conservatives do not like change. Conservatives want to conserve their own traditions and institutions even if that means trading off innovation and progress.

Liberalism (of the classical variety) starts with the fundamental belief in human autonomy, which means being self-directed and free to govern oneself in accordance with rules to which one willingly submits. The most basic principle of liberalism, according to Koyzis, is that everyone possesses property in his own person, and must therefore be free to govern himself in accordance with his own choices provided that those choices do not infringe on the equal right of others to pursue the same. Human persons should be free from coercion that favors one person or group's preferences for another. As such, true liberals have a consistent aversion to government coercion in ways that conservatives do not.

The liberal/conservative distinction may explain why many conservatives do not mind expanding the size of government to maintain their own values and traditions. Many conservatives have no problem using the coercive nature of government to enshrine "traditional values" in America in ways intolerable to liberals. For example, conservatives and liberals would disagree about having prayer in (formerly Protestant) public schools. Conservatives lament the absence of prayer while liberals see no place for prayer in that setting, or even for the idea of public schools.

We saw this distinction clearly in the politics of Ron Paul during the last presidential campaign. Paul stood out among the other Republican candidates because he was more concerned about liberty than using government to preserve traditions and preferences. At the end of the day, I have more affinities with liberals than conservatives because there are some American conservative cultural traditions that America has benefited by extinguishing.

Inaugurating Presidential Disappointment

In late 2008, the world was waiting to see if Americans would elect a president who would bring about sweeping social, cultural, and political change. As Sen. Barack Obama became President Obama it brought a mix of ridiculous expectations and unfounded fears regarding what "Superpresident" would accomplish. I was so captivated by the spectacle of it all after Election Day that I committed to attend the presidential inauguration ceremony.[39] Here's what I had to say about it.

Although I strongly disagree with the way then-House Speaker Nancy Pelosi views America, and with many policy initiatives of the Obama administration, in the spirit of honoring the office of president (1 Peter 2:17) and recognizing the legitimacy of government (Romans 13:1), I met family members and friends in Washington, D.C. to witness the transition from President Bush to President Obama. As I stood in front of the Washington Monument, I felt the magnitude and weight of the office in ways I had not experienced before. It was fantastic to witness all the pomp and circumstance. Watching the procession of congressional leaders, Supreme Court judges, and so on, was thrilling. I was particularly surprised by the cold interactions between Presidents Clinton and Carter witnessed by millions on JumboTrons before they took their seats. These two families obviously do not like each other.

Many voters on Election Day and at the inauguration were excited because "change" was coming. We were supposedly ushering in a new era of governance. But not much has changed since then. The Obama administration as continued to expand the tentacles of government into areas which government is neither designed nor equipped to manage. Oddly, there has been much disappointment among many liberals because Obama has not gone far enough in bringing about "change."

In November 2009, *The New York Times* wrote about how Europeans were growing critical of Obama because "Mr. Obama has not broken clearly

39. Bradley, "Ain't No Stoppin' Us Now."

enough with Bush administration policies that they dislike."[40] I say if the Europeans are frustrated with Obama, then he must be doing something right. Why then has there not been "change" enough to satisfy liberal critics? The answer is found in the reality check President Obama encountered when his campaign rhetoric was met with real facts about the world and by the independent agenda of Speaker Pelosi.

The Rasmussen Reports' daily Presidential Tracking Poll shows that, from July 2009 to January 2012, Obama has had a negative approval rating. What does this mean? The honeymoon phase had ended by that point. People had finally realized that Obama is just a politician.

A $9,000,000,000,000 National Deficit?

I wish we lived in a country where national debt actually alarmed voters. In 2009, the White House predicted a 10-year federal deficit of $9 trillion![41] We are told that is more than all previous deficits since America's founding combined. Additionally, the White House also said that by 2020, the national debt will equal three-quarters of the entire U.S. economy. And yet in 2015 the debt has already surpassed our GDP. Why are Americans not absolutely outraged and pressuring lawmakers to cut the government credit card? Perhaps we don't mind because we all live this way in our personal lives, with credit cards, home-equity loans, and so on.

One must wonder if people really understand what $9 trillion dollars means. Here's what it looks like: $9,000,000,000,000. This is what Americans need to see in order to understand that this is where the nation's debt is headed unless we take radical steps to stop borrowing money to spend on hunches, social experiments, and programs we know will not work. To do otherwise is nothing less than grossly irresponsible.

According to The Associated Press story cited above, the public national debt, made up of amounts the government owes to the public, including foreign governments, stood at $7.4 trillion in 2009. Excuse me, I should have written, "$7,400,000,000,000." In the private sector only a banker who was hoping to get fired would allow an institution with this much-leveraged debt to borrow one penny. Politicians, however, are more than willing to put future generations of Americans at risk of national bankruptcy for soundbites and reelection.

Wouldn't it be great if the Obama administration, in light of these asinine numbers, announced an end to deficit spending, saying, "OK, America,

---

40. Erlanger, "Europe Still Likes Obama," lines 9-11.
41. Mason, "Obama to Raise 10-Year Deficit to $9 Trillion," lines 1-9.

we have to develop a better approach to solving America's problems other than allowing politicians to shackle future generations to monumental debt"? I know this may sound radical, but perhaps Americans should consider voting out of office any politician, regardless of party, who believes that the best way reduce the national debt is to slow the economy further by increased spending on untested programs, borrowing more money, and spending even more money than the nation has access to use.

As such, a $1,000,000,000,000 ($1 trillion) healthcare reform initiative makes absolutely no sense—even if it's smoked-screen as "increasing competition." What is most pathetic is having to listen to gut-wrenching political spin from proponents of big government who will argue (1) that everything is George Bush's fault, and (2) that we need to spend more money. "Serenity now! Serenity now!"

Yes Friends, "Axis of Evil"

It seems President George W. Bush, in his January 29, 2002, State of the Union address was correct in describing Iran, Iraq, and North Korea as an "axis of evil." President Bush used the phrase to describe governments believed to be promoting terrorism and seeking weapons of mass destruction. Just over a year after those remarks, there was an international invasion of Iraq to dismantle that despotic regime.

At the time, President Bush received a considerable amount of criticism for the remarks, including from the Chinese government. "The Chinese side does not advocate using this kind of language in international relations," foreign ministry spokesperson Kong Quan told a news conference in 2002.[42] Of course, now the Chinese government has led in the building of sanctions against North Korea for their latest round of nuclear bomb posturing.

Michael Klare, professor of peace and world security studies at Hampshire College in Amherst, Mass., writing in a February 1, 2002, column, suggested that Bush's words would crumble under scrutiny. Klare said that we need to ask more accurate questions, like "How real is this threat?" and "Do we really face an 'axis of evil'?"[43]

Given what has been happening in North Korea and Iran, how could it be otherwise? On balance, North Korea and Iran continue to pose the most dangerous threat to human dignity and freedom for their own citizens, as well as threatening peace around the world. However, with the international

42. "China Berates 'Axis of Evil' Remarks." CNN.
43. Klare, "Bush's 'Axis of Evil' Crumbles under Scrutiny," lines 4-6.

rise of socialism and totalitarian regimes, there are several nations whose citizens and neighbors are threatened, as well, but North Korea and Iran are currently leading the pack.

In 2009, the Associated Press reported that North Korea threatened to wipe the United States off the map, as Washington and its allies watched for signs that the regime would launch a series of missiles in the coming days. "If the U.S. imperialists start another war, the army and people of Korea will . . . wipe out the aggressors on the globe once and for all," the official Korean Central News Agency reported.[44]

At the same time, the world watched citizens of Iran protest their dissatisfaction with the Iranian presidential election. At least 17 people were murdered, and who knows how many were injured by government law enforcement personnel as Iranians took to the streets for justice. The Associated Press reported that Iran's supreme leader said that the government would not give in to pressure over the disputed presidential election, effectively closing the door to compromise with the opposition.

I wonder what the 2002 critics of President Bush's phrase think when they watch the YouTube footage of bloodied women in the streets of Tehran or when they read about China and Russia taking the lead in imposing sanctions on North Korea. Perhaps President Bush's 2002 words were somewhat prophetic.

Youth Movement Revolutionizing Guatemala

Guatemalan Gen Xers and Millennials have taken to the streets to stand up for justice in light of a nation riddled with violence and corruption. In the summer of 2009, I spent time with a few leaders of "Un Joven Más (One More Youth)," an organization pulling together all the isolated efforts in Guatemala to move from its current environment of exemption from punishment, injustice, and fear to an environment in which freedom and justice drive the country's growth, progress, and future. One of the movement's central themes is "Guatemala, we will never abandon you."

The movement's main blog features this call to action:

> La juventud guatemalteca apela a tu responsabilidad, como ciudadano, como guatemalteco, como ser humano, de organizarte y manifestarte pacíficamente, para exigir a nuestras autoridades que cumplan con las obligaciones para las que fueron designados: defender y proteger la libertad, la justicia y la vida de los guatemaltecos. (The Guatemalan youth appeal to your sense of

44. "North Korea Threatens to 'Wipe Out' U.S." CBS News.

responsibility as a citizen, as a Guatemalan, as a human being to organize and peacefully demonstrate to demand that our authorities fulfill the obligations to which they were elected for: defend and protect the freedom, justice and life of all Guatemalans.)[45]

Certain events and conditions, including a rash of murdered bus drivers; the murder of Rodrigo Rosenburg, a respected corporate lawyer; a startling murder rate of 17 people per day, and more, motivated a few young leaders to say "enough" and organize a national movement that, if sustained, could have the impact of the American civil rights movement. These young people are determined not to be driven by fear of retribution in order to pursue what is best for the country.

In just a few weeks, using Facebook, Twitter, blogs, and text-messaging, the movement had grown from a few dozen concerned youth to over 30,000 at a recent demonstration promoting justice at La Plaza Italia, the main plaza in front of Guatemala City's City Hall. Other organizations involved in coordinating efforts include Me Importa Guatemala and Christian youth organizations like Emergente.

Many of these young leaders have bravely approached Guatemala's congressional leaders directly to promote justice and peace. Phone taps, being followed, police harassment, and restructuring time spent in public are among many of the new realities these young leaders are experiencing in their quest for justice. Spending a few days in Guatemala encouraged me to understand the true power of a few men and women willing to risk safety and comfort to suffer for the promotion of human dignity.

Republicans and Judge Latina

President Obama's choice of Sonia Sotomayor, a woman of Puerto Rican descent, for the Supreme Court was politically brilliant. Republicans needed to do enough public political grumbling to appease the party base, but wisdom demanded them to go "protest light" on opposing the 54-year-old even though she has made racially reasoned statements like this:

"I would hope that a wise Latina woman with the richness of her experiences would more often than not reach a better conclusion than a white male who hasn't lived that life."[46]

---

45. Un Joven Mas, "Juventud Guatemalteca." Website no longer available.
46. Sotomayor, "A Latina Judge's Voice."

I have given up all hope that Supreme Court justice nominees will ever be chosen for their ability to rule according to the original intent of the U.S. Constitution. Maybe conservatives should stop whining about the "good ol' days" and accept the fact that the whole process is now 100 percent political. For example, "Sotomayor" could also be translated as "re-election security" for President Obama.

Is she qualified? Yes. Sotomayor's credentials are solid and are well beyond what the Constitution requires—i.e., that the person simply be nominated by the president and confirmed by the Senate. Sotomayor graduated from Ivy League schools so she's obviously more qualified than those of us who graduated from football factories, some might joke. I wonder why people march around ranting about the "qualifications" for Supreme Court nominees when, technically, President Obama could have chosen an NBA referee.

I certainly expect Sotomayor to be an activist judge. Like any other judge, her experience may lead to forming opinions different than, say, a "white male." Her opinion, of course, presumes truth to the myth among many minorities that all white men are homogeneous and have the same set of experiences, most of which are not abounding in value. However, an additional myth claimed by those critical of Sotomayor's confession of extra-constitutional influence is that conservative judges are not activist judges. If an anti-abortion, anti-affirmative action, anti-all-things-liberal judge was nominated, conservatives would be pleased and the nominee could conveniently hide his or her judicial activism behind "constitutionality." Besides, is it really possible to be a non-activist judge in America?

Maybe Sotomayor will surprise us and do what Justice David Souter did after he was nominated by George H.W. Bush by ruling in ways ideologically opposite than the nominating president. Because this Souter/Sotomayor swap is a one-to-one liberal replacement, the court's ideological shift will not change. Moreover, since the Republican Party is slowly becoming the party of white congressional leaders, complaints against Sotomayor will be interpreted as either sexist or racist. As such, unless something strange occurs in the confirmation process, conservatives should not waste other people's money fighting too aggressively against the nomination. The time will come for rallying soon enough.

Gun Control and Teen Shootings

In March 2009 at a secondary school in Winnenden, Germany, a 17-year-old gunman went on a rampage, killing fifteen people before taking his own life.[47] Many Germans report being surprised at such tragedies because of the country's very strict gun-control laws. In 2002, Germany tightened its already tight restrictions on weapons: People purchasing a hunting rifle, for instance, must undergo background checks that can last up to a year, and those seeking a gun for sport must already be a member of a sporting club and obtain a license from police. Gun collectors also need a permit for possession of guns.

It seems that many in the gun-control debate continue to ignore the fact that criminals who intend to do serious harm will do so regardless of the level of gun control. This German student allegedly used a weapon he obtained from his home to commit this heinous crime. Therefore, tighter control laws would not have prevented this tragedy.

Perhaps the real problem is that we live in a world that has grown accustomed to solving problems and working through emotional issues by inflicting violence on others. Perhaps teens need alternative ways to work out their anger and rage without hurting themselves and other people.

In this country, the gun-control battle is on the verge of heating up again as the Obama administration considers new restrictions. In a letter to Attorney General Eric Holder, the two senators from Montana, Max Baucus and Jon Tester, wrote that the Justice Department should enforce existing laws rather than propose additional ones that could infringe on Second Amendment rights.[48]

It is important that we consider that blaming the gun might not be the best place to start when it comes to instances of gun violence, and hopefully lawmakers will discontinue the practice of using stories like the one of this school in Germany to attack the Second Amendment.

David Brooks vs. Rush Limbaugh

So what is a conservative today anyway? The reaction to Louisiana Gov. Bobby Jindal's response to President Obama's description of our expanding government in his 2009 State of the Union Address seems to have created some tensions within the conservative community. David Brooks, the conservative columnist for *The New York Times*, said on PBS that Jindal's speech represented "the stale conservatism of a bygone era."

The next day on his radio program, Rush Limbaugh proceeded to throw Brooks under the conservative bus, sautéing him for saying that he admired Obama in the beginning and has only recently been surprised by

47. "German School Gunman 'Kills 15,'" BBC News.

48. You can find the letter at www.tester.senate.gov/?p=press_release&id=2482

what the president has been offering lately. Limbaugh concluded his segment by saying:

"Well, if you want to be proved wrong by Barack Obama and you're going to call yourself a conservative columnist, Mr. Brooks, you need to drop conservative from your title, 'cause the two don't go together."

Limbaugh's questioning the conservatism of David Brooks has somewhat of an extended history, but this particular attack seems to come from Limbaugh's assessment that Brooks no longer believes that the principles of Ronald Reagan will strengthen the Republican Party in the future. So when Brooks gave a non-complimentary assessment of Jindal's speech, calling it "a disaster for the Republican Party," Limbaugh suggested that Brooks does not want Republicans sounding like Reagan as the party moves forward. Brooks' conservatism may have shifted, Limbaugh intimated.

This began to raise the question in my mind: "What is a conservative?" Brooks believes that the American people will vote only for a Republican that sounds more moderate than those who sound like Reagan. So in order to be a conservative, must one align oneself with the views of Limbaugh or Reagan? Is not Rep. Ron Paul more conservative than Reagan on some issues? Are true conservatives more libertarian in their views? Can one be a conservative politically and not morally?

Is it "OK" to be a "Brooks conservative," who seems to be more moderate in the eyes of some by virtue of wanting Obama to do well? Or is a true conservative a "Limbaugh conservative," which Brooks would say represents the rhetoric of a "bygone era"?

Is it likely that future battles in the Republican Party will be between those who think more like David Brooks and those who think more like Rush Limbaugh? Is a more moderate conservatism the future or do Republicans need to lean more toward classical liberalism or libertarian views? My own view is that we may need to resurrect the Federalist Party and hope voters will re-learn what federalism is meant to obtain.

Lame Anti-Government Preaching

Ranting against the government fails to persuade anxious voters to consider a different approach to addressing America's problems. Anti-government language may be a perfect strategy to galvanize a shrinking American demographic of "conservatives," but the rhetoric will not resonate with a generation of voters who have demonstrated a preference for government involvement in too many things. For instance, Louisiana Gov. Bobby Jindal's response to President Obama's address to Congress and the nation on February 25, 2009 seemed to employ the same rhetorical strategy that resulted in many Republicans in Congress losing their seats, as well Sen. John McCain's losing the presidential election.

Those who support the limited government described in the U.S. Constitution, restraint in government spending, and a de-centralized economy are desperately in need of a new lexicon in order to persuasively communicate these principles to an American public who misunderstand these ideas as merely "conservative," instead of ideas that provided the context for America's federalist success.

The rhetoric of "we want to put money and decisions in the hands of the American people and not the government" is not going be persuasive in the future. The majority of Americans see a positive role for government to play in many aspects of our civil society. Preaching the rhetoric of "lower taxes," "welfare state," "individual responsibility," and so on, further isolates political conservatives from America's center.

At one point, Gov. Jindal said:

"The strength of America is not found in our government. It is found in the compassionate hearts and enterprising spirit of our citizens."

While we understand the sentiment behind this principle, this type of language is unappealing to most Americans and sets up a false dichotomy. Whoever wrote this sentence for Jindal may have inadvertently narrowed the appeal to this historical fact: The strength of America *is* found in our government knowing exactly what its limited positive contribution is to create conditions for peace and human flourishing—a role that frees its compassionate and enterprising citizens to personally do more, not less.

Pitting government against the taxpayer will all but guarantee future election losses. A better approach would be to speak about the positive role of government in a republic coupled with a compelling vision for strengthening the nation's mediating institutions to sustain our flourishing so that the burden of our nation's recovery is shared by all of us as citizens.

Perhaps, it would have been better to say, "The strength of America is found in its government being free to do the things that governments do well while also freeing the compassionate hearts and enterprising spirit of our citizens to personally involve themselves in leading other effective institutions to create a context for sustainable progress." Speech writing is not my gift, but campaigning against government alone only appeals to a generation of folks putting the final touches on their wills and their bow-tie wearing Burkean grandchildren.

Tax Hypocrisy

Members of the Democratic Party should be outraged at the fact that their own leaders do not seem interested in contributing their own taxes to "care for Americans." Is it not odd that top Democrats like Tom Daschle and Timothy Geithner had tax "errors" that were magically found and remedied *after* they were nominated to head government agencies? What about President Obama's nominee for White House chief performance officer, Nancy Killefer? She withdrew her name from consideration because of tax problems as well. What gives? Are these not the same people who support using tax money to pay for bank bailouts, welfare programs, farm subsidies, and the like? How can we "help" Americans through tax-funded programs if the elite don't contribute to the pot?

Is this not hypocrisy? A hypocrite is "a person who acts in contradiction to his or her stated beliefs or feelings," according to Merriam-Webster; could not these leading Democrats be charged with acting in contradiction to the policies they promote?

I journeyed over to the Democratic National Committee website to read up on the resignations, but the party didn't seem to consider this news. Would it not be of interest to the party to note that the president's cabinet is falling apart one non-tax-paying wealthy nominee at a time?

Again, why aren't Democrats raging mad that many of the party's wealthy elites do not participate in the very process to which lawmakers expect the rest of us to submit? I totally disagree with President Obama that the cascade of resignations was his responsibility. I sincerely respect the president's embracing the fact that "the buck" stops with him, but there was no way he could have known. If a person is willing to hide money from the government and break the law, one must assume that those persons would also be the type of people who wouldn't disclose this during nomination conversations last year. In a CNN interview President Obama said this about the Daschle debacle: "I think I screwed up. And, I take responsibility for it and we're going to make sure we fix it so it doesn't happen again."[49]

President Obama did not "screw up." It's not his fault that there is a culture of tax avoidance among elites in a party of tax creators. The president is too new to Washington, D.C., to have been seduced into this brand of tenured political hypocrisy. Perhaps the president was naive to assume that the professional politicians he tapped were behaving differently than all the others (on both sides of the aisle).

49. "Obama: 'I Screwed Up' on Daschle Appointment," CNN.

Since the president seeks to bring change to Washington, I am more than willing to volunteer for various positions in his administration. I've been broke all of my adult life, especially during my 14-year graduate school stint, and I pay my taxes because it is the law and I have very little interest in going to jail.

Of course, some have argued that one way around tax evasion schemes in our convoluted system is to replace the current system with a flat tax. However, my sense is that human nature will prevail in a flat tax system as well and some will find new ways skirt even that system.

SECTION THREE

Education

Tweeting for Better Grades

IN A NEW STUDY, "Twitteracy: Tweeting as a New Literary Practice," co-author Christine Greenhow, a Michigan State professor, reports that students regularly in contact with fellow classmates and instructors on Twitter received higher grades because they were more interested in the content of the course, suggesting that one of the markers of a good course is its use of social media.

The study says research on the use of Twitter outside the field of education has emphasized its "communicative, informational, and organizational properties." On Twitter, people tweet to develop and maintain relationships through conversation beyond in-person contacts. Research has also focused on how Twitter is used for "mobilization and social protest" by gathering groups to take action without centralizing initial contact in one location. For example, the entire Occupy Wall Street movement was launched and organized on Twitter and Facebook by the socialist Canadian magazine *Ad Busters*.

The study's authors present research recommending instructional strategies for using Twitter by professors, including "answering students' questions, encouraging discussions, helping students connect, and providing support for learning and achievement." According to Greenhow, with Twitter "students get more engaged because they feel it is connected to something real, that it's not just learning for the sake of learning. It feels authentic to them." In the end, the authors note, "Twitter use in higher education may facilitate increased student engagement with course content and increased student-to-student or student-instructor interactions—potentially leading to stronger positive relationships that improve learning and to the design of richer experiential or authentic learning experiences."

As a college professor, I struggle with the notion that Twitter makes students feel more engaged and authentic. I am wondering if Twitter is as useful in small classroom settings. It seems that perhaps students feel disconnected and disengaged with classmates and professors in large university classrooms where those relationships are more difficult to foster and students are merely numbers. It seems to me that the best way to have students engage and feel connected with each other and their instructors is personal face-to-face interaction. If higher education needs Twitter to get students connected and increase performance, then perhaps there is something else wrong with how we educate in the 21st century.

Affirmative Action for Conservatives

Unless you believe that ever-expanding government programs and centrally planned economies are the solution to all of life's contingencies and social problems, you will not likely get a faculty position in the humanities, social sciences, or education at an American college or university. A prevailing myth in America is that our colleges and universities are bastions of diversity. This is laughable. To believe the diversity myth one must ignore the fact that American higher education seems to care very little about students being introduced to diverse ideas and perspectives. When American colleges talk "diversity" they only seem to mean it along the axis of race, gender, and class. The notion that a robust learning community requires students be exposed to multiple perspectives has no value in the modern academy. What matters today on most campuses is intellectual homogeneity—also known as tribal "group think."

In the August issue the journal *Inside Higher Ed*, a large survey of psychologists reported the following:

> Just over 37 percent of those surveyed said that, given equally qualified candidates for a job, they would support the hiring of a liberal candidate over a conservative candidate. Smaller percentages agreed that a 'conservative perspective' would negatively influence their odds of supporting a paper for inclusion in a journal or a proposal for a grant.[1]

---

1. Jaschik, "Admitting to Bias," see chart.

In another major study, research by Yoel Inbar and Joris Lammers demonstrates that social psychologists, for example, openly admit they would bypass conservatives in the hiring process. When the authors surveyed a large number of social and personality psychologists they discovered several not-so-surprising facts:

> First, although only 6 percent described themselves as conservative 'overall,' there was more diversity of political opinion on economic issues and foreign policy. Second, respondents significantly underestimated the proportion of conservatives among their colleagues. Third, conservatives fear negative consequences of revealing their political beliefs to their colleagues. Finally, conservatives are right to do so: In decisions ranging from paper reviews to hiring, many social and personality psychologists said that they would discriminate against openly conservative colleagues. The more liberal respondents were, the more they said they would discriminate.[2]

What's the moral of the story? It seems that there is proven discrimination against conservatives in America's colleges and universities, and this will not likely change anytime soon without radical intervention. Will colleges and universities be as proactive in securing intellectual diversity as they have been for racial and gender diversity? Do we need affirmative action hiring programs for non-liberals and progressives because conservatives are not given access to faculty opportunities? If so, that's something that even President Obama might truly call "forward."

Inner-city Education Fails without the Church

As Congress moved toward reauthorization of the Elementary and Secondary Education Act in 2011,[3] the problem was not that the Department of Education was not doing enough, but rather that it suffered from an acute case of what psychologists call "organizational narcissism." If they really wish to address America's inner-city public school crisis, federal education officials must look beyond the boundaries of their own agencies and recognize the crucial role of churches.

Steven Churchill of the Center for Organizational Design explains that organizations can have a grandiose sense of self-importance and an inflated judgment of their own accomplishments, leading to "an unreal,

---

2. Inbar and Lammers, "Political Diversity in Social and Personality Psychology," 496–503.

3. See report at "A Blueprint for Reform," United States Department of Education.

self-defeating preoccupation with the company's own image." For example, even with overwhelming evidence that, besides family support, church involvement is the most consistent predictor of academic success for inner-city children, the organizational narcissism of the education industry prevents it from tapping into the resources of black and Latino churches.

In 2008, President Obama rightly acknowledged that "[t]here is no program and no policy that can substitute for a parent who is involved in their child's education from day one." This is an indisputable truth. What should baffle every American citizen is that the role of inner-city ethnic churches is ignored in the Obama administration's education reform vision.

A series of 2010 studies in Howard University's *Journal of Negro Education* (JNE), one of America's oldest continuous academic journals focusing on black people, reported how church involvement increases education success in inner-cities. In "Faith in the Inner City: The Urban Black Church and Students' Educational Outcomes," Dr. Brian Barrett, an education professor at the State University of New York College at Cortland, describes the unique role black churches play in cultivating successful students in the inner-cities. He observed that "religious socialization reinforces attitudes, outlooks, behaviors, and practices . . . particularly through individuals' commitment to and adoption of the goals and expectations of the group" that are conducive to "positive educational outcomes."[4] In fact, back in 2009 Barrett reported that for black inner-city youth who reported attending religious services often, the black/white achievement gap "was eliminated."[5]

Barrett reports that one of the most important advantages of inner-city churches is that they provide "a community where Black students are valued, both for their academic success and, more broadly, as human beings and members of society with promise, with talents to contribute, and from whom success is to be expected."[6] Churches also affirm inner-city youth as trusted members of a community that celebrates academic success and the practices that produce it, which overrides the low expectations communicated at school. Additionally, Barrett highlights the ways in which black churches, because they are equipped to deal with families, are effective at sustaining and encouraging parental educational involvement from the heart as well as providing contexts where youth can have regular contact with other adults for role-modeling and mentoring.

Barrett is not alone. In another JNE study of 4,273 black students titled, "How Religious, Social, and Cultural Capital Factors Influence Educational

4. Barrett, "Faith in the Inner-city," 251.

5. Ibid., 250.

6. Ibid., 253.

Aspirations of African American Adolescents," Hussain Al-Fadhli and Thomas Kersen, sociology professors at Jackson State University, report that "family and religious social capital are the most potent predictors for positive student college aspirations."[7] These scholars explain that "students who attend church and believe religion is important in their lives may be more likely to interact with more adults who can help them with their school work and even provide guidance about their future goals and plans."[8] The authors conclude that students with an "active religious life, involved parents, and active social life have greater opportunities and choices in the future."[9]

Since W.E.B. DuBois wrote in the 1890s about the black church, dozens of studies confirm this truth: low-income black kids will not achieve academic success without strong families and the church. Strengthening these institutions, however, is beyond the expertise of any government agency or education program or policy. Using President Obama's phrasing, if parents need to be involved in a child's education from day one, in the inner-city the church must be involved from day two. Without thriving inner-city churches, low-performing schools are simply cultivating the next generation of crime and welfare statistics. We owe it to children to place them in contexts that are sustainable and effective.

Inner City Churches Sustain Educational Success

Christian leaders who are interested in helping inner city kids to graduate from high school should read two articles by Brian D. Barrett, assistant professor in the Foundations and Social Advocacy Department at the State University of New York College at Cortland. First, in a 2009 study called, "The 'Invisible Institution' and a Disappearing Achievement Gap," published in the journal *Religion and Education*, Barrett reported that an achievement gap that existed between white and black students was eliminated among those black students who reported that they attended church often. Moreover, those black students had higher grade-point averages than those who did not. In other words, involving kids in a church community is key to academic success. But churches and ministries that offer tutoring programs and are not integrating kids and their families into the life of the church rob kids of a proven pathway to long-term success.

---

7. Al-Fadhli and Kersen, "How Religious, Social, and Cultural Capital Factors," 386.

8. Ibid., 386.

9. Ibid., 387.

Second, in a 2010 study called "Faith in the Inner City: The Urban Black Church and Students' Educational Outcomes," published in Howard University's *Journal of Negro Education,* Barrett provides compelling data confirming that, for inner city youth, involvement in the life of a good church is second only to the family as a predictor of academic success. While there are well-intentioned parachurch ministries that provide good tutoring programs, nothing can match the success of inner city kids loved well in a church community. Nothing.

From Barrett's 2010 research we can see the specific advantages of black churches addressing the needs of inner city children in low-performing schools:

- Religious socialization occurs that reinforces attitudes, outlooks, behaviors, and practices among students-particularly through individuals' commitment to and the adoption of the goals and expectations of the group.

- Black students are valued, both for their academic success and, more broadly, as human beings.

- Regular preaching challenges the mind and heart to create a peer culture of success with different attitudes and behaviors.

- Churches reach the entire family at once by providing context to nurture and encourage and challenge loving reciprocity between parents and their children.

- The church can challenge parents and children to address the moral issues that undermine successful families and students.

- Black churches tend to be more socio-economically heterogeneous so at-risk youth can have regular interactions with high-achieving blacks for mentoring and role modeling.

- Black churches have intergenerational networks that invest in young people over the long term and provide regular adult reinforcement of good values.

- Churches invest money in creating scholarships for children that significantly humanizes the giving process and provides some informal accountability.

In light of Barrett's research, and a voluminous number of other studies for over 30 years corroborating his findings, I would be in favor of shutting down stand-alone inner city tutoring programs that do not integrate children and their parents into the life and holistic whole family ministry of the church. Why would a church offer a tutoring program but not integrate the child and family into the life of the church? What's the point?

Common Grace and Social Studies

People who have the ability to conjecture about patterns and trends in society have helped me think critically about the ways in which the effects of the Fall continue to manifest themselves as well as the ways in which God's common grace is actively at work in the world.[10] So I was surprised by the response from friends after I encouraged them to read a social science article written by a non-Christian. Some focused more on the article's non-Christian components than the author's main point. I find it disheartening that many Christians seem incapable of appreciating the work of non-Christians to gain insight into our world. Christians should be able to easily "eat the meat and spit out the bones" when reading non-Christians sources.

R.C. Sproul explains that "the word science means 'knowledge.' We tend to have a restricted view of the word as if knowledge only applies to the realm of empirical investigation." If this is true then it give us permission to see social science as social knowledge—knowledge about culture and society. While social studies may not be science in the same way that physics and chemistry are science, there is still good and true insight to be gleaned from those who study culture.

The National Council for Social Studies defines social studies as:

> 'the integrated study of the social sciences and humanities to promote civic competence.' Within the school program, social studies provides coordinated, systematic study drawing upon such disciplines as anthropology, archaeology, economics, geography, history, law, philosophy, political science, psychology, religion, and sociology, as well as appropriate content from the humanities, mathematics, and natural sciences. In essence, social studies promotes knowledge of and involvement in civic affairs.[11]

Is it not possible that God, because of common grace, could use all of the above disciplines to teach Christians and non-Christians alike the truth about our world—the good, the bad, and the ugly? Taking common grace seriously means reading secular sources with discernment, keeping those

10. For more information about common grace, see http://www.crcna.org/welcome/beliefs/position-statements/common-grace.

11. "About," National Council for the Social Studies, paragraph 2..

insights that cohere with God's truth and pitching those that do not. We acknowledge the presuppositions driving certain positions for what they are and move on. For example, we can assume that, in 2011, non-Christian evaluations of society and culture are going to have a measure of moral relativism. Given the presuppositions of unbelief, we should not be too surprised. But because of common grace God can use those with secular presuppositions to teach us true things.

Because some Christians fail to recognize that "all truth is God's truth," as Augustine famously quipped, we actually forfeit opportunities to see what God is doing despite the effects of the Fall, as well as miss opportunities to explore complex new ways in which God can use His people to be "salt and light" (Matthew 5:13) as far as the curse is found. And without civic competence it is very difficult for the church to fulfill her mission in the world.

Celebrating African-American Women Scholars

In an earlier column, I noted the growing number of black male scholars across the country but completely ignored a number of black women scholars—an unfortunate oversight on my part. I'm no historian, but it seems like we currently have more African-American women professors and administrators at traditionally Christian institutions than ever before. This is amazing and should be celebrated.

Examples include Dr. Larycia A. Hawkins, an assistant professor of Politics and International Relations at Wheaton College in Illinois; Dr. Alicia Jackson, an assistant professor of History at Covenant College in Lookout Mountain, Ga.; and Dr. Cheryl E. Williams, vice president for International and Cultural Relations and dean of Global Programs at Concordia University in Irvine, Calif.

What encourages me is that these women are doing a great job disproving the false, popular stereotypes of African-America women, which are "(1) highly maternal, family oriented, and self-sacrificing 'Mammies'; (2) threatening and argumentative 'Sapphires'; and (3) seductive, sexually irresponsible, promiscuous 'Jezebels.'"[12] Given the pervasiveness of these stereotypes, these women are doing some heavy lifting. It would be fantastic to hear their stories and learn how they have had to work against these stereotypes.

The United States is likely the only country in the world that could provide opportunities for individuals from a population racially marginalized for centuries to rise to assume the roles that these women have embraced

12. "Mammy, Sapphire, and Jezebel," *Black Women's Blueprint*.

within evangelicalism. It's still the case that most evangelical organizations have few, if any, blacks in leadership roles, but the institutions that hired these women provide encouraging signs about the future. The liberties and progress afforded minorities in the United States, compared to other countries, is simply unprecedented in Western history. We live in a great country!

A Missional Approach to Education

One of the weaknesses in the current missional emphasis in urban church planting is the lack of commitment to planting Christian schools. Too many missional Christians equate Christian schools with withdrawing from the culture. But Christian schools also can be a way to serve society by providing education alternatives for people who need them.

Outside of a church, there is no better way, institutionally speaking, to demonstrate love for our neighbors than to provide education that surpasses failing public schools in quality and virtue, especially in inner cities. Planting churches simply is not enough to effect social change. By not having "salt and light" Christian schools (Matthew 5:13-16) we are squandering an opportunity to do much good for our society. It is strategic to note that whoever teaches the nation's children shapes the future of the culture.

Puritan pastor Cotton Mather explained the justice implications of Christian education in this way:

> A Good School deserves to be call'd, the very Salt of the Town, that hath it: And the Pastors of every Town are under peculiar obligations to make this a part of their Pastoral Care, That they may have a Good School, in their Neighbourhood.
>
> A woeful putrefaction threatens the Rising Generation; Barbarous Ignorance, and the unavoidable consequence of it, Outrageous Wickedness will make the Rising Generation Loathsome, if it have not Schools to preserve it.
>
> But Schools, wherein the Youth may by able Masters be Taught the Things that are necessary to qualify them for future Serviceableness, and have their Manners therewithal well-formed under a Laudable Discipline, and be over and above Well-Catechised in the principles of Religion, Those would be a Glory of our Land, and the preservatives of all other Glory.[13]

Think about it. Children spend more time at school, from kindergarten through 12th grade, than they do at church-related activities. Because of the time kids spend at school, salt-and-light Christian schools can serve

13. Mather, "The Education of Children."

Christians and non-Christians alike in radical ways in an inner-city context. This is education as missions. How can you plant a church in a community for renewal and not also have a vision for renewing the neighborhood's education system?

Historically, the Christian tradition considered moral formation in the church and education in schools as two sides of the same coin. How wonderful would it be, then, for Christian and non-Christian children to see that, as Calvin College's James K.A. Smith puts it, a confession and understanding of "'Jesus is Lord' has a radical impact on how we see every aspect of God's good creation." Moreover, he writes, "the curriculum of Christian schools [enables] children to learn about everything—from algebra to zygotes—through the lens of Christian faith." Why not expose all children to the best possible lens for looking at reality?

The good news is that more Christians are catching the salt-and-light vision for Christian education and taking action. For example, Philadelphia area Christians joined hands and wallets in 1993 to launch the Children's Jubilee Fund (CJF), which sends inner-city kids to Christian schools and supports the flourishing of urban Christians.[14]

Because of the strong connection between education and family life, churches must also build and strengthen families, as well as create alternative education opportunities for inner-city children that form and shape them to be knowledgeable and virtuous citizens.

What is happening in Philadelphia is innovative, and more cities could benefit from missional partnerships of this nature. Missional urban church planting efforts will have little sustaining effect in our cities without missional, salt-and-light Christian schools.

Atlanta's Shame and Disgrace

When a news story would disgust my grandmother she would refer to it as being a "shame and a disgrace." This is the least we can say about the profound mess that is the Atlanta Public Schools system.[15] Riddled with scandal and poorly performing teachers, there is a generation of students whose future is at stake because of the wild antics of adults.

To start, in 2010, there were dozens of school employees suspected of changing standardized test answers to improve scores for schools in the name of helping children. The cheating scandal involved the scores on

14. You can find them at http://www.jubileefund.org/.
15. See the full story at Severson, "Scandal and a Schism Rattle Atlanta's Schools."

the Criterion-Referenced Competency Tests at 58 Atlanta elementary and middle schools, and the adults involved faced criminal charges.[16]

There are also problems with the group leading the schools, the Atlanta Board of Education, which is poisoned with factions, infighting, and coups. Dr. Beverly L. Hall, who had been with the school district for 11 years as superintendent and was named the 2009 Superintendent of the Year by the American Association of School Administrators, finally resigned from her $340,000 job in 2010 amid the scandal and financial losses for the district. She was eventually indicted for her involvement in the cheating scandal mentioned above.

The Southern Association of Colleges and Schools, the district's regional accreditation agency, even had to visit the Atlanta Public Schools to assess whether or not the nine-member board could effectively govern the district and remain accredited. Fortunately, the district kept its accreditation after months of probation. Had it not done so, the diplomas of hundreds of recent graduates would have been rendered essentially useless for college admissions.

To add to the circus, the Atlanta Concerned Black Clergy coalition held a press conference pleading for educators charged in the cheating scandal to be pardoned on racial grounds. If you watch the video it seems as if the clergy are suggesting that white racism is the root cause of the scandal and may be the reason why the school district is under attack.[17] Maureen Downey of *The Atlanta-Journal Constitution* reported that the Concerned Black Clergy's president, the Rev. Richard Cobble, in fact believes the cheating investigation smacks of racism, explaining, "Cheating on tests is one of the means in which the system designed to keep us unfocused, to keep us distracted and keep us at each other throats." Did racism and test score disparities really cause the teachers to change test answers? What confuses me is why the clergy coalition is not championing truth, integrity, and justice by challenging adult behavior within the school district.

The Atlanta public school system is, to say the least, chaotic. For the sake of the nearly 50,000 children whose futures are on the line we can only hope that many tough decisions will be made, including the removal of adults who are doing more to sabotage children than to help them.

16. See the full story at Lohr, "Atlanta Public Schools Under Fire."

17. "Concerned Black Clergy Opposes Teacher Targeting in CRCT Probe," *AJC.com*, 2:04.

The Entitlement Generation

High schools and colleges are flooded with students who confuse busyness with performance. They have been misled to believe that they deserve A's for turning in anything, and that the burden of proof is on the professor to defend why a student has not been "given" an A.

This group of teens and 20-somethings is known as the Entitlement Generation, "who believe they are owed certain rights and benefits without further justification," according to Dictionary.com. Unfortunately for teachers, this entitlement includes the expectation of A's without having to prove that one's work warrants it, which introduces interesting frustrations in education today.

First, students assume that if, for example, they do not receive an "A" on a paper, then points must have been "taken off" for something done incorrectly. I've had to explain to students repeatedly, *ad nauseam*, at every level in my teaching career—high school, seminary, and now college—that they did not earn an A because their papers were not impressive. I would tell them, "You did nothing *wrong*; the paper simply wasn't stellar." What kind of world do we live in where students are nurtured to believe that if they did not receive an A it was only because of an error? Why would students expect an A in the first place unless it was warranted? Staying up late and working hard, at the last minute, does not mean you are owed anything.

Second, students confuse memorizing with understanding. Many students have been nurtured to memorize and regurgitate data as a demonstration of acumen. Therefore, when I ask students to explain and apply what they've memorized, I often see white space on paper or hear crickets. Memorization is neither knowledge nor understanding. Memorization does not translate into application.

Third, students assume that if they easily can find information on the internet, or from some other readily available source, they don't need to know it. The objection goes something like this, "Why are you making us learn this stuff when we can just Google it?" I wish I were kidding when I tell you that the Entitlement Generation balks at the idea of being made to learn things that are available online, but it's true. It is similar logic that asks, "Why do I have to learn math when I can perform those functions on my cell phone?"

Fourth, if the going gets tough, quit. One could also name this group the "Quitter Generation." Virtues like patience and perseverance are absent from many in this age bracket. Coddled by affluence and sinfully flattered by parents and nice-guy teachers using speech meant not to hurt a child's "feelings" or damage "self-esteem," coupled with parents that refuse to let their children fail at anything, this generation bails quickly when the going gets tough or if there's no guarantee for success. I had a student drop one of my classes once because he realized that he wasn't going to receive an A. I've known students to give up and fail a class after receiving a series of bad grades instead of buckling down and working harder to raise their grades. It's pathetic.

I particularly feel bad for businesses that employ young workers who believe that they are entitled to non-performance-based high salaries and will quit when things get tough. I don't know what could change this attitude but, in the meantime, I'll have to continue to serve as the reality check that "you're not as awesome as you were told" and that you'll never succeed in life, or in my class, with a poor work ethic and a quitter's attitude.

Teachers Unions and Civil Rights Groups Block School Choice for Black Students

Teachers unions, like the National Education Association (NEA), and many civil-rights organizations inadvertently sabotage the potential of black males by perpetuating failed educational visions. Black males will never achieve academic success until black parents are financially empowered to opt out of failed public school systems.

The American public education system is failing many groups, but none more miserably than black males. The numbers are shocking. In 2010, the Schott Foundation reported that only 47 percent of black males graduate from high school on time, compared to 78 percent of white males.[18] This revelation is beyond disturbing because it exposes the fact that many public schools serve as major catalysts for the desolation of unemployment and incarceration that lies in many black boys' future.

In many places, the disparity between whites and blacks is nearly unbelievable. In Nebraska, for example, the white/black graduation gap is 83 percent compared with 40 percent and in New York 68 percent compared with 25 percent. The way urban city school districts fail black males is more disconcerting considering that black professionals are in charge. Urban districts are among the worst at graduating black males: Atlanta, 34 percent; Baltimore, 35 percent; Philadelphia, 28 percent; New York, 28 percent; Detroit, 27 percent; and St. Louis, 38 percent.

18. "Yes We Can," *The Schott Foundation.*

There are surely many reasons for such failure, and family breakdown must rank high among them. Schools may be powerless to transform black family life, but they should not be left off the hook for turning in a dismal performance. In an interview, Dr. Steve Perry, principal and founder of Capital Preparatory Magnet School in Hartford, Conn., repeatedly places the blame for the black achievement gap at the feet of the partnerships between the teachers unions and the NAACP, "a civil-rights relic." The places where black students excel, says Perry, are those where students have access to choice. Sadly the NAACP and the NEA have long undermined the push for low-income black parents to exercise freedom to choose the best schools as a national norm.

For example, even with mounting evidence demonstrating that single-sex education for blacks males from low-income households represents one of the best opportunities for graduation, the NEA petitioned the Department of Education in 2004 to prevent single-sex options from becoming nationally normative, balking because "the creation of an artificial single-sex environment [will] ill prepare students for life in the real world." What? The Eagle Academy for Young Men, a charter school in the Bronx comprised of primarily black and Latino students, the first all-male public school in New York City in 30 years, boasts a high school graduation rate of 82 percent. In 2010, Chicago's Urban Prep Charter Academy, with a 100 percent graduation rate, graduated a class of 107 black male students, all of whom began attending college in the fall of that year.

The NEA exists, it seems, only to overfund failed systems and the non-performance-based salaries of adults at the expense of black students. Nothing prepares black males for life in the real world like graduating from high school and attending college, yet the NEA consistently lobbies against parent choices that lead to black male success.

Civil-rights groups including the NAACP, the National Urban League, Rainbow PUSH Coalition, recently released a joint statement objecting to the Obama administration's education reform proposal, which includes the closing schools of failing schools, increasing use of charter schools, and other commonsensical moves toward choice and accountability in education.[19] These groups reject Obama's so-called "extensive reliance on charter schools," expressing dismay about "the overrepresentation of charter schools in low-income and predominantly minority communities."

Even though there is overwhelming evidence supporting the success of charter schools for children from low-income households, the civil-rights groups resist the opportunity for parents to exercise freedom to choose

19. "Our Six-Point Plan for Educational Equity," NAACP.

those schools. Perry highlights the cost of such blindness, observing "that our nation's urban public schools have prepared more children for poverty, the penitentiary, and premature pregnancy than they did for college."

Even though charter schools, vouchers, and tax-credit programs reflect some progress, black parents need brand new and creative options that empower parents with absolute freedom to choose the best schools. In addition to school closings and faith-based options, "mass firings" like the ones in Washington, D.C., "home schools," and other bold and innovative measures, are all important components of rescuing black males from the betrayal of teachers unions and civil-rights groups that refuse to acknowledge the dignity of low-income parents by blunting their right to choose what is best for their children. As long as teachers unions have influence in the black community and in institutions pledged to black empowerment, and black parents are not financially empowered to opt out of failing public schools, black males are doomed.

God Expelled from School District

In January 2009, the ACLU won an injunction in Florida that officially removes prayer, God, and religious activity from the Santa Rosa County School District. U.S. District Court Judge Casey Rodgers made the ruling after school officials admitted to the religious activity. The ACLU, on behalf of two high school students, sued the district, Pace High School Principal Frank Lay, and former Superintendent John Rogers.

According to Carmen Paige writing in the *Pensacola News Journal*, the injunction states the Santa Rosa County School Board and its employees are prohibited from:

- Promoting, advancing, aiding, facilitating, endorsing, or causing religious prayers or devotionals during school-sponsored events.

- Planning, organizing, financing, promoting, or otherwise sponsoring religious baccalaureate services at all schools within the Santa Rosa School District, including at Pace High School.

- Holding school-sponsored events at religious venues when alternative venues are reasonably available.

- Permitting school officials to promote their personal religious beliefs and proselytize students in class or during school-sponsored events and activities.

- Otherwise unconstitutionally endorsing or coercing religion.

According to the Pensacola paper, the ACLU says the school district violated the First Amendment when it allowed elementary graduations and middle school Christmas concerts to be held at churches, when teachers and staff at Pace High School preached about "Judgment Day with the Lord," and when teachers and staff offered Bible readings and biblical interpretations during student meetings.

This ruling might actually be a blessing in disguise for all of us. Protestants tend to forget about the religious persecution endured by Roman Catholic families attempting to put their children in America's public schools in the 19th century. The parochial school movement was started, in part, to give the children of Catholic families a persecution-free place to learn. This was during an era where Catholics were seen as enemies of Protestants.

The type of Protestant today who might object to the Florida ruling would also likely raise objections to the following: elementary schools holding graduations in Mosques; classroom instruction being interrupted to pray during Ramadan, the Muslim spiritual holiday; and teachers reading and interpreting passages from the Koran in student meetings.

My guess is that the same Protestants who might object to the Florida court ruling would also object to an elementary school principal reading the Buddhist "Daily Affirmation Prayer" over the school's intercom system every day before school begins. The prayer reads:

> Entrusting in the Primal Vow of Buddha,
>
> Calling out the Buddha-name,
>
> I shall pass through the journey of life with strength and joy.
>
> Revering the Light of Buddha,
>
> Reflecting upon my imperfect self,
>
> I shall proceed to live a life of gratitude.
>
> Following the Teachings of Buddha,
>
> Listening to the Right Path,
>
> I shall share the True Dharma with all.
>
> Rejoicing in the compassion of Buddha,
>
> Respecting and aiding all sentient beings,
>
> I shall work towards the welfare of society and the world.

Since the Bible charges the church, not the public schools, with task for spreading the Good News, perhaps this injunction will help some Christians not to rely on the state to do what the Bible calls them to do (Matthew 28:18-20). Perhaps this injunction will help some Protestants understand that if you want "prayer in school" in a secular and pluralistic society like the United States is today, you must be willing to accept the fact your neighborhood's children also could be praying to Allah, Buddha, Sulevia, Sirona, Rosmerta, or Epona. Protestants can no longer assume that Christians will always in be in positions to determine which religious activity is allowed and which is not.

If you want your children to have an education that is uniquely tied to a Christian worldview in the classroom, then send them to a good Christian school or teach that to them yourselves (Deuteronomy 6:1-25). If you want your children's non-Christian friends to learn about Christianity, love them well personally and bring them to church. If you want your son's teammates, for example, to learn about Jesus, have them over to your house for breakfast once a week before school starts to hear about the Kingdom. This is the work of the church.

Some Protestants will see such rulings as scandalous while others will welcome them. In the end, they point all the more to the fact that America is not a Christian nation.

SECTION FOUR

Contemporary Culture

It's Not Only the Poor
Who Need Moral Leadership[1]

ORAL HISTORIES OFTEN PAINT a rosy picture of the moral fiber of previous generations, in which divorce was unheard of and out-of-wedlock births rare, and in which Christian civilization kept societal immorality in check, especially among a more virtuous elite. But close attention to history reveals the truth about human condition: that regardless of our social status, everyone is in need of moral formation—and thus it has always been.

The universal need for moral leadership is illustrated in the deplorable marital culture on display in the lives of the parents of British Prime Minister Winston Churchill. In *The Last Lion*, William Manchester's best-selling biography of Churchill, we learn of Winston's parents' active participation in the rampant infidelity of the British upper class in the 1800s. Randolph Churchill was a syphilitic and Jennie Churchill was renowned for the number of affairs in which she participated. "Jennie Churchill was in and out of lovers' beds all her life . . . and she was not exceptional," Manchester observes. "[Randolph] accepted his lot. He dined with men who had lain between his wife's thighs; he played cards with them; he rode to hounds with them and entertained them in his club." Both Randolph and his son Winston were aware of her adultery, but it continued. Even more, Randolph remained friends and business partners with those sleeping with his wife.

More broadly, Manchester explains, some women of the upper class were known to request men's wives to set up an affair between them. "The affairs which were joyously celebrated during weekends were sometimes

---

1. This essay was co-authored by Sean Spurlock.

launched in wife-to-wife conversations. 'Tell Charles I have designs on him,' one would tell Charles's lady, who would acknowledge with a nod and an amused smile; she herself already had a lover or had designs of her own on someone else's husband." These blatant requests show that the general level of tolerance for extramarital promiscuity was high.

Even if a woman wasn't brave enough to ask the man's wife, she could easily find other means. Large parties where the guests stayed the night were famous for their debauchery. The guests would settle in and "after lights were out, shadowy figures would glide through the darkened hall and everyone would settle in for the night's pleasure. An hour before dawn the butler would appear in the hall bearing a gong. He would strike it once and depart. The same tiptoeing figures would reappear. Presently they would all meet at the breakfast table." The unspoken law was that no one mentioned the evening's festivities, and one should even be rude to the individual who had been his or her partner for the night.

Our imagination's revisionist history would have us believe the land of Winston Churchill's parents, mid-19th century Britain, was a time of Victorian purity and faithfulness. Nearly all Britons attended church and believed in God, right? But surprisingly, the most debased were those who prayed loudest, lauded moral scruples, gave inspiring speeches, and led the country politically, militarily, and socially. British PM William Gladstone said that he had known "eleven prime ministers and ten were adulterers." It is easy to look at our promiscuous and sex-saturated culture and wish for a return to a past filled with self-controlled, faithful spouses, but the moral culture of Churchill's parents was not one to which we should look yearningly.

Why does this matter? The Churchill anecdote reminds us of the need for religious leaders and all believers to be people of integrity.

In Britain and elsewhere, as the contrast between the publicly held moral code and private behavior became clear, the code itself was discredited. The need for repentance and reform among today's aristocratic elite—in Hollywood, on Capitol Hill, on Wall Street—is obvious. Thanks to the media, private indiscretions held in secret among the elite in a previous era are now part of the daily news cycle. Couple these stories with America's high divorce rate and we begin to see why confidence in the virtues of marriage among our youth is on the decline.

It is imperative that those of us who recognize the value of a culture of fidelity and respect—and the manifold personal, social, and economic effects that flow from it—proclaim a message that is not diluted by our own moral failings. As imperfect human beings we will all fail to live up to the ethical standards we strive to honor. But the strength of our witness lies less in what we say than in how well our actions match our words.

The End of Tackle Football?

I have friends with sons under 7-years-old who have decided their boys will never play organized tackle football. For them, the risk of long-term brain damage is too great.

It seems that we hear every week about college or NFL players leaving the game because of a blow to the head. On a single Sunday, three NFL starting quarterbacks—Philadelphia's Michael Vick, San Francisco's Alex Smith, and Chicago's Jay Cutler—all suffered concussions. Because of the frequency of such injuries in the NFL, many are beginning to wonder if children or adults should still play the game at all.

Even former NFL quarterback Terry Bradshaw doesn't think it's worth the risk for children. "If I had a son today," he said, "I would not let him play football."

According to a Center for Disease Control and Prevention (CDC) national study of athletes ages 19-and-under between 2001 and 2009, 25,376 football players suffered concussions, second only to bicycling (26,212).[2]

Overall, because of these numbers, it's time to reassess the utility of the entire sport. Something has to change in the game or the way it is played. And football fans need to be prepared for the day when, for the sake of saving our children's brains, tackling may be permanently replaced with the pulling of colorful little flags.

Hip-Hop With a Conscience

One of the things I learned from Francis Schaeffer was to celebrate truth and virtue wherever it is found. With so much of commercial hip-hop music promoting narcissism, consumerism, and misogyny, it is refreshing to find artists who challenge listeners to higher virtues. Mr. J. Medeiros, a Los Angeles-based rapper and producer, is a great example of an artist who promotes wisdom and virtue. I caught up with "Mr. J" to ask him about his music as he plans to produce a new album with his recently reformed group, The Procussions.

> *Having grown up in Colorado Springs, Colo., how did you get introduced to hip-hop?*

Colorado Springs is sort of a hub in its own way. There are numerous military bases which pull people from all over the country. Hip-hop

2. "Nonfatal Traumatic Brain Injuries," United Stated Department of Health and Human Services, 1340.

is definitely there and, with all its different arms of influence, it's diverse enough that any inspiring rapper could choose his own sound free from the pressures of regional cultural expectations. However, my first experience with hip-hop was in Rhode Island [where his family is from] at age 8. I lived in a big apartment complex—those types full of different aged kids all hanging out together. I also had babysitters with older brothers. I would sneak into their room while they were blasting their boom box listening to the Run DMC *King of Rock* album. Between those two social environments I fell in love with hip-hop.

> *As an artist, you made a conscious decision to write lyrics that are not as lucrative in our current media environment. Why take the risk?*

If you write music centered on misogynistic material, for example, you will have more "success" I am sure. However, if you're trying to write music in an attempt to connect to some truth within yourself or in the world, it requires a certain type of honesty and introspection that has no time to worry whether or not it will "sell." If I have any values at all, I'm sure it has something to do with faith, family, friends, great song writers, and some awesome books!

> *On your first solo project you wrote a powerful song honoring your parents. Why dedicate so much space to them?*

I wrote "Call You" around 10 years ago. When I think about it, now, I feel that I didn't say anywhere near enough about them. I still feel anxiety when I think about writing about my parents. They are just too big of characters to fit inside a 3- to 4-minute song. My parents fought really hard to keep the family out of poverty. They are self-educated, extremely hardworking, and would never let me lie, not even to myself. They still don't, ha! My father, as stated in the song, is an ex-Marine. He works at a pizza place. He rides his motorcycle and plays his original songs at bars around town. My mother has had two jobs my whole life as a waitress. For one of her jobs she runs a restaurant. They are still married and they hide nothing, blush at nothing, and still have room for faith. When it came to rapping, they'd always push me to "be about it" not just dream about it. They gave me just enough of what I needed to find my own way, and I'm truly grateful for that.

A Congratulations and an Open Apology
to Andy Roddick

At the beginning of the U.S. Open in 2012, then 30-year-old Andy Roddick announced he was retiring. Admittedly, I had mixed feelings. It took me years to grow to appreciate Roddick and his style of play because I had been an avid fan of Pete Sampras. Roddick had burst onto the professional scene with an explosive serve that was second to none. His controversial on-court presence did not sit well with me because I interpreted it as arrogance. I recognized it, I guess, because it takes one to know one. Whenever Roddick argued with an umpire or a line judge I saw myself. Instead of pointing out my own flaws I spent years talking about his on social media. I was happy to see him lose matches, especially to Roger Federer. My poor attitude continued for years, but then something happened.

A few years ago I began to notice how reporters showed no mercy toward Roddick, constantly pressuring him to talk about not winning more majors, his rankings, and retiring. The post-match press conferences were painful to watch. I began to wonder if these reporters had souls. So when Roddick played his final match, losing to Juan Martin del Potro in the fourth round of the U.S. Open, I was torn. Why? Because looking back at his career I finally started to appreciate just how much he did for American tennis. I began to care less about his outbursts and more about the fact that Roddick had been the last American standing in the Association of Tennis Professionals (ATP) top 10 for a number of years. In fact, as I write this, there are no Americans in the ATP men's top 10. America is desperate for a new generation of players with Roddick's skill.

In light of this, I was happy to hear that the Andy Roddick Foundation raised about $1 million to help fund youth programs at a new 10,000-square-foot, eight-court tennis and learning facility in Austin, Texas. With one of its chief goals "to teach character and life skills through sports-based mentoring and education," the foundation will make a difference in Austin. And teaching virtues through such mentoring will not only serve society but will also introduce a new generation to the game of tennis.

In the end, it turns out that Andy Roddick is a better man than I allowed myself to believe, and if I had an opportunity to meet him in person I would congratulate him on a great career quickly followed by an apology for the slander and mockery I've directed at him over the years. It would be a great punctuation to his legacy if the opportunities afforded youth at this new Austin facility would cultivated a new generation of American players with good skills and virtuous character. What a great way to serve the game of tennis in the United States and around the world.

Puritans and Propaganda

Rapper Propaganda created a tornado of criticism with the release of "Precious Puritans" on his album *Excellent*. In the song, Propaganda reminds his audience to increase their cultural intelligence by caring about the black experience in America and to recognize the fact that, like the Puritans, we all have blind spots and need to have our minds constantly renewed (Rom. 12:2) by God's word. The song also challenges those who uncritically treat the Puritans as a protected class that stands outside of the Bible's command to "test everything" (1 Thess. 5:21).

For those who may be unfamiliar, Puritanism was a Christian reform movement that arose within the Church of England in the late 16th century. The movement spilled over into New England well into the 17th century and had a significant influence on the mores of America's founding. Theologically speaking, the Puritans were committed to the doctrines of grace that emerged from the Protestant Reformation, with their particular emphasis on the intersection of sound doctrine and personal piety. In recent years, many young white Baptists and non-denominational evangelicals have been looking for substantive, theologically driven, analytic approaches to personal piety rooted in a tradition they found lacking in their own backgrounds. Thirsting for depth and history, these "new-Calvinists," with the help of well-known pastors like John Piper, have found spiritual enrichment by studying the Puritans.

"Precious Puritans" simply raises a caution about loving the Puritans too much because, although they had sound doctrine on issues like personal piety, that tradition was complicit in perpetrating injustice against Africans and African Americans. The song opens with these words:

> *Pastor, you know it's hard for me when you quote puritans.*
> *Oh the precious Puritans.*
> *Have you not noticed our facial expressions?*
> *One of bewilderment and heartbreak.*
> *Like, not you too pastor.*
> *You know they were the chaplains on slave ships, right?*
> *Would you quote Columbus to Cherokees?*
> *Would you quote Cortez to Aztecs?*
> *Even If they theology was good?*
> *It just sings of your blind privilege wouldn't you agree?*
> *Your precious Puritans.*
>
> *They looked my onyx and bronze skinned forefathers in they face,*
> *Their polytheistic, god-hating face.*
> *Shackled, diseased, imprisoned face.*

And taught a gospel that says God had multiple images in mind
when he created us in it.
Their fore-destined salvation contains a contentment in the stage
for which they were given which is to be owned by your forefa-
thers' superior image-bearing face.

Says your precious Puritans.

The song continues to highlight ways in which the black experience in the Puritan tradition is mishandled within white conservative evangelicalism. However, instead of leaving it simply at critique and dismissal, like we might find among some black liberation theologians, Propaganda ends the song by confessing that he is no less flawed than the Puritans, as his wife can attest, and offers praise to God because "God really does use crooked sticks to make straight lines." That is, Propaganda is calling for humility in recognizing that, in the end the noetic effects of sin are present in the Puritans, in himself, and the rest of us. As such, what is to be praised is not any class of men but the providence and sovereignty of God that He fulfills his mission through messed up people.

What's been so odd to me is the tribalist attacks from those who fear that Propaganda is in some way throwing the Puritans under the bus to never be read again. A lamentable example of this is a blog post by Professor Owen Strachan, Assistant Professor of Christian Theology and Church History at Boyce College. In his post, Strachan suggests that the song might be dangerous because he wonders "if Propaganda isn't inclining us to distrust the Puritans. He states his case against them so forcefully, and without any historical nuance, that I wonder if listeners will be inclined to dislike and even hate them."

Is this a slippery slope? Does testing and critiquing lead to this? Did Martin Luther's comments about Jews incline people to hate him and reject him? Or John Calvin's execution of Michael Servetus? Or Abraham Kuyper's racism? Or Jonathan Edwards' slave owning? I could go on.

The answer, of course, is "yes" and "no." Those who would reject the Puritans because of their white supremacy will themselves struggle to find much of anyone in Western Christianity to embrace. All have sinned and fall short of the glory of God in some way (Rom. 3:23), including all of those we hold in high esteem. There is an obvious "no" because this is not how the Bible teaches Christians to engage in cultural and historical analysis. We are to eat the meat and spit out the bones. This includes those who are both inside and outside the tribe. There is much meat in the Puritans but there are also massive bones.

Propaganda's point is that if white evangelicals do not talk about the bones of their heroes they run the risk of doing great harm to people of color. Many of us are beginning to wonder why white evangelicals do not seem to care much about this and seem willing to trade off "honoring" their forefathers for their own comfort over doing what is necessary to build racial solidarity. Some of my liberation theology friends, in the end, would see Strachan's critique as a dismissal of acknowledging the importance of caring about how the Puritans are presented to African Americans and would constitute a racial microaggression or a micro-invalidation.

The largest concern is the seemingly tribal nature of many of Propaganda's Puritan-loving critics. Could this be an example of confirmation bias? As Jonathan Haidt explains in the book *The Righteous Mind*, confirmation bias is "the tendency to seek out and interpret new evidence in ways that confirm what you already think".[3] In general, according to Haidt, we are good at challenging statements made by other people but when it comes to one's own presuppositions facing opposition the tendency is to protect it and keep it. Therefore, "if thinking is confirmatory rather than explanatory . . . what chances is there that people will think in an open-minded, explanatory way when self-interest, social identity, and strong emotions make them want or even need to reach a preordained conclusion?"[4] In this sense, Propaganda broke a tribal code: never critique anyone within the tribe.

Strachan considers the Puritans "forefathers" and in a tribalist way, some would argue, seeks to protect their legacy. Had Propaganda dropped a track critiquing Roman Catholics, Jeremiah Wright, Rob Bell, Brian McLaren, or preachers of the prosperity gospel, he'd be called a hero. During my seminary years I was never rebuked for mentioning Martin Luther King Jr. in a sermon because of his sins. Why? Because King, like the others, are outside the tribe and are fair game to be critiqued in any form. Since they are not "one of us" there is no expectation of extending grace. Grace is reserved for those with whom we agree.

I experienced this tribal protectionism when I challenged Doug Wilson's poor historiography of the antebellum South. Theologians Carl Trueman and Scott Clark experienced this recently when stating that complementarianism is not a "gospel issue." The bottom line is that the Bible provides a model for the importance of confessing the sins of our fathers (Neh. 9:2) and testing everything (1 Thess. 5:21). Why? Because if we do not

3. Haidt, *The Righteous Mind*, 80.
4. Ibid., 81.

hold those in the past accountable to God's Word we will repeat their sins. "Precious Puritans" is the iron that sharpens us. It keeps us from making the Puritans a golden calf. Racism and white supremacy is the other Reformed tradition so we need regular reminders to hold God and his Word in high esteem over the works of mere men.

After reading Strachan's post I was left wondering if he had ever read Joseph Washington's books on Puritans and race.[5] In light of Washington's research, what Propaganda did in this song is minimal. Candidly, it is difficult for me to see why Propaganda's song stands out in light of the thousands of pages of published writings of Puritan white supremacy that seems to have had no effect on people treating them as a protected class. In the new Calvinist world, there seems to be a growing trend that you can have "hard-hitting exhortation" as long as it is directed at those who are not beloved within the new-Calvinist tribe. The best critique of Strachan's tribalism comes from Pastor Steve McCoy, so I will not repeat his excellent points here but McCoy concludes that Strachan completely misses the point of Propaganda's song.[6]

Lastly, it seems that as a rapper himself, Strachan would not expect much "nuance" in a genre that normally uses hyperbole as a rhetorical device. After all, it is a rap song. Since when does anyone expect "rhythm and poetry" (a.k.a. RAP) to have nuances and qualifications? I wonder why Strachan is not treating the song according to its genre.

Strachan's defensiveness of his forefathers, who get it right, demonstrates exactly why Propaganda needed to produce this song. In fact, perhaps we need more rhythm and poetry to help us test and confess. If artists like Propaganda are not given freedom to call us to critique our theology and culture, we cannot achieve true racial solidarity in the kingdom. Songs like "Precious Puritans" keep our eyes fixed on Jesus.

Human Nature: the Question behind the Culture Wars

Culture wars can produce nasty rhetoric. Political discourse quickly becomes emotionally charged and divisive. We are tempted to view those with whom we disagree as not only irrational but evil. The culture of demonization of our political opponents is what moral psychologist Dr. Jonathan Haidt sought to dismantle with his 2012 book, *The Righteous Mind: Why Good People Are Divided by Politics and Religion.* Haidt, Professor of Ethical

5. See Washington, *Puritan Race Virtue.*
6. See McCoy, "Missing the Point of Propaganda's 'Precious Puritans.'"

Leadership at New York University's Stern School of Business, believes that we demonize opponents because we do not recognize that everyone values fairness. Moreover, we justify our positions from antithetical moral foundations.

In one sense, Haidt is not saying anything that religious leaders and economists haven't been saying for centuries, namely, that at the root of our understanding of politics are fundamental beliefs about human nature and definitions of morality. In recent decades, Americans have increasingly turned to psychologists as experts on morality and human action. As such, religious and economic texts like Pope John Paul II's *Centesimus Annus*, Abraham Kuyper's *Problem of Poverty*, and even Thomas Sowell's *Conflict of Visions*, all of which explain political conflicts as extensions of contrary views of human nature and morality, are ignored. However, Americans are willing to listen when a psychologist remixes these themes.

Haidt's research team identified six moral foundations to analyze and thus explain the differences between progressives (modern liberals) and conservatives: care, liberty, fairness, loyalty, authority, and sanctity. After several years of research, Haidt's team discovered that progressives scored high on their commitments to care, liberty, fairness, and low on loyalty, authority, and sanctity, whereas conservatives value all six roughly evenly. The result is that progressives and conservatives do not understand each other. They usually talk past each other because issues like welfare, universal health care, and the like, are not where the real disagreements lie. Each side fails to understand the other's definition of fairness.

Conservatives, for example, value fairness in terms of whether or not free people are able to take advantage of the same processes made available to them in society. Progressives tend to define fairness in terms of equality of material outcome or equality of proportion. Conservatives, then, are more concerned about whether all citizens are free to exercise their gifts and talents, under the law, to meet their own needs through participation in free markets. Progressives, on the other hand, conceptualize fairness as whether people have similar incomes, whether people have the same luxuries in life. They envision a world where the force of government intervention eliminates disparities.

In an interview with Bill Moyer, Haidt, a self-proclaimed "centrist" confessed that, "When I began this work, I was very much a liberal. And over time, in doing the research for my book and in reading a lot of conservative writing, I've come to believe that conservative intellectuals actually are more in touch with human nature. They have a more accurate view of human nature. We need structure. We need families. We need groups. It's okay to have memberships and rivalries." Competition creates the conditions for economic growth, Haidt says, because "cooperation and competition are opposite sides of the same coin. And we've gotten this far because we co-operate to compete." In other words, competition has moral implications.

In the book, Haidt concludes that conservatives have an advantage in connecting with American values because conservative morality equally rests on all six moral foundations. They are more willing to embrace the reality of trade-offs and sacrifice in order to achieve "many other moral ob-jectives." Moral psychology, says Haidt, also explains why the Democratic Party has struggled to connect with the American people since the 1980s because Democrats have no compelling moral case for their ideas. The lop-sided morality of progressives in the Democratic Party is something that Haidt hopes moral psychology can address.

If Haidt's moral psychology research is right, then progressives will be forced to reject long-held presuppositions about human nature. Perhaps moral psychology can help call a truce to the nasty culture wars so that we can stop and discuss what it means to be human—a discussion conducted in the hope that conservatives and progressives can return to sharing the moral foundations that shaped America's liberty and prosperity.

Nice People, Good Food in Small Town America

Eric Bergeson of the *Crookston Daily Times* (a small town Minnesota news-paper) wrote an opinion column in 2011 lamenting that talented young people leave small towns. Because of a recent personal experience, I was left thinking, "There may not be many opportunities in small towns, but the people are so nice. Why leave?" I have no scientific proof to substantiate this claim but it seems that small-town folk are more genuine than city folk. After living in New York City now for a couple years—where people simply don't have time to be nice—I have been trying figure out why it seems that people seem to be more personable in small-town America.

For example, in my recent travels I was having breakfast at the Three Squares Restaurant in Waupaca, Wisc. (population 5,887) when I noticed that patrons not only said "hello" as they walked by my table but they also asked, "How are you?" At first glance, this may sound like no big deal, but there was something different about the way people asked me that I've only experienced in small towns. I could be wrong but I felt like people really wanted to know. It was as if I had permission to ask one of them to pull up a chair so I could tell the details of how I was doing that day. It seemed so genuine. I say this having grown up in the South (Atlanta) where people would say, "Hey, how are you," give you a hug, and 20 minutes later will slander you at church to your friends. The Waupaca "how are you?" made my pancakes, scrambled eggs, bacon, and home fries taste even better.

When I pulled my rental car into the parking lot of Burgertown Dairy Freeze in Bigfork, Mont., (population 1,658) I was rendered speechless by a guy who parked just as I did and nearly walked over to me to say, "Hey there, how are you?" I stuttered back in a confused tone, "I'm fine, how are you?" As I sat down to eat the one of the best hamburgers I've ever had in my life, with a fantastic huckleberry milkshake, a family of three approached my table with their 5-year-old son waving enthusiastically and saying, "Hi, hi." I felt like I was in a movie or something. Where I'm from kids do not say "Hi" to strangers even when they are with their parents.

I've been trying to put my finger on why I was engaged so genuinely is these towns. I'm not sure if I could live in a small town, but they are certainly now my preferred destination when I need a break from the city. Is there anything better than down-to-earth, genuine people and good food? Three cheers for small towns!

The Death of Marriage

If interviews my college students conducted in New York this semester are any indication, marriage in America is dead. I don't mean "in trouble" or "struggling," I mean dead. Many of the New York 20-somethings questioned have no confidence in matrimony and have reduced it to merely a contracted long-term dating relationship. When my students, in asking about cultural views, came to the topic of marriage, these New Yorkers in their 20s responded with some of the most heart-wrenching descriptions of the institution, which to me signals trouble for the future of American family life.

Here are just a few of the sample responses:

- 24-year-old male from Manhattan:

  Don't even get me started! Well, marriage is a piece of paper. It's a certificate. I mean legally, that's what marriage is. Marriage was not originally supposed to be about love, the way it is understood now. I think it was largely about families given tax benefits and now it's become completely distorted. What does it mean to be married? It doesn't mean anything anymore. It doesn't mean [expletive]. It used to be about commitment but people get divorced all the time now.

- 27-year-old male from Queens:

Traditionally it has been a man and a woman who are in love, and, under God, are brought together, to live the rest of their lives together and have a family. This is ideal. For me, well, you might call me a hopeless romantic, but it's when you find someone you love and you get to know everything about them and they know everything about you, and you grow old together. It's possible, I think. It could be a man and an elephant, although I don't think the elephant could have the same feelings. It's just two people, not just a man and a woman, could be a man and a man, could be three men. Ideal is monogamy, I think it's possible, but it doesn't really happen.

- 21-year-old female from Midtown Manhattan:

  I actually kinda don't really believe in marriage. People can be happy just being with another person they love for the rest of their lives without being married. I think marriage is something that society kinda says that when you get to a certain age you're just like 'Oh, I have to get married; that's the right thing to do,' and I think a lot of people kinda look down on you when you're not married. So, I think it's just a societal thing.

These three are not even close to being the most extreme examples, but they do best represent the overall beliefs shared by most in the 50 to 60 surveys we conducted.

What Christians should find troubling is (1) their definition of marriage seems to have little or nothing to do with procreation, and (2) marriage to them is nothing more than a relational contract between people with strong feelings for each other. If young Americans only believe feelings and a contract to be the essence of marriage, then it will be increasingly difficult to convince them that things like same-sex marriage or polygamy should not be legal.

Truthfully, supporters of traditional marriage between one man and one woman will likely lose the public debate about alternative forms of marriage until they can successfully tie marital sex to procreation as normative and stop divorcing themselves. But in the end, if moral norms do not define the practice of marriage in America, then we can't be surprised when young adults say that marriage "doesn't mean anything anymore." Honestly, can we blame them?

Showing No Empathy

Some have argued that since the 1960s, baby boomers have destroyed every cultural institution in America they have touched: marriage, family, public education, government, financial markets, healthcare, and more. Many argue that one of the most tragic legacies of the baby boomer generation is its narcissistic offspring who now dominate high schools, college campuses, and the world of 20-somethings. Children of boomers, who tend to have been raised under the delusion that the world revolves around them, have recorded the lowest rates of measured empathy in American history, according to new research.

This is not the typical generational angst over youth coming of age; there is something quantifiable and different about the children of baby boomers. Paul Anderson and Sara Konrath, both professors at the University of Michigan, report "that American college students have been scoring lower and lower on a standardized empathy test over the past three decades."[7] They add:

> In fact, a research paper published in May in *Personality and Social Psychology Review* shows that since 1980, scores have dropped 34 percent on 'perspective taking' (the ability to imagine others' points of view) and 48 percent on 'empathic concern" (the tendency to feel and respond to others' emotions). The standardized empathy questionnaire included questions like, 'I often have tender, concerned feelings for people less fortunate than me,' or 'I sometimes try to understand my friends better by imagining how things look from their perspective.'[8]

While researchers are not certain of the causes, Anderson and Konrath point out a combination of factors that may play a role, including delaying adulthood's traditional markers like marriage and family in order to attend graduate school, popularization of reality TV shows and the narcissistic exhibitionists who appear in them, the focus of primary education on the problem of low self-esteem rather than low empathy, and the relative decline of face-to-face interaction and emotional communication due to increased online socializing.

The lack of empathy for others confirms what psychologists have reported about the implications of baby boomers treating their kids like royalty, raising them to think about themselves and their success above anything else. In *The Narcissism Epidemic* Jean Twenge and Keith Campbell write:

7. See Anderson and Konrath, "'Why Should We Care?"
8. Ibid., lines 29–36.

A focus on individual achievement that leaves out feelings, love, and caring is a recipe for narcissism. The missing piece of caring for others cascades into many of narcissism's negative outcomes, such as lack of empathy, incivility, entitlement, and aggression. In raising superachievers, today's parents may have, perhaps unintentionally, raised super-narcissists[9].

Although America's young narcissists have radically changed college culture, Anderson and Konrath have not given up hope, citing that many young people today *do* have empathy and suggesting that change is possible as professors teach empathy in the classroom through role playing and doing exercises that develop interpersonal skills.

But change through behavior modification will have limited long-term success because, in my experience, true empathy only comes from the humility resulting from an encounter with the Triune God. In fact, the only way to correct how baby boomers have raised their children is to have a society with a vibrant and healthy church. Nothing destroys narcissism and establishes true empathy better than staring at the cross of Jesus Christ.

American Men Aren't Tough Enough for Hollywood

If you're looking for a man to be cast as the lead role in an action-packed Hollywood thriller, then don't expect him to be an American, says Amanda Fortini. Because Americans raise weak and wimpy men Hollywood producers have no other choice than to look for Europeans or Australians.

In a recent *Details Magazine* article titled, "Why All of Hollywood's Toughest Stars Wear Stilettos," Fortini says:

> For years we've been on first-name terms with our male action stars: Sly. Bruce. Jean-Claude. *Ah*-nold. But until recently, you could count the memorable female action heroes in mainstream American movies on one hand: Sigourney Weaver as the smart, self-possessed Ellen Ripley in the Alien franchise; Linda Hamilton as the reluctant, super-buff Sarah Connor in *Terminator 2*; Uma Thurman as the barbarously vengeful Bride in *Kill Bill: Volumes 1 and 2*. Women were usually on the receiving end of the action—rescued, ogled, or swept off their feet—but now they're often the instigators. In addition to *Hanna* (Saoirse Ronan plays a teen assassin; Cate Blanchett, the agent trying to capture her), there's Zack Snyder's *Sucker Punch*, a hyper-stylized tale about a

9. Twenge and Campbell, *Narcissism*, 86.

group of young women (Emily Browning, Abbie Cornish, Jena Malone, and Vanessa Hudgens) who must battle samurai and serpents to escape a mental hospital.[10]

There was a time in Hollywood when women were swept away and rescued by strong leading American men. Those days are apparently over. Part of the explanation for why American women today dominate action hero roles is that, in America, women are simply tougher than men. Americans raise boys to be soft. Fortini highlights that "some blame squishy, effete American culture for the mysterious lack of plausibly masculine specimens." Movie producer Joseph Papsidera, who cast the last two Batman movies, says that "American men aren't men on the screen."

Moreover, "Kids are raised like veal," Papsidera says in the article. Fortini notes that Philip Noyce, the director of *Salt*, "looking for some masculine man" to cast in an ABC pilot, said that "the best candidates he's seen have been Australian." According to Noyce, Australians "grow up less protected and with the ability to express themselves physically in daily life, which makes them more in touch with their athleticism."

Wow. Is it that bad? Are the toughest "men" in America actually women? Or is that America's tough men do other things than become actors? Fortini concludes that the action hero movie, "notorious for its chauvinism has become an unlikely advertisement for feminism." Does Fortini have a point? I'm not sure how to explain the trend but it's true that we are much more likely to see an American man in a comedy movie acting like a buffoon than an action thriller cast in one of the tough roles now given to "tough guys" like Angelina Jolie.

From Hymns to Hip-Hop

If you are looking for theologically saturated Christian music that has the greatest potential for widespread appeal, your best option may be Christian hip-hop. Because of its form—a high volume of words with little repetition—hip-hop may provide one of the best modes of music to convey propositional truths and doctrinal content that at the same time connects to a younger generation. Contrast that with Contemporary Christian Music (CCM), which is often criticized for being shallow, theologically light, and generally lacking content that inspires the mind and the heart.

---

10. Fortini, "Why All of Hollywood's Toughest Stars Wear Stilettos," lines 7-17.

It is important to keep in mind that Christian hip-hop, unlike other contemporary genres, generally is not intended for use during corporate worship, so rejecting its appropriateness for the liturgy is not relevant.

But even with the deep theological content found in much of Christian hip-hop, many evangelicals view it as an inappropriate medium for Christian music.[11] This objection reveals some level of ignorance about the historical development of Christian music.

Dr. David Koyzis, in his book *Political Visions and Illusions*, highlights this ignorance by noting, "Many conservatives dislike 'pop' or 'rock' music and prefer, say, the baroque pieces of Bach or Telemann. . . . The very label 'baroque' was used in a derogatory fashion by conservatives of that day to describe what they felt to be ugly music."[12] Today many hail the "ugly" church music set to baroque as the height of Christian music and a form that should be normative today.

What we consider to be "ugly" forms of music often depend on personal preferences and social location. For example, in Christian traditions that sing only the Psalms without instrumental accompaniment,[13] the worst thing for them would be to sing praise to God using lyrics not directly from the Bible and to pollute music offered to God with instruments like a pipe organ. Could Christian hip-hop simply be the "ugly" music of our era?

Let's take a look at the lyrics from the song "Triune Praise" by hip-hop artist Shai Linne and note the theological depth that is not generally found in CCM music:

> *Praise God the Father, the Immortal Creator*
>
> *For Your glory you made us, You're the Sovereign Orchestrator*
>
> *All that You decree will most surely come to happen*
>
> *You're awesome as can be and Your glory none can fathom*
>
> *Nothing could ever stain You, the heavens can't contain You*
>
> *We thank You for sending Your Son to explain You*
>
> *Otherwise we would have remained in the dark*
>
> *but You sent Your Holy Spirit to spark a change in our hearts*
>
> *According to Your eternal purpose and will*
>
> *You determined to reveal Yourself to those who deserve to be killed*
>
> *Those of us whom You foreknew adore You*

11. For an extreme example of this, see: http://www.jesus-is-savior.com/Evils%20in%20America/CCM/hip_hop.htm.

12. Koyzis, *Political Visions*, 93.

13. For example, the Reformed Presbyterian Church.

We praise You that You predestined us to be conformed to

The image of Your Son who's the radiance of Your glory

When I meditate on it, the weightiness of it floors me

So Father, we'll praise you over and over again

Because You sent Your only Son to atone for our sins

Boyce College student and rapper/producer Alex Medina even finds similarities between a Christian rapper and a beloved hymn writer in their lives and the content of their music: "[John] Newton's care for his local church in Olney and the development of 'Amazing Grace' reminded me [of] Sho Baraka." And you'll see these commonalities with rappers associated with labels like Reach, Cross Movement, and Lamp Mode, to name a few.

Given the international popularity of "ugly" hip-hop in general, and the weak content of much CCM music, Christian rap may emerge as the last bastion theologically driven Christian music for generations to come.

Bringing Truth to Struggle

Humble Beast Records, a West Coast hip-hop label that features a number of Christian rappers, is one of the most progressive record labels in America. What I find most exciting about this label is that they are producing a fair amount of free music, and the artists rap about real life situations while applying the gospel. I recently caught up with one of the pillars of the label, Braille, to discuss his life and his last album, *Weapon Aid*:

Tell us about your faith journey.

I actually wasn't raised in a Christian home. My parents were divorced and neither side raised me with any specific religion. The gospel was first preached to me by a hip-hop street evangelist when I was 14. I wasn't really searching for God, and I wasn't at a rock bottom in life. I was just a young, shy kid who liked to rap. But after the gospel was preached to me I could never leave it alone. Looking back, my understanding was pretty limited: I didn't have my own car and my family didn't go to church. I didn't really start regularly attending church or being discipled until after high school. Nevertheless, the awareness of sin, the desire to please God, and the reality that I needed a Savior, and that Jesus was the only way became evident during my teen years.

How were you introduced to rap?

I started rapping at age 13. When I was in middle school I was a fan of Michael Jackson, New Kids on the Block—yikes—and MC Hammer. I had a black-and-white checkered floor in my room and I would try to dance. I even tried singing for a little bit, but when I discovered rap the pieces finally fit together. I had a little composition notebook where I made up an imaginary crew because no one else around me rapped. When I got saved, the outlet took on a whole new meaning. For the most part I was isolated—as a hip-hop artist and as a believer—so those two worlds just gelled together for me. As I grew in my faith, I would express it in music—even when no one was listening. I didn't even call it "Christian" hip-hop. I didn't know there was such a thing.

What hip-hop artists influenced you?

The first album that made me say, "This is what I want to do," was *Midnight Mauraders* by A Tribe Called Quest. I was never a tough guy or a ladies' man. A lot of rap personas didn't fit me. When I started hearing groups like A Tribe Called Quest, De La Soul-guys who were rhyming about regular life and so forth—it helped me realize that there was a place within hip-hop for an artist like me.

Could you describe your last album for us?

I started writing the songs during a season of life during which I was betrayed and abandoned. I knew bitterness and anger weren't going to help me. I also knew that I couldn't bottle it all in. So I opened up; I cried out to God. The process forced me to dig deeper in myself and see the depth of my own fallenness. The album titled *Weapon Aid* is just a clever way of saying "healing songs." Calling out to God for healing and deliverance and ultimately confronting every area of my life with the gospel.

How has fatherhood changed you personally and your music?

My daughter is 4 years old and I've been a single father for a good portion of that time. Between age 3 and 4 I took a whole year off and just focused on her full time. When I performed at concerts, she would be on stage with me. Being full time with her changed so much in me. How I spent my time, what was important to me, and everything started to shift. After I put her to bed I would just study the Scriptures, get refreshed, and do it again the next day. I can't explain all the ways it changed me, but the Lord used that unique scenario in my life to teach me deeper levels of patience, serving, and humility. It has been a very humbling experience, but I wouldn't trade it for anything.

Now that you're approaching 30, how have your views on being a man changed over the years?

[Being a man] is bigger than handling responsibilities. It's the understanding that my life truly isn't my own. Serving God means serving your family, serving the church, serving your co-workers. It's not a "part" of my life; it's my whole life. Nothing keeps you repentant like serving, because an unrepentant heart doesn't want to serve. But when your life *requires* you to serve, you have to rely on God in order to do it. You can't rely on God or trust Him if you're beefing with him. So it pushes you towards repentance, and then you truly begin to see the depths of His grace in Jesus Christ. You see how dependent you really are, that you need Him in every area of your life. [Being a man] is seeing your sin for what it really is and realizing you can only overcome it through Jesus. You can only get back to God through Jesus because you are incapable of getting back on your own. From that comes a deep sense of gratitude. You are no longer doing anything good in order to prove your own goodness, or to earn God's favor. It's just a response to His grace with the hope that He would shine through your life and be glorified. Living by the grace of God through Jesus for the glory of God, in every area of life and repenting when you fail, that's what being a man is about.

Christianity Infused Hip-Hop

HeeSun Lee, a Korean-born poet and rapper, has opened the eyes of many people through her music, which connects the Gospel to real life. Raised in Staten Island, N.Y., HeeSun uses her gifts to share her experiences, her testimony, and her love for God. In her debut album, *Re:Defined.*, HeeSun displays special skill in communicating the mystery of redemption. I had the privilege of interviewing HeeSun to ask her about the project.[14]

You've become a prominent Christian artist, rapper, and poet on the East Coast. What parts of life have matured your faith and marriage?

I was born in Seoul, Korea, but was placed into foster care right after. I was adopted four months later and sent to Staten Island, N.Y., to live with my adoptive parents. My spiritual journey has been long and winding! I've definitely had my ups and downs, my doubts, and my "Christ-fanatic" times, and my good and bad phases. What sparked my belief in God was

14. HeeSun interview, October 30, 2010.

my grandma dying when I was 15-years-old. It was the first time I ever felt a sense of loss in my life because she lived with me and watched over me a lot.

And your husband?

I met my husband in church, actually, 12 years ago! We have had a crazy relationship ever since then, from breaking up to getting back together to breaking up again. There have been many challenges in our marriage because of that, but God has been working in us and helping us deal with our past issues. We were married in November of 2009!

What influenced your entrance into hip-hop?

I was always into writing. I've written stories since I was 13. As I was getting older, though, the stories transferred into poems and then the poems transferred into songs. Hip-hop has been a part of my life since I was in junior high school. I remember bumpin' Warren G in my mother's car and her getting at me because she kept hearing curse words. After Warren G, I started having a huge obsession with Will Smith! I memorized all of his songs on his *Big Willie Style* album, and I would even record myself rapping his verses on my cheap karaoke machine. Once I entered college, I would listen to any hip-hop that was hot. I was heavy into Tupac, and I started memorizing his songs too. His songs were harder to memorize because he has about a million joints [tracks] recorded! Hip-hop was a way for me to express myself on paper and then onto music. I never tried to be something I wasn't, and I always wrote from my heart. My whole thing is, if you can't be real in your music, why bother?

It's unusual to see a female Asian-American hip-hop artist. How has your background influenced your work?

Being adopted and growing up with identity issues has been the biggest obstacle I've ever had to face. To be honest, I'm still dealing with it, but hip-hop has helped me a lot. Trying to always fit in to a specific group is a struggle because you can live your entire life never feeling accepted, but hip-hop accepted me. It was the first culture to look at me for who I was and not care; it helped me to open myself up in my lyrics and to not be ashamed of who I was. I want to make sure that being a rapper or a poet will assist me in bringing unity to different cultures. That would be my ultimate goal as an artist.

What inspired the concept and vision for the Re:Defined. album?

Re:Defined was birthed after I was going through a lot of transitioning in my life. I was changing churches, ministries, friendships, everything, and so I wanted my album to reflect what I've been through and where I was going. As Christians, we all have our different phases, and I believe it's important to show people how you've grown and how you've changed for the better. There are a lot of topics on this album including racism, foster kids, abandonment, love, women's empowerment, my testimony, life issues, everything!

> *You have a great video for the song "Open Your Eyes" on this release.*[15] *What inspired the song?*

This song starts off by telling a story about a woman in a dead-end relationship where her boyfriend is cheating on her left and right. Instead of getting out of the relationship, she decides to lower her worth by cheating as well. I wanted to show people, especially women, that we do not need to sink to any level where it's compromising who we are as women. We should remember how beautiful and important we are, and if we're ever with a man who cannot value our worth, dump him! It's also a wake-up call to the men as well, where they need to understand how important it is to treat their women with respect.

Brie Stoner's *Delicate Hour*

Longtime music producer, writer, and performer of the soundtrack of the NOOMA series Brie Stoner released her *Delicate Hour* EP back in 2010. Having spent a decade working on the Rob Bell series, she finally let us into her own musical work with a glimpse of things to come. The experienced songwriter, who has previously worked with the likes of the late Jay Bennett of Wilco, shares her soul in beautifully crafted songs that show her maturity and depth, with solid Neil Young-ish Americana/folk/rock melodies and sweet, sleepy vocals reminiscent of Mazzy Star.

The EP, featuring performances from friends David Vandervelde (Secretly Canadian) and Evan Slamka (Marjorie Fair, Square on Square), was recorded in studios in L.A., Nashville, and even the artist's own home in Grand Rapids, Mich. Gathering friends across the country to collaborate on the record, Stoner is proudly boasting "indie" artist cred with made-in-the-Midwest gumption.

The five songs delve into everything from the precarious nature of love in relationships ("Delicate Hour") to the singer's weathered spiritual

---

15. The video is posted online at http://youtu.be/8_gJHH1j2so.

journey ("To Wrestle"). "Part Time Believer" boasts a spaghetti Western vibe to balance the heady questions she asks about the extreme dualistic natures of safe vs. wild, good vs. evil, and heaven vs. hell.

In "Edge of a Broken Heart," Stoner manages to turn Richard Marx and Fee Waybill's 1980's hair band rock anthem into a slow, dreamy song that flows seamlessly into her own. Stoner shows her bilingual/bi-cultural past with "Together Forever," a sweet live performance sung part in English, part in Spanish.

With promises from her camp of new music ahead in the fall and the holidays, Stoner seems to enter into the singer/songwriter scene with more than a tent and a backpack. She packs brick and mortar—a depth, authenticity, and talent that is sure to have staying power in an industry inundated with pop culture five-minute phenoms.

Stoner's EP can be sampled and purchased on iTunes. I have had the privilege of knowing Stoner for a few years, and it's been a treat for me to hear about the EP as a concept and then to see the final product. Music has such a powerful meaning of connection, touching us in unique ways. Stoner succeeds in producing a series of tracks that connects well to the human story with a beautiful voice and wonderful melodies to match.

The Priority of Fatherlessness

Outside of the marriage crisis, fatherlessness is the greatest social problem in America. Churches, schools, and non-profit organizations not partnering on specific initiatives to build virtuous men and strong fathers are missing an opportunity truly to bless society.

Fatherlessness affects all of us and is at the root of all kinds of evil and brokenness. According to a 2004 longitudinal study, fatherlessness is correlated with a significantly higher rate of incarceration, even when controlling for factors such as income and parental education.[16] The level of correlation between fatherlessness and social pathologies should be a call to arms. The future of civil society hangs in the balance. Churches and community organizations lacking specific, directed initiatives to build and support virtuous fathers forfeit the right to complain about America's social problems.

Sadly, elitism and ignorance about fatherlessness confine the problem to low-income communities. Growing up in a two-parent household is a

---

16. See the full story at Harper and McLanahan, "Father Absence and Youth Incarceration."

significantly better predictor for academic achievement than a higher income level, as indicated by a 1992 study.[17]

The problem of fatherlessness is bigger and broader. To understand it requires a proper definition: Fatherlessness is not defined as children with *deceased* fathers, but rather children with *absent* fathers. Men who are absent physically, emotionally, and spiritually from the lives of their children are everywhere and all contribute to the pathologies related to fatherlessness.

The data are overwhelming. Sixty-three percent of youth suicides, 90 percent of all homeless and runaway children, 85 percent of all children who exhibit behavioral disorders, 71 percent of all high school dropouts, 85 percent of all youths sitting in prisons, and so on, all have fatherlessness in common.

What are local churches doing about fatherlessness specifically? In most cases, nothing directly. But there are bright spots. Churches such as Crossroads Tabernacle in The Bronx tackle fatherhood openly and bless their communities. "Confessions of Fatherhood" is a short video produced by Crossroads extolling the virtues of fatherhood.[18] It features men who are courageous enough to confess their imperfections and commitments to rely on all that the church provides to be the best fathers possible.

The parental humility displayed at Crossroads is a model for churches interested in addressing fatherhood specifically and locally while inviting other men to meet God there.

Looking for Eden in All the Wrong Places

In *The Culture of Cities*, published in 1938, Lewis Mumford articulated a vision for the beauty of cities that many people have failed to appreciate.[19] In contradistinction to the neo-agrarian romanticism of Wendell Berry and others, Mumford affirmed that "cities are a product of the earth." There is nothing in city life that keeps city-dwellers from experiencing nature.

Wendell Berry, for example, seemed to believe that being connected to nature assumes agricultural manifestations. Berry said, "Our model citizen is a sophisticate who before puberty understands how to produce a baby, but who at the age of thirty will not know how to produce a potato." What's

---

17. Sandefur, "The Effects of Parental Marital Status," 119.

18. "Confessions of Fatherhood," Crossroads Tabernacle, 5:27.

19. Mumford, *The Culture of Cities*, 1.

wrong with being a sophisticate who knows the good of what it means to be fruitful and multiply, but is incapable of working the land?

Mumford, however, offered a different vision of moving away from agriculture to urban life:

> [Cities] reflect the peasant's cunning in dominating the earth; technically they but carry his skill in turning the soil to productive uses, in enfolding his cattle for safety, in regulating the waters that moisten his fields, in providing storage bins and barns for his crops. Cities are emblems of that settled life which began with permanent agriculture: a life conducted with the aid of permanent shelters, permanent utilities like orchards, vineyards, and irrigation works, and permanent buildings for protection and storage.[20]

To be in a city is to be in nature. The city and the countryside represent the abundant handiwork of God. Cities represent concentrated activities of people living out their human vocation to be rulers and subduers of creation—a priestly function to manage creation well, create conditions for flourishing human life, and bring glory to God. Mumford reminded us that "cities arise out of man's social needs and multiply both their modes and their methods of expression." The management of social needs is the privilege and distinction of being human. We call this stewardship.

Instead of the nostalgia of withdrawing to agrarian lifestyles, Mumford explained that cities provide the refining advantage of cultural clashes: "In the city remote forces and influences intermingle with the local." He continued:

> [T]heir conflicts are no less significant than their harmonies. And here, the concentration of the means of intercourse in the market and the meeting place, alternative modes of living present themselves: the deeply rutted ways of the village cease to be coercive and the ancestral goal cease to be all-sufficient: strange men and women, strange interests, and stranger gods loosen the traditional ties of blood and neighborhood . . . .[21]

Cities provide an image of the type of scattering that God rebuked his people for resisting when they built the Tower of Babel. The clash of cultures provides opportunities to bring the best contributions to social life from various peoples: skills, art, food, techniques, music, religion, and so on. Christians in cities bring the Kingdom to the nations in ways that other

20. Ibid., 1.
21. Ibid., 2.

contexts cannot. Cities also test our understanding of human solidarity on the basis of our common humanity and commands to love our neighbor. Additionally, economic markets promote multi-ethnic, multi-racial interaction.

Mumford went on to say that "the city is a fact in nature." Understanding cities as nature keeps us from mystically longing for a context that gets us back to some better, more communal, less sustainable, homogeneous shire. As a fact in nature, said Mumford, cities allow the flourishing of human social needs as "both a physical utility for collective living and a symbol of those collective purposes and unanimities that arise under such favoring circumstances."

There is nothing wrong with having a preference for smaller towns or more rural contexts, but to set rural life—"simple living," or the mythology of small town solidarity and the like—against urban living is to introduce a twisted distortion of nature and is foreign to the world of the Bible. Alternatively, those who argue that urban life is the best way to live miss the diversity represented in the providence of God using rural and urban contexts to fulfill his good intentions for the whole creation. So the next time you want to "get back to nature and see God's creation," skip the mountains and visit your nearest major city.

"White Messiah" Films

The movie *The Blind Side*, which depicts a white family's successful adoption of an at-risk black male, has elicited charges of "racism" from many in the black community. The word "silly" comes to mind as the most charitable word I would use in response to such a charge. A movie depicting the true story of what the white Tuohy family actually did for a kid in need, who happened to be black, does not contain what we normally think of as racial dehumanization. It seems that many blacks are confusing "racism" with our distaste for "White Messiah" movies.

The Blind Side—which picked up Oscar nominations for best picture and best actress (Sandra Bullock)—is not racist, but it does depict the often told story of white people coming to the aid of some indigenous, needy ethnic person. My guess is that many white people appreciate movies like this because they help defend against the constant charge that all problems in America have a direct causal link to white people. Movies like *The Blind Side* tell the world that, even with America's complicated history, white people are not necessarily bad people.

Ironically, such movies can be convicting to middle-class blacks because, outside of family members, they are just as unlikely to take in at-risk black males as whites. If suburban blacks had a regular cultural habit of doing what the Tuohys did, it would change America.

Alternatively, movies like *Avatar*, also nominated for the best picture Oscar, elicit suspicions of racism because they depict a common Hollywood fiction that white people are here to save the universe. *The New York Times'* David Brooks explains the racism of *Avatar* clearly:

> *Avatar* is a racial fantasy par excellence. The hero is a white former Marine who is adrift in his civilization. He ends up working with a giant corporation and flies through space to help plunder the environment of a pristine planet and displace its peace-loving natives. The peace-loving natives—compiled from a mélange of Native American, African, Vietnamese, Iraqi and other cultural fragments—are like the peace-loving natives you've seen in a hundred other movies.[22]

Must it always be the case that a white male comes to save the day (again)? Perhaps this may explain the movie's popularity. There are those who believe that *Avatar* affirms white supremacy—the same kind of white supremacy that juxtaposed Christian missions with the African slave trade and colonialism in Africa, Asia, and elsewhere, for example, in India, South Africa, and Haiti. Brooks explains that this type of white supremacy:

> . . . rests on the stereotype that white people are rationalist and technocratic while colonial victims are spiritual and athletic. It rests on the assumption that nonwhites need the White Messiah to lead their crusades. It rests on the assumption that illiteracy is the path to grace. It also creates a sort of two-edged cultural imperialism. Natives can either have their history shaped by cruel imperialists or benevolent ones, but either way, they are going to be supporting actors in our journey to self-admiration.[23]

While movies like *The Blind Side* are clearly not racist in the least, fictional films like *Avatar* may explain the growing consternation caused by stories involving minorities that depict white people as the heroes. I guess this means we need more Will Smith-as-hero movies than Keanu Reeves ones. Who knows? The debate continues.

---

22. Brooks, "The Messiah Complex," A27.

23. Ibid.

Hope for "Precious"

Child sexual abuse cases are reported up to 80,000 times a year, but the number of unreported instances is far greater, according to the American Academy of Child Adolescent Psychiatry.[24] Why? Children are afraid to tell anyone what has happened, and the legal procedure for validating an episode is difficult. The frequent occurrence of child sexual and physical abuse makes films like *Precious* reflect more truth than they should.

The movie, set in 1987, is a story of an obese, illiterate, black 16-year-old Harlem girl named Claireece "Precious" Jones and her not so uncommon dysfunctional family. Precious, played by Gabourey Sidibe, in her acting debut, has been raped and impregnated twice by her father, Carl, and suffers constant physical, mental, and sexual abuse from her unemployed mother, Mary. Precious' first child, known only as "Mongo" (short for "Mongoloid"), has Down syndrome and is being cared for by her grandmother. After Precious becomes pregnant a second time, she is suspended from school. *Precious* is a film adaptation of the award-winning 1996 novel *Push: A Novel* by Sapphire.

This movie will make you cry. I was particularly moved by its depiction of those who tried to give Precious a chance at improving her life, including an amazing schoolteacher and a social worker. My personal dream one day is for this level of brokenness to be handled well by the church.

One of great ironies about evangelicals is that churches that have the most resources—pastoral counseling, clinical Christian counseling services, attorneys, empty nesters, nurses, doctors, teachers, etc.—tend to be located in communities far removed from the rural and urban contexts where we find high concentrations of openly needy kids who are handed over to the government to deal with levels of sin and brokenness that desperately need supernatural intervention. We complain about "welfare" programs but don't live near people in need to offer them better alternatives.

I wish I had good answers about connecting Christians with the most gifts and resources to people with the most desperate needs—a situation that's often called a "spatial mismatch." The problems of the physical and sexual abuse of children are everywhere, but those hurting in communities with resources have the greatest access to help. What brought me to agony in this film was the lack of options Precious had in terms of knowing where to go for help.

Many Christians will not like this film because of its accurate portrayal of verbal and physical abuse, but *Precious* is true for many rural and urban

---

24. "Sexual Abuse," American Academy of Child and Adolescent Psychiatry, line 2.

girls. I long for the day when movies like this will show the church function-ing as a normal part of the help narrative. But that will require two things: (1) Christians with the best resources living in openly broken communi-ties, and (2) a strong Christian presence in the film industry. Until then, the imagination of film audiences will be left with stories of hopelessness and despair at the brokenness of the world.

Everybody's (not) Fine

It seems that every Christmas there is a family flick depicting conflict and reconciliation. Robert De Niro leads a great cast in one such film, which also stars Drew Barrymore, Kate Beckinsale, and Sam Rockwell. A 2009 remake of the 1990 Italian film *Stann Tuttie Bene*, *Everybody's Fine* features De Niro as a widower who tries to improve his relationships with his complicated adult children. The movie is a sad reminder of the long-term consequences of family members who routinely keep secrets from one another.

Marvin Olasky wrote a review of the movie from the perspective of a parent. I viewed the film from the perspective of an adult child. As the movie accurately depicts, in most families parents do not know their adult children like they might assume. In the 14 years during which I worked in youth and college ministry, I was routinely amazed at the naïveté of parents who believed that they "knew everything" about their adolescent and young adult children. I was shocked at parents who would say that they have a "great relationship" with the same teen or young adult who would, in turn, lament to me the exact opposite. How could this be?

Power dynamics and love distortions are so prevalent in most fami-lies that relational honesty is nearly impossible. *Everybody's Fine* is a hard reminder that, in most families, everybody's not fine. Too often honesty is catalyzed only in juxtaposition to crisis—death, suicide, divorce, drug abuse, religious shifts, and so on. I'm beginning to wonder more and more how many of my friends' parents have any idea how much their adult chil-dren loathe being around them and what it would look like for these adult children to break the silence and explain why. I'm beginning to wonder what it would take for siblings to reconcile the differences that destroyed their relationship 10, 20, or even 30 years ago. Why are we so unwilling to be honest?

I am encouraged, however, by a few of my friends' parents who have taken courageous steps to encourage honesty with their adolescent and adult children. It is a wonderfully painful experience of confession, repentance, and reconciliation, bringing both tears and joyful intimacy. I wonder if we really want to know the truth. Are we sadly content with the façade?

The weeks that span Thanksgiving through New Year's are often difficult for families because of concealed tensions, pain, and disappointments. In the end, I encourage families with adult children to watch movies like *Everybody's Fine*, *The Family Stone* (2005), and *Little Miss Sunshine* (2006) because they seem to be great opportunities to "get some stuff out on the table" so that future gatherings can be context of respite and joy instead of tension and guardedness.

Honoring a Navy SEAL

I don't know how much active duty Navy SEALs get paid, but it's not enough. I arrived at this conclusion after reading the story of Marcus Luttrell in the book *Lone Survivor: The Eyewitness Account of Operation Redwing and the Lost Heroes of SEAL Team 10*. It is the most moving and personally transforming story I've ever read about someone of my generation.

In early July 2005, four U.S. Navy SEALS departed for the mountainous Afghanistan-Pakistan border for a reconnaissance mission. Their mission was to document the activity of an al-Qaeda leader believed to be very close to Bin Laden with a small army in a Taliban stronghold. Five days later, after heavy fighting, only Marcus Luttrell made it out alive. After being wounded and presumed dead in a firefight that took the lives of his teammates, Luttrell crawled for miles through the mountains and was taken in by sympathetic villagers who risked their lives to keep him safe from surrounding Taliban warriors.

Luttrell's story recounts not only the events surrounding the dreadful days before and after losing his teammates, but it also invites readers to understand the years of training and preparation necessary to produce warriors like Luttrell. It's a story about discipleship, camaraderie, courage, commitment, wisdom, and mercy.

Readers will be challenged by Luttrell's brutal honesty describing how the "liberal media" and "rules of engagement" put soldiers' lives at risk because terrorists have figured out how to disguise themselves as civilians and how to contact the media to give the appearance that U.S. soldiers have murdered "innocent" people. War is ugly and has costly spillover effects. According to Luttrell, terrorists use politician-drafted rules of engagement to exploit soldiers' lack of freedom to protect themselves and prevent murderous situations from occurring in the first place. Luttrell writes:

The truth is, any government that thinks war is somehow fair and subject to rules like a baseball game probably should not get into one. Because nothing's fair in war, and occasionally the wrong people do get killed. . . . Faced with the murderous cutthroats of the Taliban, we are not fighting under the rules of Geneva IV Article 4. We are fighting under the rules of Article 223.556mm—that's the caliber and gauge of our M4 rifle. And if those numbers don't look good, try Article .762mm, that's what the stolen Russian Kalashnikovs fire at us, usually in deadly, heavy volleys.

Overall, not only was I brought to tears in some parts, and aroused to anger at terrorism in others, a few moments after closing the book, I seriously thought through what it would look like for me to drop what I'm doing and join the Navy. I was previously unaware of the specialized training as well as the nature of SEAL teams. These men are simply amazing. If I ever meet a SEAL in person I'll consider it a real honor. Because I am constantly thinking about applications for the church I couldn't help but imagine what a formidable force of good the church in America could be if we raised boys to be men with Navy SEAL levels of camaraderie, courage, and wisdom. What if we really understood what it meant to train others to "take up their cross"? Read the book. You'll be inspired.

iPod Reservations

Until I started walking around New York City and noticed that every third or fourth person seemed to have one, I was blissfully unaware of the popularity of iPods. When this late adopter walked into the Apple Store the other day to buy an iPod Nano, I likely became one of the last of my friends to buy one of the devices. I had resisted over the years mainly because I have psychological issues about paying $150 or more for a something barely larger than a credit card.

On April 9, 2007, Apple announced that the 100 millionth iPod had been sold, making it the fastest selling music player in history.[25] According to eWeek.com, during its July 21, 2009 earnings report, Apple announced iPod sales had declined since the year before, but only by 7 percent.[26] That still meant that 10.2 million units were sold, and millions and millions of people are walking around with buds in their ears.

25. "100 Million iPods Sold," Apple.
26. Kolakowski, "Apple Slashes Apple TV Price," lines 1-4.

I have a few concerns about introducing this device into my life. I have yet another device to worry about losing. Adding a cell phone to the wallet and keys I already carry around is burdensome enough. Plus, how are ear buds going to affect my hearing in the long run? I am so paranoid about making my hearing loss worse, I'll likely turn the volume down so much that I can barely hear the music.

Is this going to make me less of an extrovert and more of an isolationist? When my iPod is on and I'm lost in a world of music and podcasts, am I going to stop talking to strangers? I used to regularly strike up conversations with people I don't know and eventually get to the topic of religion. Now I don't have to talk to anyone while I'm watching my nephew's soccer game or walking through the park. I can also freely ignore the beggars I see nearly every day because I can act like I don't hear them saying, "Do you have any spare change?"

I was trying to imagine Jesus plugged into his iPod mediating on the Psalms and walking right past all those folks asking him for help. In some ways it is a ridiculous question to ask: "Would Jesus have an iPod?"

I am aware, as with all other technologies, that this is not a matter of "if" but of "how much," "how loud," "when," and so on. The great irony of acquiring new technology to enhance my quality of life is that the devices seem to do little more than bring on new complications.

50 Years Makes a Difference

One Saturday, I took the subway to Madison Square Garden in New York City to attend a concert celebrating Polito Vega's 50 years as "El Rey de Radio" (the King of Radio). Vega was honored for his half-century on the airwaves with a two-day concert series organized by two radio stations, WPAT and WSKQ. The evening featured a star-studded Latin music lineup, with artists like Gilberto Santa Rosa, Víctor Manuelle, Millie Quesada, Olga Tañón, Oscar de León, José Alberto "El Canario," India, and Tito El Bambino.

Polito Vega, 71 at the time, was born and raised in la Playa de Ponce, Puerto Rico, and journeyed to New York in the late 1950s to launch a singing career. Instead, Vega found himself on radio beginning in 1958, and became a historic figure in American music by popularizing the Latin sound along the East Coast and beyond.

Fans of *I Love Lucy*, featuring Cuban-born Desi Arnaz, might recall an era in music when Latin sounds were being introduced to the American mainstream through television, movies, and jazz. In the mid-1960s, Vega was one of the first radio personalities in United States to identify and align himself with the commercial potential of the musical style that came to be known as salsa.

In 1964, when "The Motown of Latin Music," Fania Records, was launched, salsa music exploded in the United States and the Caribbean, and Vega found himself in the middle of music history as the most prominent salsa DJ in the world. Vega can still be heard on WSKQ, Mega 97.9, playing classic Latin favorites on weekends from noon until 8 p.m. Vega's radio programs are also syndicated and can be heard throughout the United States and in the Caribbean.

While the music at the Madison Square Garden event was spectacular, I found myself returning to the realization that these types of celebrations will not be in America's future, because gone are the days when people will have 50-year careers in one vocation. Those in my generation were not raised to think that way. When I see men like Vega and the impact he has had in the music industry, I wonder what is lost when Gen-Xers and Millennials continue to spend three to five years, on average, pursuing every new career "opportunity."

In Praise of Barbershops

When I was a kid, I didn't understand that the experience of visiting the barbershop was just as much about the social experience as it was about the haircut. I used to hate going. Now, I'm tempted to go once a week. I feel sorry for two types of guys: (1) those who grew up being dragged to a "salon" and (2) those whose mothers cut their hair past kindergarten.

I fully understand that some people wisely avoid barbershops for financial reasons. And there's nothing wrong, of course, with a man going to a salon, especially if his haircuts are complicated. Nevertheless, there is wonderful socialization that occurs during regular barbershop visits.

I was once shopping near 181st Street and St. Nicholas Avenue in New York, in desperate need of bed linens and a haircut. After purchasing linens, I walked past Jorge's barbershop, and as I stood there not sure if I should enter, I was asked, "Hey, do you need a haircut?"

I was quickly reminded why I love barbershops. I can remember as a kid not wanting to get a haircut by a man I didn't know holding shiny metal weapons and buzzing machines. At the time, of course, I didn't realize what I was learning. What do men talk about? Why are they watching this game on television? What athletes are playing well or not playing well? Why is that new government policy a bad idea? What's that boxer's name? Women usually do what? How does my father interact with his peers? These were all the questions and more that I didn't realize I was engaging in over the years of regularly getting my haircut.

As I walked into Jorge's shop and sat down, a baseball game was on the TV, without the sound turned down, and music was playing at just the right level to permit sing-alongs. I did get a few stares walking in with a huge comforter and bed linens, but I didn't care. What mattered to me is that for 30 minutes or so I was about to join a community.

My haircut was happily interrupted when the barber offered a short proposition, watched an amazing play in progress during the baseball game, or belted out the portion of a chorus of a popular song. When Héctor Lavoe's song "El Cantante" started playing and everyone broke out in unison singing "Hoy te dedico mis mejores pregones," I thought, "This solidarity and camaraderie is so cool." I know the song well but was humming with group. I was reminded of my appreciation for a former era when American barbershops formed social and musical centers for men that launched the barbershop quartet music harmonic genre.

Norman Rockwell has a number of fantastic paintings depicting the barbershop experience that remains alive and well in a few neighborhoods in America. I suppose I am somewhat of a traditionalist, but it just seems odd that some guys will grow up in America never experiencing something so important to the masculine journey, all for the expediency of having their hair "done" by "Suzy" the "hair stylist" in a salon.

Water Toys of the Wealthy

In March 2009, I boarded a $1.6 million boat, and it felt really good. Sitting in the air-conditioned lounge area, I was reminded that the boat would sell for more than most people's lifetime earnings. The 24th annual Palm Beach International Boat Show sailed into West Palm Beach, Fla., and I was there for my first look at the water toys of the wealthy. More than 1,000 boats valued at more than $350 million were on display along Flagler Drive and the Intracoastal Waterway.

I was socializing with a group of 20 and 30-somethings who have the capital to drop $2 million on recreational boats. The ethos among those in my age demographic seemed to be this: Do whatever it takes to get people together, have the most fun possible, and do it with the best toys. It was truly one of the few times in my life during which I was absolutely speechless in conversation. I was completely out of my element.

During lunch with my wealthier peers I mentioned what "I did." I tried to avoid it but soon I was asked, "So Anthony, what do *you* do?" The sighs of "Ahhh, isn't that cute?" I received after confessing my vocation made me wonder if I said that I was teaching kindergarten. I was also wracking my brain trying to figure out how one of my new best friends in his late 20s could afford to scout million dollar boats as a "first boat" because he didn't "want to get too carried away." I sat there and chuckled, saying, "Yeah, I know what you mean."

From what I could tell, plastic surgeons in South Florida must be very, very busy. If collagen were illegal, the police would have needed several buses to remove all the Barbies prancing around in Versace sunglasses and Hermès handbags. I also got the sense that this is a community of people where marriages do not last very long. Or, maybe I simply witnessed a culture where fathers like hanging out with their daughters? At any rate, this is where the beautiful people hang out.

I should have known it was going to be an interesting day when the closest marina parking lot was packed not with middle-class and "new money" cars like Audis, BMWs, and Mercedes Benzes but cars driven by rich people like Porsches, Rolls-Royces, Lamborghinis, and Maseratis. Overall I felt like I was on the set of the 2002 reality TV show *Single in the Hamptons.*

Many of these people were beyond coveting. One of my friends spoke of people down there not thinking twice about dropping $1,000 to $2,000 per night hanging with friends on the weekends at bars and restaurants. Near the end of my weekend I decided that it is good that I don't live there. I couldn't afford it now, and if I was wealthy, I'm afraid the toys might seduce me.

I'm oddly thankful for my negative net worth of $52,000 with my $72,000 school loan constraints. It certainly forces me to keep life simple and makes a community like this one that I can visit for only a few hours each year.

Loving *House*

I have a confession: I was once addicted (kinda) to watching *House*. The Fox TV show, starring Hugh Laurie as Dr. House, was a provocative take on the medical drama genre. According to the network's description, Dr. House solves medical mysteries where the villain is a medical malady and the hero is an irreverent, controversial doctor who trusts no one, least of all his patients.

The show came to a close in December of 2012. Over the course of eight seasons, it was nominated for 25 Emmy Awards, winning 5, including one for Outstanding Writing for a Drama Series for its creator and executive producer, David Shore.

Here's why I think I love the show so much:

- Dr. House says whatever he thinks about people. He has no filter. I'm so jealous of that at times. I would love to be able to tell people, "You're an idiot." His bedside manner is horrible, and he usually says offensive things to his coworkers and patients. I do this all the time. If you use your mouth to communicate to people, eventually you're going to say something that offends someone. House, however, is such a brilliant clinician, the hospital puts up with his inappropriate comments and actions.

- Dr. House is a workaholic. Me too! I don't even want to count the number of hours I actually work. It's depressing.

- Dr. House looks for any psychological or emotional reasons for the actions of his patients and coworkers. House explores reasons behind the symptoms and enjoys pointing out the huge plank in the eyes of others. Occasionally, Dr. House will acknowledge that he has a speck of dust in his own eye.

Overall, the show was brilliant. The medical maladies may not have even been real. I have no way of knowing, but the production team did a fantastic job of mixing suspense and comedy. I wonder if I and others are so enthralled by the show because Dr. House says what everyone thinks but no one will say—which is not always good. Maybe we like the show because too many of us are workaholics. Maybe we like the show because many of us are keen to the notion that people's irrational actions are often motivated by past bad experiences.

I am not promoting the above characteristics as necessarily "good," but they are compelling to watch. To be honest, I'm much more like Dr. House than I should be, and I wonder whether, I'd be interested in the show at all if I had a different set of personal weaknesses. In the meantime, thanks to re-runs on cable, I will continue to watch several hours of *House* every week.

Renting Way Underrated

There is nothing wrong with being a long-term or permanent renter. Don't believe the hype. One of the reasons we are in the midst of a housing depression is the misguided belief that owning a home is always a good investment and that home ownership is key to experiencing the "American Dream."

Both are false. Owning a home is not a good investment if you cannot afford to maintain it or if you are not the home-owning type. Owning a home does not necessarily create a better quality of life.

Pushing home ownership on those who are probably better suited to be long-term or permanent renters sets many people up to fail. The home ownership idol does not deliver, as we now see.

I have an engineer friend who earns a great salary and sold his house a few years ago because he didn't like being a homeowner. He disliked doing maintenance work, mowing the grass, dealing with all the extra bills, worrying about security issues, and so on. He sold his house and is now a renter with no plans to buy another home anytime soon. He invests his money in other areas instead of property because, as we have now seen, housing investments are not guaranteed to appreciate.

Renters are people who want a certain lifestyle. They prefer the freedom of mobility, free from the hassle and worry of house maintenance, etc. For older generations, home ownership made more sense because of their romantic vision of "settling down" in marriage, buying a house with a fence, raising a family, and remaining in the same house for 30 years before retiring to a place that they really enjoy. For younger generations—most of whom will have four to six career changes during their lifetime—renting long-term often makes more sense.

There are many people stuck in towns they hate and working jobs they no longer want because they bought a house that they cannot afford to sell. The value has tanked or they do not have the cash to prepare it for sale. How sad is it to have to turn down a fantastic job opportunity because your house has you in residential shackles? Moreover, to be "house rich" and "cash poor" can no longer be sold as a "good investment." Is it not irresponsible to buy a house that you cannot afford, hoping that "someday" it'll pay off? What if your "someday" never comes?

People who are truly wealthy are not so because of home value appreciation. There are other areas to invest money and people should be free from the cultural mythology that harasses them to buy a house. Leave renters alone, because they are not throwing their money away as the myth portrays. If renters choose to rent, the economic trade-off is theirs and theirs alone to absorb.

Renters, I know you all value other things and the home-owning types just don't understand. When your family and friends ask you, "When are you going to buy a house," feel free to chuckle and say, "Maybe never." If you're not the home-owning type, there is nothing wrong with you.

Personal Blogging is Dead

If you have a personal blog, shut it down. Nobody cares what you are mus-
ing about, and few people can even find it. This is the advice of Paul Boutin,
writing about the end of personal blogging for *Wired Magazine*.[27] Twitter,
Flickr, and Facebook have made personal blogging obsolete, he argues, adding that posting personal pictures and your "random thoughts" to be read
by those surfing the blogosphere is a waste of time and bandwidth.

Blogging has now become professionalized and formalized into a
cheap way to launch a website. Originally, weblogs provided a platform for
the common person to journal online for any passerby to read, but now it
has become a place to sell advertising, as magazines, newspapers, professional organizations, well-known public figures, and so on, have redefined
the genre and taken it over. I started blogging back in 2003, but most of
the folks who began when I did have terminated their blogs and moved on
to Facebook and Twitter.

Boutin writes:

> Cut-rate journalists and underground marketing campaigns
> now drown out the authentic voices of amateur wordsmiths. It's
> almost impossible to get noticed, except by hecklers. And why
> bother? . . . Scroll down Technorati's list of the top 100 blogs and
> you'll find personal sites have been shoved aside by professional
> ones. Most are essentially online magazines: The Huffington
> Post. Engadget. TreeHugger. A stand-alone commentator can't
> keep up with a team of pro writers cranking out up to 30 posts
> a day.[28]

Nowadays, the only people left in the blogosphere to comment on your
posts are hecklers and trolls, what Boutin calls "the Net's lowest form of life:
The insult commenter." If you unwisely pour your heart out in a post, some
anonymous troll with an obscure first name or bizarre screen name, like
"tko4zr," will gladly offer venom like: "This post is weird. Why don't you just
leave the country then." Because of the haters back-stroking in cybersludge,
many of the professionalized and media blogs have to moderate comments.
When you post a comment on CNN's website, this message pops up: "Comments are moderated by CNN and will not appear on this story until after
they have been reviewed and deemed appropriate for posting."

Christian blogging has really deteriorated over the last few years, with
folks posting slanderous personal attacks on leaders they do not like, or

27. See the article at Boutin, "Twitter, Flickr, Facebook Make Blogs Look so 2004."

28. Ibid., lines 23-36.

those armchair theologians who seem to believe that their commentaries on Bible passages are worth the rest of us reading, or that sad person who thinks it's clever to be nothing but a contrarian, or the end-times fanatic who sees every news story as one of "the signs."

As personal blogging approaches the fate of the rotary phone, whenever I get an email announcing, "Hey, we just started a family blog" or "Hey, I now have a blog posting my thoughts," I roll my eyes and assume the person is likely new to the internet. I'm often tempted to write back: "Cool, welcome to 2000. I'll be sure to check it out on Xanga."

Blogging is definitely here to stay, in general, although its future is clearly headed in the direction of online magazines. Boutin is correct that Twitter—which limits each text-only post to 140 characters—is what blogging was in the early 2000s. Happily, Twitter brings something to the internet that is recommended in James: brevity. Personal blogging had a good run.

Common Sense Results

From time to time, I like to survey new health studies to add to the long list of things to say "oops" to. I found three interesting studies from the past month or so that I have to share. According to the latest research, I am glad I didn't do any of the following: play high school football, head soccer balls, or eat fast food as a child. (My family ate nearly all of our meals at home—thanks Mom!)

First, according to a new study, high school football players have a high risk for strokes. Jared R. Brosch and Meredith R. Golomb examined teens who had suffered a stroke and discovered a high correlation with playing football. Bioscholar reports that researchers found "some of the potential risks include an increase of hyperventilation, repeated neurological injury, use of anabolic steroids, use of highly caffeinated energy drinks and an increase in obesity of young players."[29]

Second, one of the coolest tricks in soccer is to watch a player score a goal by heading the ball pass the goalie. But heading the ball may not ever be a safe way to play the game. New research indicates that it may, in fact, lead to brain damage. Researchers used an MRI machine to analyze changes in brain activity of 32 adult amateur soccer players who headed balls 436 times a year on average. Those players that headed the ball 1,000 or more times a year presented abnormalities similar to traumatic brain injuries suffered in car accidents. That can't be good.

29. "Adolescent Football Players at Higher Risk for Stroke," Bioscholar.

Finally, we know that childhood obesity is a major problem in the United States and that children today eat fast food more than any previous generation. Unfortunately, all of the quick and easy food given to kids these days may be shortening their lives. The *Northwest Indiana Times* reports a new study from Northwestern University where researchers sampled thousands of teens, ages 12 to 19, and found that "they are more likely to die from heart disease at a younger age than today's adults."[30] This means that today's teenagers are expected to have more heart-disease-related deaths than previous generations. This should not come as a surprise.

How can we summarize the moral of these health studies? I was thinking of this: Use common sense. Getting big really fast for sports may not be worth it in the long run, God didn't make our heads to hit things, like balls, with it, and eating bad food is bad for your health. This is may seem like basic common sense, but it's become the American way to fund studies to tell us things that we already know.

Leaders are Developed, Too

Many are familiar with the old adage: "Leaders are born, not made." I am beginning to doubt the accuracy of this statement. While it's true that many leadership skills are God-given gifts, it is also true that natural-born leaders need to have their skills developed by others.

A few years ago, James Dobson said we are facing a leadership void. I agree that is partly true, but the void is actually his generation's fault. We have several "Pauls," but very few "Timothys." When I was in seminary, a group of us fervently prayed for mentors, hoping we would have someone to show us the way. After a few years we faced the hard reality that, for the most part, baby boomers are not really into mentoring and leadership coaching. We realized we were on our own.

As many boomers transition out of leadership positions with some of the nation's largest churches and religious organizations, many are finding there is no next president/CEO or senior-level leader in the pipeline. In the October issue of *The Harvard Business Review*, Claudio Fernández-Aráoz, Boris Groysberg, and Nitin Nohria offer great ideas for organizations on how to create a leadership pipeline. They note that "promising managers are attracted to companies known for strong development opportunities, and a well-managed talent pipeline dramatically increases the odds that a company will appoint great leaders at the top." That is, if organizations want

30. "Teens More Likely to Die from Heart Disease at a Younger Age than Today's Adults," nwitimes.com.

to keep and attract talented people, then it is important to make a verbal, programmatic commitment to develop emerging leaders into great leaders. Being committed to talent management is key to maintaining institutional growth and longevity.

One important finding of the author's research was that the effective management of the next generation of leaders always encompasses three sets of activities:

> The first involves the establishment of clear strategic priorities, which shape the way companies groom high-potential leaders. The second involves the careful selection of high-potential candidates-and communicating who they are to others in the organization. This can be touchy. And the third comprises the management of talent itself-how high potentials are developed, rewarded, and retained.

For several years I have been consulting Christian organizations, encouraging them to grow their own leaders instead of trying to find some leader "out there." The risk, time, and investment to adopt this approach will be worth it in the long-term. When looking for someone with leadership "potential," as the authors note, managers should look for a person who demonstrates the "ability to grow and to handle responsibilities of greater and scale and scope." The authors note that this is that type of person who can do four things well: (1) manage a vast range of information, (2) lead and encourage others, (3) demonstrate resolve and consistency in meeting goals, and (4) seek out new experiences, ideas, knowledge, and constructive feedback. This is the type of person organizations should do whatever is necessary to retain.

In recent years, I have known several friends who quit their jobs and moved on to other organizations because they had demonstrated leadership potential but their managers had no idea how to develop them. Whenever I serve on the board of directors for an organization I look for evidence of internal leadership development opportunities and on-going succession planning for senior leadership, because organizations that do not invest in developing leaders will have none in the long-term. I do this because I don't think we simply have a leadership void these days but a leadership development vacuum that will sadly result in the folding of several organizations as key leaders approach retirement. If you want leaders, then invest in them.

Better than Being 'Less Bad'

What do future generations need for us to do today with respect to the environment? Do we need to reduce the amount of toxic waste we release? Do we need to consume less? To date, our dialogue about environmental stewardship has fallen short because it seems that the best we can do is be "less bad." What if there were a way to manufacture and consume that actually replenished the earth? What if the waste from our production processes actually provided nutrients for ecosystems instead of toxins? God knew what He was doing. Why don't we simply mimic His processes?

In 2002, architect William McDonough and former Greenpeace chemist Michael Braungart published *Cradle to Cradle: Remaking the Way We Make Things*, which introduced a revolutionary way of thinking about environmental stewardship that remains relatively unknown among Christian ethicists today. The authors explained the basic premise of the Cradle to Cradle (C2C) approach this way: "When designers employ the intelligence of natural systems-the effectiveness of nutrient cycling, the abundance of the sun's energy-they can create products, industrial systems, buildings, even regional plans that allow nature and commerce to fruitfully co-exist." In other words, the problem isn't that we don't "reduce, reuse, and recycle" enough. The *real* problem is that our entire industrial complex does not mimic nature. After all, in the natural world all waste is food.

McDonough and Braungart believe that looking to nature for our design and manufacturing processes is the only way to be good stewards of the earth in the long run. The authors even suggest looking at ants as a model (Proverbs 6:6), gleaning principles not only about work ethic but also how to use natural resources.

Our entire infrastructure is simply too linear, according to McDonough and Braungart: "It is focused on making a product and getting it to a customer quickly and cheaply without considering much else." But would recycling help? Not exactly. Recycling is just another example of being "less bad." People don't think about the fact that recycling is a *manufacturing* process that uses fossil fuels and produces toxic waste. As such, the net gain for the environment is negligible because the recycling process is no less harmful to the environment than a production process from raw materials.

Much of the Christian rhetoric about the environment seeks to make a persuasive case that we should care. OK, we get it. We should care. Now it's time to move on and think about how to do this in practice. Thankfully, the answers are not far from us if we would only apply what God has already programmed in nature. Who would have imagined that sound environmental stewardship might literally begin with ants?

When Trauma Doesn't Heal

Living in the aftermath of trauma can be described as nothing less than a life of suffering. For people with post-traumatic stress disorder (PTSD), the church can be a hard place to be. Well-meaning friends try to help by offering platitudes like "we're praying for you" or "you need to believe the gospel" or "give it over to the Lord," but they just don't seem to understand that the suffering just doesn't go away. Thankfully, theologians are trying to discern biblical truth for trauma survivors who live in a world full of triggers and misunderstanding.

For example, Dr. Shelly Rambo, professor of theology at Boston University, challenges Christian leaders to think theologically about trauma survivors in *Spirit and Trauma: A Theology of Remaining*.

A traumatic event is not like a death of a loved one or being rejected by a friend. Instead it involves activities that were life-threatening, either physically or in one's perception, creating a sense of unrecognizable fear, utter helplessness, or horror. Rambo points out that trauma is a wound that "remains long after a precipitating event or events are over," and it "exceeds categories of comprehension" related to an event. Trauma is an encounter with death that exceeds the human capacity to take in and process the external world. In fact, because of trauma, what one knows about the world is shattered. What is true and safe are ruptured. "The event becomes the defining event beyond which little can be conceived," writes Rambo. Life is not the same anymore. The trauma interprets life for the sufferer. There is no life after the storm. It hovers. The rain may stop but the clouds threatening rain always remain.

Surviving post-trauma is a life of navigating one's way through a minefield of triggers that remind the sufferer of the traumatic event or events. Triggers can lead to random bouts of sobbing, irregular and disturbed sleep patterns, outbursts of anger, depression, anxiety, loss of hope, loss of interest in things once loved, thoughts of suicide, self-medicating with drugs or alcohol, as well as running away from thoughts, conversations, people, and places that might arouse traumatic memory. Because trauma survivors re-experience the event in ways outside of their control, healing is not a matter of believing the right things about God. Or getting the gospel right. Time does not heal traumatic wounds. Traumatic memory is something only God can heal. The Holy Spirit must empower trauma sufferers to re-imagine their future.

Is there hope for healing PTSD in this life? Maybe. There are no easy answers or guarantees. But what I do know is that those limping around in life after experiencing trauma need people who love them enough to realize that they may never "get over it" and that their on-going struggle does not represent weak faith. Come, Lord Jesus (Revelation 22:20)!

Silent Suffering

Bill Zeller's suicide is a tragic story of a Christian home, sexual abuse, and a man trying to make sense of his pain. According to Rachel Jackson in *The Daily Princetonian*, Zeller died on the night of Jan. 5, 2011 from injuries resulting from a suicide attempt. He was a fifth-year Ph.D. student in computer science at Princeton University and was already a nationally known computer programmer.

Zeller left behind a 4,000-word suicide note (warning: contains some profanity) that details his agony of dealing with being sexually abused:

> My first memories as a child are of being raped, repeatedly. This has affected every aspect of my life. This darkness, which is the only way I can describe it, has followed me like a fog. . . . I've never been able to stop thinking about what happened to me and this hampered my social interactions.[31]

Zeller wrote that he never shared what happened to him with anyone, including professionals. Instead he tried many things to soothe the pain—drugs, alcohol, relationships, success—but nothing seemed to work. Zeller wrote about having nightmares about his abuse three to four nights a week. He also expressed hatred for his family and for Christianity:

> I despise everything they stand for and I truly hate them, in a non-emotional, dispassionate and what I believe is a healthy way. The world will be a better place when they're dead—one with less hatred and intolerance. If you're unfamiliar with the situation, my parents are fundamentalist Christians who kicked me out of their house and cut me off financially when I was 19 because I refused to attend seven hours of church a week. They live in a black and white reality they've constructed for themselves. They partition the world into good and evil and survive by hating everything they fear or misunderstand and calling it love.

Zeller went on to describe his family as one where "church was always more important than the members of their family. . . . A house where the love of music with any sort of a beat was literally beaten out of me." When he was 8 years old his parents told him that his grandmother was going to hell because "she was Roman Catholic." His parents claimed not to be racists

31. Johnson, "Agonizing Last Words," lines 8-15 of Zeller's letter.

but "[talked] about the horrors of miscegenation [interracial marriage]." If Zeller's description of his parents' faith is accurate there are many concerns. And some have blamed religion, at least in part, for Zeller's death.

But what compounded his agony was how he felt uncomfortable going to anyone for help. No one was safe. No one could be trusted. There was too much shame. I can't imagine how painful it must have been for his family and friends to learn of his struggles along with the rest of us in his note.

As I've written before, men like Zeller suffer in silence because they doubt the frequency of this type of abuse and rarely talk about it within the church. In the end, my hope is that the Holy Spirit will give hurting people like Zeller courage to seek help and provide people to listen so that this type of suffering can be relieved through the grace of Christ.

Zeller's note is one of the most difficult things I've ever read. I'm encouraging people to read it with the hope that it will foster good discussions about handling abuse, trauma, trust, friendships, parenting, Christianity, and more.

Ending Online Anonymity

Maintaining an anonymous internet persona tends to bring out the worst in online behavior and can lead to hostile and insulting interactions, including flame wars. *New York Times* columnist Stanley Fish proposes that online anonymity be terminated to bring civility to internet conversations, and I agree with him completely. If you are not willing to stand behind your words, in your name, you should not speak. Fish writes:

> The practice of withholding the identity of the speaker is strategic, and one purpose of the strategy . . . is to avoid responsibility and accountability for what one is saying. Anonymity, Martha Nussbaum, a professor of law and philosophy at the University of Chicago observes, allows Internet bloggers 'to create for themselves a shame-free zone in which they can inflict shame on others.' The power of the bloggers, she continues, 'depends on their ability to insulate their Internet selves from responsibility in the real world, while ensuring real-world consequences' for those they injure.[32]

Fish raises important concerns about the character and integrity of those who prefer anonymity in order to avoid being held responsible for their public speech, but what is the solution?

32. Fish, "Anonymity and the Dark Side of the Internet," lines 30-39.

Taylor Brooks, co-founder of SpeakerWiki, says that internet flame wars have led some websites to require commenters to register using their Facebook accounts or have employed systems where participants can vote off those who comment with offensive speech. "The problem is not with anonymity, the problem is with people," Brooks said. "When [commenters] know that they can't be caught they are more likely to have flame war conversations." Brooks recommends "Y Combinator" as a good example of a website that self-polices speech. The site avoids flame wars and increases participation by other users by expecting civility and allowing commenters to vote off others who use speech that does not promote civil discourse through "downmodding."

Over the years, it has been my habit not to respond to commenters who do not to take public ownership of their public comments by name. If commenters are not willing to be held accountable to the same standards of public speech as I am, I find little incentive to take them seriously. If commenters were expected to open themselves up to accountability by putting a real name with comments, the need to report inappropriate comments to website administrators would sharply decline.

Billable Hours Enslave Lawyers

Let's us say your hypothetical cousin Emily gets accepted into Vanderbilt University's School of Law. Should you rejoice or despair? If law school leads to working in a large law firm, which is often the only viable option for graduates, Emily's future might not look as bright as you think.

For one thing, lawyers in large firms tend to have very low job satisfaction ratings, with a life driven by the billable hour being the main culprit of discouragement. That's because today's law firm makes its money by billing clients by the hour. As the Yale Law School Career Development Office points out: "In order for you to be profitable to your firm, you must make enough money from your billable hours not only to cover your salary and your overhead, but also to generate revenue for the firm. It's not a complicated equation—the more hours you bill, the more revenue for the firm. As a result, the incentive is to keep you working and billing your time."[33] It's no wonder that young attorneys in large firms find themselves becoming slaves to the billable hour.

Large law firms also tend to place more distance between the managing attorneys and their young associates. Because of this lack of personal contact, tracking billable hours becomes the most efficient way to keep tabs

33. "The Truth about the Billable Hour," Yale Law School.

on the work of these young attorneys. Therefore, the best way to get the attention of your superiors is to bill more hours.

Enslavement to billable hours has not always been the normative law firm culture, but the recent rise of large firms, some with more than 200 lawyers on staff, changed all that. Back in the early 1960s, as Notre Dame law and theology professor M. Cathleen Kaveny points out in her article on the billable hour culture, only 38 U.S. firms had more than 50 lawyers; today, more than 500 firms are at least that large. Also during the '60s, attorneys at large firms billed about 1,500 hours annually on average. Today they average 2,000 hours a year, which requires working 10 hours a day, six days a week.[34]

For lawyers on the ever-elusive and competitive partnership track, that means that they have very little or no time for family, friends, or public service. Moreover, lawyers in large firms are tempted to reduce and value all of life in relation to opening up space for billable time. Why not eat lunch at your desk while you bill hours? Why not work through your kids' soccer games and dinner with the family? They'll understand. Becoming a partner is really important, right?

Because of law school-related debt, much of this culture is sadly unavoidable. In order to pay back loans, many young attorneys are driven to practice law in large firms where the earning potential is greater. This is how many get trapped. In the end, in light of the billable hour-standard, perhaps you should be sobered by Cousin Emily's acceptance to Vanderbilt's law school. It could be the beginning of well-paid, prestigious, and miserable life.

Men Suffering in Silence

In 2005, a major study on sexual abuse reported that one in six adult men reported being sexually molested as children, and, surprisingly, nearly 40 percent of the perpetrators were female.[35] In America's gynocentric practice of Christianity, men suffer in silence as they are often overlooked as victims of sexual abuse. In many evangelical churches men are usually steered into "accountability groups" while women are provided support groups and healing opportunities for past pain. Perpetrators are men, victims are women. That's the dominant paradigm with good rationale, statistically speaking. But every church in America is populated with scores of male victims of sexual abuse in need of help.

---

34. Kaveny, "Billable Hours in Ordinary Time," 173–220.
35. For more information, go to https://1in6.org/the-1-in-6-statistic/.

I offer this in no way to discount or dismiss the horrible suffering of the high percentage of women who were sexually abused. Thankfully, there are many, many resources for women to get help. But boys and men do not have as many, if any, opportunities within the church to openly process and receive help with abuse. Shame and silence about this issue prevail. Thankfully there are some groups beginning to alert parents about, for example, the overlooked problem of predatory female teachers and others who target boys.

Organizations like 1in6.org focus on men who have had unwanted or abusive sexual experiences. Although this is not a Christian organization, most Christian male victims of sexual abuse may want to start there because I am unaware of any Christian platforms like this that offer such help. I have only attended one church that has ever openly put men in the category of "sexual abuse victim." Men's ministries, which tend to focus on Bible and theology knowledge, fellowship, entertainment, and keeping men "accountable," are usually not a safe place for the one man out of the six to get help. As I asked a couple of years ago, "Do men hurt?" or are men just seen as the problems that need to be constrained and rebuked?

At 1in6.org you'll read stories like that of Aaron Gilmore, who from age 11 to 17 was abused by a woman who was a family friend. By his early 20s, Gilmore was a key figure in the passage of a landmark law in New Zealand that recognizes that women can sexually abuse and rape boys, which created provisions for prosecution. Or like that of Theoren Fleury, who developed a substance abuse problem, which ultimately forced him out of the National Hockey League in 2003, driven by his struggles with the pain and agony unleashed by a hockey coach's sexual abuse in his teenage years. There are many other courageous stories on the website as well.

Every Sunday, pastors stand in front of an audience of abused men and rarely mention it. Do not expect to see this as a topic at a men's conference anytime soon. Because of the pain and shame, many men do not even share these stories with their spouses or friends. I'm glad for organizations like 1in6.org that provide resources for male victims and those who want to help them. Hopefully, one day, more churches will openly recognize this as a reality so males in need of help and restoration (Luke 4, Isaiah 61) can receive the holistic healing that comes because of the active work of God the Father, and the Son, and the Holy Spirit. May the silent suffering end.

Biomimicry: Design Inspired by Creation

God designed the world so that natural systems produce no waste. One organism's waste is another organism's food. This is God's cradle-to-cradle design.[36] What if humans were able to unlock the mysteries of God's design of nature so that the things we manufacture and produce for human flourishing also create food for other organisms instead of creating waste that sits in landfills or is incinerated? How much more sustainable would our lives be? How much better would we be at managing our impact on creation? These are central questions behind an area of environmental sustainability called biomimicry.[37]

Biomimicry is an emerging discipline that studies nature's best designs and then imitates those designs and processes to solve human problems. After all, God has already provided a model for us to follow. And God's creation can serve as an appropriate measure of the quality of our innovations while also serving as a credible guide. Therefore, we can look to creation not simply to discover what we can extract from it but also what we can learn from God's design.

Do we really need another book or conference on "environmental stewardship?" The case has been made ad nauseam that Christians ought to lead conversations about "caring for the environment" and that we are a "bad witness" by not being involved in initiating those discussions. The stewardship conversation can help make a case for *why* we should care, but stewardship does not tell us what we should actually do. It does not move us beyond stage-one thinking. Biomimicry is a good area for Christians to serve as leaders in design so that what we produce simultaneously is good for human flourishing and blesses creation.

Environmental stewardship is not a battle against the "liberals," "tree huggers," "atheist environmentalists," and "evolutionists," it's an opportunity to lead by designing our environments with a conscious emulation of God's genius. In the book *Biomimicry: Innovation Inspired by Nature*, Janine Benyus describes what such leadership could look like:

> In a biomimetic world, we would manufacture the way animals and plants do, using sun and simple compounds to produce totally biodegradable fibers, ceramics, plastics, and chemicals. Our farms, modeled on prairies, would be self-fertilizing and pest-resistant. To find new drugs or crops, we could consult animals, and insects. . . . Even computing would take its cue from

36. For further reading, see McDonough and Braungart, *Cradle to Cradle*.
37. See http://biomimicry.org/what-is-biomimicry/.

nature, with software that "evolves" solutions, and hardware that uses the lock-and-key paradigm to compute by touch.[38]

In other words, we would look to God's good creation and His design of natural systems to direct our innovation and production processes for food, buildings, automobiles, furniture, clothing, toys, and so on. God shows us what works and what lasts. Innovation inspired by creation is beyond the rhetoric of conservation or preservation; it gets to the heart of co-creation. Creation not only gives a sense of the normative standards for conduct but also wisdom to live well (Proverbs 1:22–23, 8:4, 22–23, 27–30; Job 38–41). In the book *Creation Regained*, theologian Albert Wolters reminds us that "the Lord teaches the farmer his business. There is a right way to plow, to sow, and to thresh, depending on the kind for grain he is growing" (Isaiah 28:23-29). The Lord also teaches us how to design.

Sadly, with the rise of modernism and industrialization, even Christians have forgotten the advantages of consulting God's design in nature for wisdom on best principles for how we should make things. Because we are God's representatives on earth, we are cultivating creation where God left off and we must try our best to make our waste food for something else in the short-term. After all, that's how God designed his world and biomimicry can guide our role in it. It's time to move beyond stage one.

All Moms Aren't "Great"

The holidays and birthdays can be difficult for some because of severe family dysfunction. In recent years, fathers have been faulted for complicity in emotionally wounding children, but little attention is paid to the role of emotionally abusive and unstable mothers. On Mother's Day, women are praised. On Father's Day, men are reprimanded. Christine Ann Lawson in her book *Understanding the Borderline Mother* makes the case that much family dysfunction originates with a child's intense, unpredictable, and volatile relationship with mom.

According to Lawson, adult children wounded by toxic mothers often have these common thoughts in her presence: "I never know what to expect," "I don't trust her," "She says it didn't happen," "She makes me feel terrible," "Everyone else thinks she's great," "It's all or nothing," "She's so negative," "She flips out," "Sometimes I can't stand her," and "She drives me crazy."

While the book is primarily targeted towards adult children with mothers that have borderline personality disorders, I find that looking at

---

38. Benyus, *Biomimicry*, 2–3.

the four types of mothers Lawson describes can be helpful in understanding most difficult mothers:

1. Waif. The waif mother presents herself as helpless. She is primarily a victim and seeks to evoke sympathy and care from others, especially her children. On the outside, the Waif may appear strong, but internally, she feels like an impostor. Waifs tend to have been a victim of childhood abuse or neglect, were treated as inferior, or were emotionally denigrated. The primary message to her children is, "Life is so hard."

2. Hermit. Hermit behavior evokes anxiety and protection from others. The Hermit fears letting anyone in because she was likely hurt by someone she trusted. She tends to be overprotective of her children and lives in fear of bad consequences. The primary message to her children is, "Life is too dangerous."

3. Queen. The queen's inner experience is one of deprivation and her behavior demands compliance and allegiance. She is the demanding mother who often intimidates to get her way. She can be vindictive, greedy, manipulative, flamboyant, and greedy. Her emotional message to her children is, "Life is all about me."

4. Witch. The witch mother is angry. She takes her anger out on others. Her behavior evokes submission. She actually is filled with self-hatred and may single out one of her children to bear the brunt of her rage. Her emotional message to her children is, "Life is war."[/NL 1–4]

These mothers have different public and private personalities, and only their children know the truth and roll their eyes when they hear, "Your mom is great!" The verbal assaults coupled with passive-aggressive guilt manipulation corners children into embracing their mother's twisted emotional messages. This can make being around her unbearable. What makes Lawson's book so valuable is that, in addition to explaining difficult mothers, she also gives fantastic advice for adult children so that they can simultaneously love their mothers while creating healthy boundaries that thwart future conflict.

No Romantic Past for Children

There has never been a time in human history better for children than the era in which we currently live. In a Western culture like ours that worships children and idolizes youth, the low social status of children in antiquity seems foreign. Given the reality of the Greco-Roman world, it makes

Judeo-Christian teaching on children and parenting a powerful counter-cultural witness.

In his book *When Children Became People: The Birth of Childhood in Early Christianity*, O.M. Bakke reminds us that in the Greco-Roman world children were considered the lowest form of human beings. The social pecking order went something like this: free male citizens, women, older men, slaves, barbarians, and then . . . finally . . . children. This was because it was believed that children had the least capacity, among all others, for *logos*—word, speech, and reason.

Children symbolized the absence of *logos*. The idea that they lack reason is consistently found in sources ranging from the time of Homer to that of Cicero. Bakke recalls a popular Greek aphorism that said, "Old men are like children once more." In both Platonic and Aristotelian thought, the opinions of children were seen as no more of consequence than those of animals. To refer to an adult as a child was to issue a major insult.

Moreover, to call someone a "boy" in the Greco-Roman world was perceived as an egregious insult because children were associated with stupidity: *pueritia amentia*. This is a very interesting point considering the way in which white Southerners routinely and publicly referred to black men as "boy" from the time of chattel slavery through the 1960s. Is it possible that the South retained much of the Greco-Roman perspective on children? If so, to call a black man "boy" was more than an assault on his masculinity; it was also an assault on his dignity.

The Romans were also particularly dismissive of children because they were physically weak, vulnerable, and exposed to sickness. Given the mortality rate in the Greco-Roman world, it is not too surprising that children became symbols of human weakness. Children also were not valued because they were seen as lacking courage and subsequently became a symbol for human fear. In fact, Cicero made a well-known point that it is difficult to find any reason to praise a child for his inherent qualities.

This is the cultural context in which Jews in the Greco-Roman world lived before and during the time of Jesus. Many may find that this understanding of children sheds new light on Jewish and Christian teachings on value of a child. Respecting the dignity of a child in antiquity was socially counter-cultural. This is a reminder that the good ol' days may not have been that good after all.

Put Down that Glass of Milk
and Eat Your Vegetables

Most Americans have bought into the propaganda that we need milk for strong bones and teeth. I don't believe it anymore. A serving of many kinds of green vegetables contains more calcium than a glass of milk. Moreover, the connection between strong bones and cow milk simply does not hold up to science and history. In America we have all been conditioned to believe that milk contributes to strong bones throughout a child's life. In the end, could this rhetoric be nothing more than the dairy lobby taking advantage of government intrusion into the world of business?

According to a *New York Times* article, the dairy industry is struggling.[39] Dairy farmers are now using a technique to discard sperm with Y-chromosomes to produce more female cows for milk production. The problem today, however, is that demand is low and dairy farmers are being paid to discard milk they produce, as well as being compensated to send cows for slaughter. I am wondering, however, if demand is down in part because American families are "wising-up" to the fact that children and adults don't need to drink milk to stay healthy. Maybe it's time that we say "good-bye" to the government-supported dairy industry.

The dogs I've owned over the years had strong bones, and they didn't drink cow's milk. Lions have strong bones, and they don't drink cow's milk. Gorillas have strong bones, and they don't drink cow's milk. Grizzly bears have strong bones, and they don't drink cow's milk. I am not saying it is forbidden as a beverage, but I'm not convinced that anyone ever needs to drink milk from a cow—ever.

Walter Veith, former professor and chair of the Department of Zoology at the University of Western Cape, South Africa, has this to say:

> Mother's milk is essential for infants, but then infants are specially designed to cope with this growth-promoting food. Prior to weaning, the necessary enzyme systems needed for the digestion and assimilation of milk components are active, but they are progressively deactivated with age. The milk of other mammals also differs in composition from human milk, and this, together with the potential danger from ingested antigens, makes cow's milk unsuitable for human consumption.[40]

If we don't need a cow's milk then why is it in the government food pyramid? An interesting study published a few years ago in the medical

39. See the article at Neuman, "From Science."
40. Veith, "Lactose Intolerance," lines 7-13.

journal *Pediatrics* titled "Adult Female Hip Bone Density Reflects Teenage Sports-Exercise Patterns but Not Teenage Calcium Intake" demonstrates that, for women, bone density has more to do with early exercise than calcium intake.[41]

It's pretty well-known that many vegetables—for example, dark green leafy vegetables like spinach, Swiss chard, mustard greens, and collard greens—have higher levels of calcium than milk. Shredded cabbage, also common in many salad bars, is also a good source of calcium. If parents want to make sure their children get good amounts of calcium perhaps it's better to stick with old saying, "Honey, eat your vegetables."

A Family that Bikes Together. . .

Several years ago, Bill and Amarins Harrison, of Mount Vernon, Ky., took their children, Cheyenne, Jasmine, and Robin (respectively aged 6, 4, and 3 and the time), on a bike ride across America. Now that's what I call "a memorable family road trip." The Harrisons have said that they enjoy traveling and embraced the biking idea as a great way to see the country. The family planned to arrive in Fairbanks, Alaska within several months, covering about 7,000 miles and traveling through Texas, New Mexico, and California on a bicycle built for five.

I am intrigued by this story because I myself purchased a bike shortly before hearing it, not to become a cyclist, but to use it as a regular form of transportation and recreation. It seems like I'm seeing more and more people riding bicycles than I did a few years ago, and I'm hoping that my town adopts a practice that has been prevalent in several Latin American cities: opening up major city thoroughfares to pedestrians and cyclists on Sundays.

I have seen major streets reserved in such a manner firsthand in Quito, Ecuador, and I'm aware of the practice in Guatemala City and Bogotá, Columbia. These cities actually keep cars from accessing miles and miles of main city streets to open them up to pedestrians and cyclists. The result of the temporary car ban is scores of families riding bicycles or walking together. It was absolutely wonderful to witness families enjoying time together this way. I'm not a psychologist but there must be something emotionally healthy for families when parents spend leisure time together with their children and other families and friends.

I would love it if community bicycling became a cultural norm worldwide in large cities where families may not have opportunities to do such

41. Lloyd, "Adult Female Hip Bone Density," 40–44.

activities during the week. I would love to bicycle on Sundays along with others in my neighborhood. Moreover, the traffic changes force sections of the city to shut down and lessen the incentive for businesses to remain open.

When I ride my bicycle I see different things and run into different people. It's great!

While something like the Harrison family's journey is a bit extreme, it's interesting to think about how the effects it could have on families that try it. Worldwide, it would be even more interesting to see if there are any long-term effects on families and communities when commerce shuts down on Sundays and families are free to get out and enjoy being together without having to spend much money. In addition to praying, perhaps in the future we will witness some town boasting a slogan about the importance of families biking together.

Sons Loved by Fathers

"Fathers are really close to their sons down here," I thought as I walked around Guayaquil, Ecuador, watching fathers and sons with their arms interlocked or draped over one another as they walked, having one-on-one lunches together, or simply having afternoon coffee. Initially, the level of physical closeness struck me as isolated, but as I moved around the Guayaquil, and later on in Quito, I noticed that it was a recurring pattern. It seemed that fathers displaying physical and emotional closeness with their sons is simply a normative cultural value and likely a parental expectation.

As I thought about the United States, I began to wonder why it seems that this level of relational closeness is not the norm here. I was at a sushi restaurant one night with friends in Quayaquil and I saw an older teen arriving late to join his family for dinner. He greeted them all by kissing and hugging his mother, father, and middle school-aged younger brother. Kissing the mother was normal, but kissing his dad and brother on the cheek in public is something I don't normally see here in the States, not even among Christians.

Most guys in America grow up with their fathers never really paying too much attention to them emotionally. Most guys I know can't have sustained conversations with their fathers unless it pertains to work, sports, the weather, a theology lecture, or the like. Why is this?

As I sat in the Quito airport, I saw a father and son chatting. There was something different about this conversation. The son looked to be about 20-years-old and the father looked to be in his late 40s or early 50s. They were sitting next to each other, but the father was turned at an angle toward his son and doing nothing for about 40 minutes other than looking at this son right in the eye, and giving him affirmative head nods and pats on the back. The father made occasional comments. The father wasn't on his Blackberry and his son wasn't sending and responding to text messages or hooked up to an iPod or a game system. They were talking to each other uninterrupted. The look on his dad's face communicated something like, "You're the apple of my eye and I'm interested in everything you have to say no matter what." It was encouraging to see.

Of course, this is not exclusive to Ecuador. I've seen similar things when I travel to Guatemala among my friends and their own families there. I am also certain that some families in the United States have similar patterns, as well. The difference in Latin America is that this level of relational connectedness between fathers and sons seems very public.

When a father, then, tells his son that God, his heavenly father, loves him, he has a very good context for understanding what that means when his father teaches his son about the Scriptures: physical, undivided, affirmative, unconditional love and affection. "You know son," a father might say, "kinda like the way I treat you, but without sin" (Deuteronomy 7:7-13).

Home-Wrecking, Army-Style

I used to be neutral on the issue of women in combat, but after hearing about the amount of deployment adultery that takes place, I am starting to care. In mid-2009, two of my close friends were redeployed for Iraq—one divorced and one recently married. At a farewell dinner, my divorced Army friend, Ben (not his real name), told me that after his first Iraq tour every guy in his squad divorced his wife months after returning home. Every one of them. With the exception of Ben, all these guys were having sex with female soldiers during their deployment. In Ben's case, his wife was cheating on him back here in the States.

Ben hated the fact that his wife left him but was glad to be single on this second tour because of the strain that deployment puts on young marriages. Ben told me the general pattern is that male and female soldiers would spend lots of time together working, and within a few weeks pairs would form. "You knew what was going on," Ben said. We then discussed whether or not it is wise to put both men and women in such a difficult position. We arrived at no conclusion.

These "hook-ups" are not new, of course. It happens every summer with teenage camp counselors all over America. (You remember. In June they are at camp to "serve kids" and by early August they have met "the one.") The difference, of course, is that married adult men and women are committing painful sin against themselves and others. Maybe we should not be surprised. I seem to be getting more cynical every year.

I am in no way blaming women for men cheating, but I am beginning to wonder more and more if it is wise to have young men and women together in a combat theater for 12 to 16 months at a time. Are we introducing struggles that would not be there normally? Does deployment set young marriages up for failure? Should married guys be deployed at all? (By the way, it also would be unwise, and inaccurate, to assume that all these couples were not Christians.) I do not know the answers to these questions, having had many married friends shipped out on 12-month deployments, my views on this issue have begun shifting away from neutrality.

Bibliography

"About." Hustle University. http://hustleu.org/about-us/.

"Acton Institute Core Principles." Acton Institute. http://www.acton.org/about/acton-institute-core-principles.

Adams, Stephen. "Heading a Football 'Could Lead to Brain Damage.'" http://www.telegraph.co.uk/news/health/news/8920625/Heading-a-football-could-lead-to-brain-damage.html.ß

"Adolescent Football Players at Higher Risk for Stroke." Bioscholar. 9 December 2011. http://news.bioscholar.com/2011/12/adolescent-football-players-at-higher-risk-for-stroke.html.

"The AFCARS Report." United States Department of Health and Human Services, Administration for Children and Families, Administration on Children, Youth and Families, Children's Bureau. http://www.acf.hhs.gov/sites/default/files/cb/afcarsreport16.pdf.

Al-Fadhli, Hussain and Thomas Kersen. "How Religious, Social, and Cultural Capital Factors Influence Educational Aspirations of African American Adolescents." The Journal of Negro Education 79 (2010) 380-89.

Allen, John. "Benedict in Cameroon: a Tale of Two Trips." http://ncronline.org/blogs/all-things-catholic/benedict-cameroon-tale-two-trips.

Alliance Defending Freedom. "Pulpit Freedom Sunday." http://www.alliancedefendingfreedom.org/pulpitfreedom.

Allport, Gordon Willard. The Nature of Prejudice. 25th ed. New York: Basic, 1979.

Alvaré, Helen. "Traditional Family Law: Connecting Marriage with Children." The Witherspoon Institute. 6 December 2011. http://www.thepublicdiscourse.com/2011/12/4397/4/.

American National Standards Institute. ANSI Announces Availability of International Social Responsibility Standard, ISO 26000." PR Newswire. http://www.prnewswire.com/news-releases/ansi-announces-availability-of-international-social-responsibility-standard-iso-26000-106441933.html.

Anderson, Melissa. "The Blind Side: What Would Black People Do Without Nice White Folks?" http://www.dallasobserver.com/film/the-blind-side-what-would-black-people-do-without-nice-white-folks-6420117.

Anderson, Paul, and Sara Konrath. "'Why Should We Care?'—What to Do about Declining Student Empathy." http://chronicle.com/article/Why-Should-We-Care-What/128420/.

Anderson, Terry L., ed. *Property Rights and Indian Economies.* Lanham: Rowman & Littlefield, 1992.

———. "Self-Determination: The Other Path for Native Americans." http://www.perc. org/sites/default/files/june06.pdf.

Anyabwile, Thabiti. "Collateral Damage in the Invitation of T.D. Jakes to the Elephant Room." *The Gospel Coalition.* 1 October 2011. http://thegospelcoalition.org/blogs/ thabitianyabwile/2011/10/01/collateral-damage-in-the-invitation-of-t-d-jakes- to-the-elephant-room/.

Applebaum, Binyamin, and Robert Gebeloff. "Who Benefits from the Safety Net?" *Economix.* 13 February 2012. http://economix.blogs.nytimes.com/2012/02/13/ who-benefits-from-the-safety-net/?_r=0.

Baccara, Mariogiovanna, et al. "Gender and Racial Biases: Evidence from Child Adoption." *CESifo,* Working Paper No. 2921. http://papers.ssrn.com/sol3/papers. cfm?abstract_id=1545711.

Barrett, Brian. "Faith in the Inner-city: The Urban Black Church and Students' Educational Outcomes." *The Journal of Negro Education* 79 (2010) 249-62.

Beattie, Robb. "Putting the Crack Baby Myth to Bed." http://www. nationalreviewofmedicine.com/issue/2005/07_30/2_feature04_13.html.

Benedict XVI. *Caritas in Veritate, Encyclical Letter on Human Development.* http:// www.vatican.va/holy_father/benedict_xvi/encyclicals/documents/hf_ben-xvi_ enc_20090629_caritas-in-veritate_en.html.

Benyus, Janine M. *Biomimicry: Innovation Inspired by Nature.* New York: Harper Perennial, 2002.

Bergeson, Eric. "Small Towns Must Value Those Who Stay." http://www.crookstontimes. com/opinions/columnists/x1954211086/Small-towns-must-value-those-who- stay.

Bishop, Bill. *The Big Sort: Why the Clustering of Like-Minded America Is Tearing Us Apart.* Boston, MA: Mariner Books, 2009.

Bishop, Greg. "In Tebow Debate, a Clash of Faith and Football." http://www.nytimes. com/2011/11/08/sports/football/in-tebow-debate-a-clash-of-faith-and-football. html.

Biskupic, Joan. "The Supreme Court Tackles Race." http://usatoday30.usatoday.com/ news/washington/judicial/2009-04-20-supreme-court_N.htm. April 21, 2009.

"A Blueprint for Reform: The Reauthorization of the Elementary and Secondary Education Act."United States Department of Education. http://www2.ed.gov/ policy/elsec/leg/blueprint/blueprint.pdf.

Boutin, Paul. "Twitter, Flickr, Facebook Make Blogs Look so 2004." http://archive. wired.com/entertainment/theweb/magazine/16-11/st_essay.

Bradley, Anthony. "Ain't No Stoppin' Us Now." *World Magazine.* 5 November 2008. http://www.worldmag.com/2008/11/ain_t_no_stoppin_us_now.

———. *Liberating Black Theology: The Bible and the Black Experience in America.* Wheaton, IL: Crossway, 2010.

Brea, Jennifer. "Africans to Bono: 'For God's Sake Please Stop!'" American Enterprise Institute. 3 July 2007. http://www.aei.org/publication/africans-to-bono-for-gods- sake-please-stop/.

Brooks, David. "If It Feels Right . . ." *The New York Times.* 21 September 2011. http:// www.nytimes.com/2011/09/13/opinion/if-it-feels-right.html.

———. "The Messiah Complex." *The New York Times*. 7 January 2010. http://www.nytimes.com/2010/01/08/opinion/08brooks.html.

Burns, Bob. "New TSA Pat-down Procedures." http://blog.tsa.gov/2010/11/new-tsa-pat-down-procedures.html.

Carter, A. J. "The Elephant Wins." http://epointchurch.wordpress.com/2011/10/04/the-elephant-wins/.

"The Catholic Intellectual Tradition: A Conversation at Boston College." Boston College. http://www.bc.edu/content/dam/files/top/church21/pdf/cit.pdf.

Chryssavgis, Johnn. "The Spiritual Way." In *The Cambridge Companion to Orthodox Christian Theology*, edited by Mary Cunningham and Elizabeth Theokritoff, 150–64. Cambridge Companions to Religion. Cambridge: Cambridge University Press, 2008.

Clark, Kendall. "Defining 'White Privilege.'" *Race, Racism, and the Law*. http://racism.org/index.php?option=com_content&view=article&id=387:whiteness05a&catid=69&Itemid=165.

"China Berates 'Axis of Evil' Remarks." CNN. http://edition.cnn.com/2002/WORLD/asiapcf/east/01/31/china.bush/index.html?related.

Collins, Jim, and Jerry I. Porras. *Built to Last: Successful Habits of Visionary Companies*. New York: Harper Business, 2004.

"Compendium of the Social Doctrine of the Church." Pontifical Council for Justice and Peace. http://www.vatican.va/roman_curia/pontifical_councils/justpeace/documents/rc_pc_justpeace_doc_20060526_compendio-dott-soc_en.html.

"Concerned Black Clergy Opposes Teacher Targeting in CRCT Probe." AJC.com. 15 December 2010. http://www.ajc.com/videos/news/concerned-black-clergy-opposes-teacher-targeting/vdHwp/.

"Confessional Statement." The Gospel Coalition. http://www.thegospelcoalition.org/about/foundation-documents/confessional-statement.

"Confessions of Fatherhood." Crossroads Tabernacle. https://www.youtube.com/watch?v=TxhTocrwRW8.

Crain, Nicole V. and Mark W. Crain. "The Impact of Regulatory Costs on Small Firms." https://www.sba.gov/advocacy/impact-regulatory-costs-small-firms.

Crawford, Nathan, ed. *The Continuing Relevance of Wesleyan Theology: Essays in Honor of Laurence W. Wood*. Eugene, OR: Pickwick Publications, 2011.

Crouch, Andy. *Culture Making: Recovering our Creative Calling*. Downers Grove, IL: InterVarsity, 2008.

Dade, Corey. "Government Job Cuts Threaten Black Middle Class." http://www.npr.org/2012/05/09/152297370/government-job-cuts-threaten-black-middle-class.

Dawson, William. *Bismarck and State Socialism: An Exposition of the Social and Economic Legislation of Germany Since 1870*. London: Forgotten Books, 2008.

DeNavas-Walt, Carmen, and Bernadette D. Proctor. "Income and Poverty in the United States: 2013." https://www.census.gov/content/dam/Census/library/publications/2014/demo/p60-249.pdf.

DeYoung, Kevin. "What's Up with Lutherans?" http://thegospelcoalition.org/blogs/kevindeyoung/2011/06/23/whats-up-with-lutherans/.

Dorland, W. A. Newman. *Dorland's Illustrated Medical Dictionary*. 32nd ed. Philadelphia, PA: Saunders/Elsevier, 2012.

Dougherty, Sean, and Juan Thomassie. "An Analysis of Salaries for College Basketball Coaches." *USA Today*. 30 March 2011. http://usatoday30.usatoday.com/sports/college/mensbasketball/2011-coaches-salary-database.htm.

Dougherty, Sean, et al. "Salary Analysis of 2010 Football Bowl Subdivision Coaches." *USA Today*. 26 December 2010. http://usatoday30.usatoday.com/sports/college/football/2010-coaches-contracts-database.htm.

Driscoll, Mark. "Emerging vs. Emergent." http://www.youtube.com/watch?v=RcbnGXSYxuI.

Duchon, Dennis, and Michael Byrns. "Organizational Narcissism." http://digitalcommons.unl.edu/cgi/viewcontent.cgi?article=1094&context=managementfacpub.

"El Paso Vending." Institute for Justice. http://www.ij.org/el-paso-vending.

"An Emotional Reunion with the Klan?" ABC News. http://abcnews.go.com/video/playerIndex?id=6819133.

Erlanger, Steven. "Europe Still Likes Obama, But Doubts Creep In." *The New York Times*. 1 November 2009. http://www.nytimes.com/2009/11/02/world/europe/02europe.html.

Evans, Rachel Held. "Mark Driscoll is a Bully. Stand up to Him." *Rachel Held Evans Blog*. 11 July 2011. http://rachelheldevans.com/blog/mark-driscoll-bully.

"Executive Branch (non-Postal) Employment by Gender, Race/National Origin, Disability Status, Veterans Status, Disabled Veterans." United States Office of Personnel Management, Central Personnel Data File (CPDF). https://www.opm.gov/policy-data-oversight/data-analysis-documentation/federal-employment-reports/demographics/2006/table1-1.pdf.

Fernández-Aráoz, Claudio, et al. "How to Hang on to Your High Potentials." https://hbr.org/2011/10/how-to-hang-on-to-your-high-potentials/ar/pr.

Filipovic, Jill. "Prosecuting Pregnant Drug-Addicted Mothers." http://www.feministe.us/blog/archives/2007/05/24/prosecuting-pregnant-drug-addicted-mothers/. May 25, 2007.

"Finding Families for African American Children." Evan B. Donaldson Adoption Institute. http://adoptioninstitute.org/old/publications/MEPApaper20080527.pdf.

Fish, Stanley. "Anonymity and the Dark Side of the Internet." http://opinionator.blogs.nytimes.com/2011/01/03/anonymity-and-the-dark-side-of-the-internet/.

Fisher, Celia B., et al. "Applied Developmental Science, Social Justice, and Socio-Political Well-Being." *Applied Developmental Science* 16 (2012) 54-64.

"'For God so Loved the World' for a $19.99 Oil Change?" CBS News. http://dfw.cbslocal.com/2011/09/28/for-god-so-loved-the-world-for-a-19-99-oil-change/.

Fortini, Amanda. "Why All of Hollywood's Toughest Stars Wear Stilettos." http://www.details.com/culture-trends/women/201104/hollywood-stars-stilettos-salt-sucker-punch-kick-ass/.

Frazier, Ryan. "What Does 'Missional' Mean?" *Real LIfe*. 15 June 2010. http://www.ryanfrazier.com/ryanfrazier.com/real_life/Entries/2010/6/15_What_Does_Missional_Mean.html.

Friedman, Milton. "The Social Responsibility of Business is to Increase its Profits." *The New York Times Magazine*. September 13, 1970. http://www.umich.edu/~thecore/doc/Friedman.pdf.

Garr, Emily, and Elizabeth Kneebone. "The Suburbanization of Poverty: Trends in Metropolitan America, 2000 to 2008." http://www.brookings.edu/research/papers/2010/01/20-poverty-kneebone.

George, Cindy. "Couples Vow Stronger Unions on Black Marriage Day." http://www.chron.com/news/houston-texas/article/Couples-vow-stronger-unions-on-Black-Marriage-Day-1702146.php.

"German School Gunman 'Kills 15.'" BBC News 11 March 2009. http://news.bbc.co.uk/2/hi/europe/7936817.stm.

Ghosh, Palash. "New York City's Abortion Rate Double the National Average." *International Business TImes.* 3 February 2011. http://www.ibtimes.com/new-york-citys-abortion-rate-double-national-average-263031.

Glaude Jr, Eddie. http://www.huffingtonpost.com/eddie-glaude-jr-phd/.

———. "The Black Church is Dead." http://www.huffingtonpost.com/eddie-glaude-jr-phd/the-black-church-is-dead_b_473815.html.

"Global Christianity—A Report on the Size and Distribution of the World's Christian Population." PewResearchCenter. http://www.pewforum.org/2011/12/19/global-christianity-exec/.

"God Loves Cities and Christians Should Too, says Tim Keller." Christiantoday.com. http://www.christiantoday.com/article/god.loves.cities.and.christians.should.too.says.tim.keller/26938.htm.

Haidt, Jonathan. *The Righteous Mind: Why Good People are Divided by Politics and Religion.* New York: Vintage, 2012.

Harper, Cynthia C., and Sara S. McLanahan. "Father Absence and Youth Incarceration." *Journal of Research on Adolescence* 14 (2004) 369-98.

Harris, Alisa. "Endangered Species." http://www.worldmag.com/2010/03/endangered_species.

Henninger, Daniel. "From Bismarck to Obama." http://www.wsj.com/articles/SB10001424052970204488304574430832455371844.

Henry, Matthew. "1 Corinthians." In *Matthew Henry's Concise Commentary,* 1706. http://www.christnotes.org/commentary.php?b=46&c=3&com=mhc.

Hilton, Elise. "Zero-Game Economic Fallacy." http://blog.acton.org/archives/24085-zero-sum-game-economic-fallacy.html.

Hinze, Christine F. "Quadragesimo Anno." In *Modern Catholic Social Teaching: Commentaries and Interpretations,* edited by Kenneth Himes, ch. 9. Washington DC: Georgetown University Press, 2005.

Holm, Jeffrey E., et al. "Assessing Health Status, Behavioral Risks, and Health Disparities in American Indians Living on the Northern Plains of the U.S." *Public Health Reports* 125 (2010) 68–78. http://www.ncbi.nlm.nih.gov/pmc/articles/PMC2789818/.

Holmes, Seth M. "An Ethnographic Study of the Social Contexts of Migrant Health in the United States." *PLOS Medicine* 3 (2006) 1776-93.

Hopkins, Dwight. "Liberating Black Theology: The Bible and the Black Experience in America." *Black Theology* 9 (2011) 117-18.

Inbar, Yoel, and Joris Lammers. "Political Diversity in Social and Personality Psychology." *Perspectives on Psychological Science* 7 (2012) 496–503.

Inglehart, Ronald. "The Silent Revolution in Europe: Intergenerational Change in Post-Industrial Societies." *The American Political Science Review* 65 (1971) 991-1017.

"Interview with Jim Wallis." PBS.org. http://www.pbs.org/wgbh/pages/frontline/shows/jesus/interviews/wallis.html.

Isidore, Chris. "College Football's $1.1 Billion Profit." http://money.cnn.com/2010/12/29/news/companies/college_football_dollars/index.htm.

Jackson, Rachel. "Zeller GS, 27, Dies in Hospital." http://dailyprincetonian.com/news/2011/01/zeller-gs-27-dies-in-hospital/.

Jaschik, Scott. "Admitting to Bias." https://www.insidehighered.com/news/2012/08/08/survey-finds-social-psychologists-admit-anti-conservative-bias.

John Paul II. *Centesimus Annus, Encyclical Letter on the Hundredth Anniversary of Rerum Novarum.* http://www.vatican.va/holy_father/john_paul_ii/encyclicals/documents/hf_jp-ii_enc_01051991_centesimus-annus_en.html.

———. *Laborem Exercens, Encyclical Letter on Human Work.* http://w2.vatican.va/content/john-paul-ii/en/encyclicals/documents/hf_jp-ii_enc_14091981_laborem-exercens.html.

Johnson, Eric. "Nightline Face-Off: Why Can't a Successful Black Woman Find a Man?" ABC News. 21 April 2010. http://abcnews.go.com/Nightline/FaceOff/nightline-black-women-single-marriage/story?id=10424979.

Johnson, Joel. "The Agonizing Last Words of Programmer Bill Zeller." http://gizmodo.com/5726667/the-agonizing-last-words-of-bill-zeller.

Johnson, Kenneth M., and Daniel T. Lichter. "Growing Diversity among America's Children and Youth: Spatial and Temporal Dimensions." *Population and Development Review* 36 (2010) 151–176.

Jones, Andrew. "Emerging Church Movement (1989–2009)?" *Tall Skinny Kiwi.* 30 December 2009. http://tallskinnykiwi.typepad.com/tallskinnykiwi/2009/12/emerging-church-movement-1989—-2009.html.

Jones, Joy. "Marriage is for White People." http://www.washingtonpost.com/wp-dyn/content/article/2006/03/25/AR2006032500029.html.

Kainz, Howard. "If Contraception, Why Not Gay Marriage?" *Crisis Magazine.* 7 July 2011. http://www.crisismagazine.com/2011/if-contraception-why-not-gay-marriage.

Kalomiris, Manolis. "Is 'Sola Scriptura' the Key to the Truth?" http://oodegr.com/english/ag_grafi/genika/sola_scriptura1.htm.

Kaveny, M. Cathleen. "Billable Hours in Ordinary Time: A Theological Critique of the Instrumentalization of Time in Professional Life." *Loyola University Chicago Law Journal* 33 (2001) 173–220.

Kee, Alistair. *The Rise and Demise of Black Theology.* Enlarged ed. London: SCM Press, 2008.

Keller, Tim. "The Missional Church." http://www.freedomchurchbaltimore.org/reading/missional-church-tim-keller.

———. "Tim Keller on Churches and Race." https://www.youtube.com/watch?v=5F2m1PepVb4.

Kirby, Alan. "The Death of Postmodernism and Beyond." *Philosophy Now.* https://philosophynow.org/issues/58/The_Death_of_Postmodernism_And_Beyond.

Kitwana, Bakiri. *The Hip-Hop Generation: Young Blacks and the Crisis in African-American Culture* New York: Basic Civitas Books, 2003.

Klare, Michael T. "Bush's 'Axis of Evil' Crumbles under Scrutiny." http://www.laprensa-sandiego.org/archieve/february01-02/BUSH.HTM.

Knopping, Greg. "Bill Belichick is the Highest Paid Coach in all of Pro Football." http://www.patspulpit.com/2010/5/23/1484333/bill-belichick-is-the-highest-paid.

Kolakowski, Nicholas. "Apple Slashes Apple TV Price to $229, Eliminates 40GB Model." http://www.eweek.com/c/a/Data-Storage/Apple-Slashes-Apple-TV-Price-to-299-Eliminates-40GB-Model-699878.

Koyzis, David. *Political Visions and Illusions: a Survey and Christian Critique of Contemporary Ideologies.* Downers Grove, IL: InterVarsity Academic, 2003.

Kravitz, Derek. "Airport Pat-downs Provoking Backlash." http://www.seattletimes.com/nation-world/airport-pat-downs-provoking-backlash/.

Ladd, George Eldon. *The Presence of the Future: The Eschatology of Biblical Realism.* Grand Rapids, MI: Eerdmans, 1974.

Landau, Simon. "Mayor Gray's Statement On Flashmob Shoplifting." http://brookland.wusa9.com/news/67060-mayor-grays-statement-flashmob-shoplifting.

"Left Behind in America: The Nation's Dropout Crisis." Center for Labor Market Studies.   http://www.northeastern.edu/clms/wp-content/uploads/CLMS_2009_Dropout_Report.pdf.

Leo XIII. *Rerum Novarum, encyclical letter on capital and labor.* http://www.vatican.va/holy_father/leo_xiii/encyclicals/documents/hf_l-xiii_enc_15051891_rerum-novarum_en.html.

"Life 'Meaningless' for Young." The Scotsman. http://www.scotsman.com/news/uk/10-of-young-people-think-life-is-worthless-1-752266.

Limbaugh, Rush. "Mr. Brooks and the Czars of Obama." http://www.rushlimbaugh.com/daily/2009/02/25/mr_brooks_and_the_czars_of_obama.

Lloyd, Tom. "Adult Female Hip Bone Density Reflects Teenage Sports-Exercise Patterns but not Teenage Calcium Intake." *Pediatrics* 106 (2000) 40–44.

Lohr, Kathy. "Atlanta Public Schools Under Fire." http://www.wbur.org/npr/131955644/Atlanta-Public-Schools-Under-Fire.

Lurie, Bob. "Wal-Mart's Green Strategy Raises Serious Issues." https://hbr.org/2010/06/why-you-should-worry-about-wal.

Lytle, Ryan. "Study: Twitter Improves Student Learning in College Classrooms." http://www.usnews.com/education/best-colleges/articles/2012/10/29/study-twitter-improves-student-learning-in-college-classrooms.

Ma, Damien. "Chinese Workers in Africa Who Marry Locals Face Puzzled Reception at Home." *The Atlantic.* 20 June 2011. http://www.theatlantic.com/international/archive/2011/06/chinese-workers-in-africa-who-marry-locals-face-puzzled-reception-at-home/240662/.

MacAdam, Alison. "TSA Head Defends 'Enhanced Pat Downs' and Safety of Scanners." http://www.npr.org/sections/thetwo-way/2010/11/16/131364772/tsa-head-defends-enhanced-pat-downs-and-safety-of-scanners.

Macon D. "Patronize Black People." http://stuffwhitepeopledo.blogspot.com/2009/12/patronize-black-people.html

Mahally, Farid. "A Study of the Word 'Love' in the Qur'an." http://answering-islam.org/Quran/Themes/love.htm.

Malewitz, Jim. "New Year Will Bring Higher Minimum Wages in 10 States." The Pew Charitable   Trusts.   http://www.pewtrusts.org/en/research-and-analysis/blogs/stateline/2012/12/20/new-year-will-bring-higher-minimum-wages-in-10-states.

"Mammy, Sapphire, and Jezebel." *Black Women's Blueprint*, 21 February, 2011, http://www.blackwomensblueprint.org/2011/02/21/mammy-sapphire-and-jezebel/.

Mason, Jeff. "Obama to Raise 10-Year Deficit to $9 Trillion." http://www.reuters
    .com/article/2009/08/21/us-obama-deficit-longterm-exclusive-
    idUSTRE57K4XE20090821.

Mather, Cotton. "The Education of Children," http://www.spurgeon.org/~phil/mather/
    edkids.htm.

McCoy, Steve K. "Missing the Point of Propaganda's 'Precious Puritans.'" http://www.
    stevekmccoy.com/blog/2012/09/missing-the-point-precious-puritans.

McCracken, Brett. Hipster Christianity: When Church and Cool Collide. Grand Rapids:
    Baker, 2010.

McDonough, William, and Michael Braungart. Cradle to Cradle: Remaking the Way We
    Make Things. New York: Northpoint, 2002.

McKnight, Scot. "From Wheaton to Rome: Why Evangelicals Become Roman Catholic."
    JETS 45 (2002) 451–72.

Mead, Walter Russell. "American Challenges: The Blue Model Breaks Down." The
    American Interest. 28 January 2010. http://blogs.the-american-interest.com/
    wrm/2010/01/28/american-challenges-the-blue-model-breaks-down/.

———."Obamageddon Coming to a City Near You?" The American Interest. 12
    July 2011. http://blogs.the-american-interest.com/2011/07/12/obamageddon-
    coming-to-a-city-near-you/.

Meade, Frederick Alexander. "Avatar: An Extension of White Supremacy." http://
    www.thepeoplesvoice.org/TPV3/Voices.php/2010/01/10/avatar-an-extension-of-
    white-supremacy.

Medina, Alex. "Amazing Grace for Lions and Liars." http://stayonpost.com/2010/03/24/
    amazinglion/.

"Mission & Vision." Union Theological Seminary. http://utsnyc.edu/about/mission-
    vision/.

"Mission Statement." Westminster Theological Seminary. http://www.wts.edu/about/
    beliefs/mission.html.

Montgomery, John Warwick, "Christian Apologetics in the Light of the Lutheran
    Confessions." Concordia Theological Quarterly 42 (1978) 258–75.

Moss, Otis, and Charles Jenkins. "The Black Church Must Stand up for President Obama."
    http://elev8.hellobeautiful.com/606240/rev-otis-moss-ii-rev-charles-jenkins
    -standing-up-for-obama/.

"Most Children Younger than Age 1 are Minorities." United States Census Bureau.
    http://www.census.gov/newsroom/releases/archives/population/cb12-90.html.

"The Movement." Radical the Book. http://www.radicalthebook.com/movement.html.

Muehlhauser, Luke. "17 Kinds of Atheism," http://commonsenseatheism.com/?p=6487.

Mumford, Lewis. The Culture of Cities. New York: Harcourt, Brace, Jovanovich, 1970.

National Council for the Social Studies. "About National Council for the Social Studies."
    http://www.socialstudies.org/about.

"NBA Salaries." InsideHoops.com. http://www.insidehoops.com/nbasalaries.shtml.

Nemeth, Charles P. Criminal Law. 2nd ed. Boca Raton, FL: CRC Press, 2012.

Neuman, William. "From Science, Plenty of Cows but Little Profit." http://www.
    nytimes.com/2009/09/29/business/29dairy.html.

"Nonfatal Traumatic Brain Injuries Related to Sports and Recreation Activities among
    Persons Aged ≤ 19 Years — United States, 2001–2009." United States Department
    of Health and Human Services, Centers for Disease Control and Prevention.
    http://www.cdc.gov/mmwr/pdf/wk/mm6039.pdf.

Norman, Joshua. "Naked Body Scan Images Never Saved, TSA Says." http://www.cbsnews.com/news/naked-body-scan-images-never-saved-tsa-says/.

"North Korea Threatens to 'Wipe Out' U.S." CBS News. http://www.cbsnews.com/news/n-korea-threatens-to-wipe-out-us/.

"Obama: 'I Screwed Up' on Daschle Appointment," CNN. February 2009, http://www.cnn.com/2009/POLITICS/02/03/obama.daschle/index.html.

Ohlemacher, Stephen. "Fact Check: The Wealthy Already Pay More Taxes." http://www.usatoday.com/money/perfi/taxes/story/2011-09-20/buffett-tax-millionaires/50480226/1. September 21, 2010.

Olasky, Marvin. "Is Everybody Fine?" http://www.worldmag.com/articles/16138.

Olasky, Susan. "Notable Books." *World Magazine*. 4 June 2010. http://www.worldmag.com/2010/06/notable_books.

"100 Million iPods Sold." Apple. 9 April 2007. http://www.apple.com/pr/library/2007/04/09100-Million-iPods-Sold.html.

"One in Ten Young in Northern Ireland 'Cannot Cope with Life.'" BBC News. 2 January 2013. http://www.bbc.co.uk/news/uk-northern-ireland-20882504.

"Otto von Bismarck." Social Security. http://www.ssa.gov/history/ottob.html.

"Our Six-Point Plan for Educational Equity." NAACP. http://www.naacp.org/blog/entry/our-six-point-plan-for-educational-equity.

Paige, Carmen. "Schools Ordered to Stop Prayer." http://pqasb.pqarchiver.com/pnj/doc/436171530.html.

Pius XI. *Divini Redemptoris, Encyclical Letter on Atheistic Communism*. http://www.vatican.va/holy_father/pius_xi/encyclicals/documents/hf_p-xi_enc_19031937_divini-redemptoris_en.html.

————. *Quadragesimo Anno: Encyclical Letter on the Reconstruction of the Social Order*. http://www.vatican.va/holy_father/pius_xi/encyclicals/documents/hf_p-xi_enc_19310515_quadragesimo-anno_en.html.

Platt, David. "My Take: Why My Church Rebelled Against the American Dream." http://religion.blogs.cnn.com/2010/12/23/my-take-why-my-church-rebelled-against-the-american-dream/.

————. *Radical: Taking Back Your Faith from the American Dream*. Colorado Springs: Multnomah, 2010.

Podles, Leon J. *The Church Impotent: The Feminization of Christianity*. Dallas: Spence, 1999.

Popken, Ben. "Full Body Scanners Don't Work, Israeli Security Expert Says." http://consumerist.com/2010/04/30/post-1/.

"Population of the United States by Race and Hispanic/Latino Origin, Census 2000 and 2010." Infoplease. http://www.infoplease.com/ipa/A0762156.html.

"Preamble." The Gospel Coalition. http://www.thegospelcoalition.org/about/foundation-documents/preamble/.

"President Exit Polls." The New York Times. http://elections.nytimes.com/2012/results/president/exit-polls.

"The Prince's Trust: YouGov Youth Index." The Prince's Trust. http://www.princes-trust.org.uk/pdf/YouGov%20Youth%20Index%20DSN%200689%20jan09.pdf.

Rah, Soong-Chan. *The Next Evangelicalism: Freeing the Church from Western Cultural Captivity*. Downers Grove, IL: InterVarsity, 2009.

————. "The Next Evangelicalism and the Changing Face of American Christians." https://vimeo.com/9302059.

Rah, Soong-Chan, and Michael Streich. "Second Great Awakening and American Religion." https://suite.io/michael-streich/22r72nv.

Rasmussen Reports. "Obama Approval Index History." http://www.rasmussenreports.com/public_content/politics/obama_administration/obama_approval_index_history.

Rector, Robert and Rachel Sheffield. "Air Conditioning, Cable TV, and an Xbox: What is Poverty in the United States Today?" http://www.heritage.org/Research/Reports/2011/07/What-is-Poverty.

Reid, Lesley W. and Robert M. Adelman. "The Double-Edged Sword of Gentrification in Atlanta." http://www.asanet.org/footnotes/apr03/indexthree.html.

Robbins, Liz. "Billboard Opposing Abortion Stirs Debate." http://cityroom.blogs.nytimes.com/2011/02/23/billboard-opposing-abortion-stirs-debate/.

Ryken, Philip Graham, and Michael LeFebvre. *Our Triune God: Living in the Love of the Triune God*. Wheaton, IL: Crossway, 2011.

Saad, Gad. "Homo Consumericus: I'm Not a Doctor, But . . ." *Psychology Today*. 1 November 2009. https://www.psychologytoday.com/articles/200911/homo-consumericus-i-m-not-doctor?collection=33901.

Sandefur, Gary D., et al. "The Effects of Parental Marital Status during Adolescence on High School Graduation." *Social Forces* 71 (1992) 103-21.

Sandoval, Edgar, et al. "Fast-food Workers Strike to Protest Low Wages at McDonald's, Taco Bell, Other Chains." *New York Daily News*. 29 August 2013. http://www.nydailynews.com/new-york/fast-food-walkout-workers-u-s-protest-wages-article-1.1440232.

Schmidtz, David. *Elements of Justice*. Cambridge: Cambridge University Press, 2006.

"Scientific Realism." *Stanford Encyclopedia of Philosophy*. http://plato.stanford.edu/entries/scientific-realism/.

Sessions, David. "'Pulpit Freedom Sunday' Pastors Don't Care about Religious Freedom." http://www.thedailybeast.com/articles/2012/10/07/pulpit-freedom-sunday-pastors-don-t-care-about-religious-freedom.html.

"Sexual Abuse." American Academy of Child and Adolescent Psychiatry. https://www.aacap.org/AACAP/Families_and_Youth/Facts_for_Families/FFF-Guide/Child-Sexual-Abuse-009.aspx.

Severson, Kim. "Scandal and a Schism Rattle Atlanta's Schools." *The New York Times*. 11 December 2010. http://www.nytimes.com/2010/12/12/education/12atlanta.html.

Silber, Kenneth. "From Bismarck to Bush." http://www.thinkadvisor.com/2008/08/01/from-bismarck-to-bush.

"Slander." D. Miall Edwards: International Standard Bible Encyclopedia Online. http://www.internationalstandardbible.com/S/slander.html.

SmartLX. "Christian Denominations." http://asktheatheist.com/?p=502.

Smith, James K. A. "The Case for Christian Education." http://www.thebanner.org/features/2011/01/the-case-for-christian-education.

"The Solid Progress of African Americans in Degree Attainments." The Journal of Blacks in Higher Education. http://www.jbhe.com/features/52_degree-attainments.html.

Sotomayor, Sonia. "A Latina Judge's Voice." Lecture given at University of California, Berkely, 2001.

Sproul, R.C. "All Truth is God's Truth." http://www.ligonier.org/learn/articles/all-truth-gods-truth-sproul/.

Starzyk, Renee. "Governor Responds to Charge CRCT Investigation is Racist." http://www.cbs46.com/story/14770360/governor-responds-to-charge-crct-investigation-is-racist-12-06-2010.

"State Graduation Report." Schott Foundation for Public Educaiton. http://blackboysreport.org/national-summary/state-graduation-data/.

Stearns, Rollin. "The Strategy Behind Same-Sex Marriage." http://www.henrymakow.com/why_were_losing_the_fight_agai.html.

Sum, Andrew, et al. "The Consequences of Dropping out of High School." *Northeastern University Labor Market Studies Report.* http://www.northeastern.edu/clms/wp-content/uploads/The_Consequences_of_Dropping_Out_of_High_School.pdf.

"Teens More Likely to Die from Heart Disease at a Younger Age than Today's Adults," nwitimes.com. 22 November 2011. http://www.nwitimes.com/niche/get-healthy/newsletter-featured-health-care/teens-more-likely-to-die-from-heart-disease-at-younger/article_1c60c604-d7d0-517f-8b53-5d64ebec02f6.html.

Thomas-Laury, Lisa. "Crisis Facing Single Black Women." http://6abc.com/archive/7305571/.

Tripp, Paul David, *Forever: Why You Can't Live Without It.* Grand Rapids, MI: Zondervan, 2011.

Trueman, Carl. "Is Nicene Christianity that Important? An Historical-Ecumenical Note." *Mortification of Spin.* 27 September 2011. http://www.mortificationofspin.org/mos/postcards-from-palookaville/is-nicene-christianity-that-important-an-historical-ecumenical-note.

———. "L'Orthodoxie? C'est Moi!" *Mortification of Spin.* 29 September 2011. http://www.mortificationofspin.org/mos/postcards-from-palookaville/lorthodoxie-cest-moi.

"The Truth about the Billable Hour." Yale Law School. http://www.law.yale.edu/studentlife/cdoadvice_truthaboutthebillablehour.htm

Tulchin, Drew, and Jessica Shortall. "Small Business Incubation and its Prospects in Indian Country." http://www.socialenterprise.net/assets/files/Small%20Business%20Incubation.pdf.

Twenge, Jean M., and W. Keith Campbell. *The Narcissism Epidemic: Living in the Age of Entitlement.* New York: Atria, 2010.

Un Joven Mas. "Juventud Guatemalteca." http://unjovenmasguate.blogspot.com/2009/05/juventud-guatemalteca.html. June 3, 2009.

Veith, Walter J. "Lactose Intolerance." https://hydrotherapyman.wordpress.com/2011/06/18/lactose-intolerance-tags-milk-dairy-products/.

Villano, David. "The Slumming of Suburbia." http://www.psmag.com/business-economics/the-slumming-of-suburbia-3941.

Vorjack. "Thoughts on Driscoll." http://www.patheos.com/blogs/unreasonablefaith/2011/07/thoughts-on-driscoll/.

———. "Our Mission and Vision." http://www.wts.edu/catalog/11_12_about_westminster/missionandvision.html.

"Washington State Teen Unemployment Rate: 34.5 Percent." *Puget Sound Business Journal.* 13 June 2011. http://www.bizjournals.com/seattle/news/2011/06/13/washington-state-teen-unemployment.html.

"What Does It Mean to Be a Sustainable Business?" http://2012books.lardbucket.org/books/sustainable-business-cases/s05-03-what-does-it-mean-to-be-a-sust.html.

Wheeler, Robert. "Voices of the Damned: A Rights-Based Analysis of Abortion in America." In *Reinventing the Right: Conservative Voices for the New Millennium*, edited by John Amble and Robert Wheeler, 97. Charleston, SC: BookSurge Publishing, 2010.

Wilkens, Steve, and Mark L. Sanford. *Hidden Worldviews: Eight Cultural Stories That Shape Our Lives*. Downers Grove, IL: IVP Academic, 2009.

Wilson, Elwin. Interviewed by Don Lemon. http://transcripts.cnn.com/TRANSCRIPTS/0902/08/cnr.05.html.

Witte, John, and Frank S. Alexander, eds. *The Teachings of Modern Christianity On Law, Politics, and Human Nature*. New York: Columbia University Press, 2006.

Wolters, Al. *Creation Regained*. Grand Rapids: Eerdman's, 2005.

Worldview Everlasting. "DeYoung, DeRestless & DeRealLiteralLutheran Ninjitsu." http://www.youtube.com/watch?v=xMCayHARWSM.

Wray, Matt. *Not Quite White: White Trash and the Boundaries of Whiteness*. Durham: Duke University Press, 2006.

"Yes We Can: The Schott 50 State Report on Public Education and Black Males 2010." The Schott Foundation. https://www.opensocietyfoundations.org/reports/yes-we-can-schott-foundation-50-state-report-public-education-and-black-males.

"Youngsters are More 'Vulnerable.'" BBC News. http://news.bbc.co.uk/2/hi/uk_news/wales/7808302.stm.

Subject Index

A

Abortion, 8, 13, 32, 48, 50, 83, 102, 110, 124, 167–169, 178, 188, 273
Abuse, 24, 25, 78, 79, 100–103, 106, 107, 148, 165, 166
  sexual, 238, 254, 257, 258, 278
  drug, 239
  childhood, 255, 261
Achievement, 56, 194, 197, 198, 207, 225, 234
African-American(s), 4, 5, 53, 54, 80, 86, 112, 113, 119, 125, 140, 148, 156, 159, 160, 168, 201
Apologetics, 28, 29, 30, 39, 44, 49, 50, 100, 276
Asians, 58, 66, 67 69, 114, 156, 168

B

Bismarck (German Chancellor), 159, 173, 174, 176–180, 271, 278
Blacks, 5, 6, 7, 8, 14, 15, 16, 43, 44, 46, 53, 71, 80, 81, 83, 109, 110, 111, 113, 116, 118–123, 125, 126, 127, 130, 131, 132, 134, 138–141, 149, 150, 151, 152, 156, 157, 159, 160, 168, 170, 199, 202, 206, 207, 236, 237, 274, 278

Black Church(es), 30, 32, 43, 53, 54, 55, 82, 83, 86, 113, 120, 124, 147, 148, 197, 198, 199, 270, 273, 276
Black Evangelical Scholars, 53, 54, 55
Black Theology, 30, 31, 54, 121, 122, 270, 273, 274

C

Calvin, John, 19, 88, 217
Civil Rights Movement, 46, 80, 109, 111, 114, 117, 118, 120, 125, 152, 187, 206, 207
Congress, 5, 31, 118, 137, 158, 160, 173, 179, 190, 191, 196
Crow, Jim, 15, 46, 111, 117, 118, 138, 140, 152

D

Delinquency, 24, 25, 26, 139, 168
Democrats, 13, 48, 51, 118, 142, 192, 221
Demographics, 12, 58, 59, 67, 80, 124, 125, 272
Discrimination, 14, 23, 121, 130, 131, 132, 151, 152, 196
Diversity, 58, 115, 123, 150, 152, 195, 196, 236, 273
Drugs, 165, 166, 253, 254, 259
  War on, 138

E

Economics, vii, xi, 10, 55, 58, 72, 74,
    101, 102, 136, 200, 279
Education, xi, 3, 19, 46, 53, 61, 69, 87,
    93, 107, 108, 111, 119, 123, 131,
    137, 144, 146, 149, 156, 168,
    169, 172, 173, 177, 178, 194,
    195–199, 201–207, 209, 210,
    215, 224, 233, 269, 275, 276,
    277, 278, 280
Empower(ed), 2, 75, 111, 148, 178, 206,
    208, 253
Empowerment, 53, 72, 74, 119, 167,
    169, 178, 208, 232
Episcopal (Episcopalean), 74, 95
    Church, 8, 31
Equality, 73, 74, 130, 131, 220
Eugenics, 8, 109, 111, 138, 139, 140
Evangelicals, 4, 5, 6, 8, 9, 10, 87, 94, 96,
    97, 98, 112, 114, 115, 166, 167,
    168, 216, 218
    progressive, 11
    conservative, 12
    church-going, 13, 16, 19
    black, 41, 44, 47, 48, 53
    suburban, 55, 58, 63
    young, 64
    Middle-class Western, 66, 67, 69,
    71, 79, 81
    non, 84
    white, 227, 238, 276
Evangelicalism, 4, 5, 8, 11, 12, 34, 40, 41,
    47–50, 53, 54, 55, 58, 63, 66, 67,
    77, 91, 97, 113, 115, 123, 166,
    202, 217, 277

F

Facebook, 1, 22, 32, 35, 43, 92, 118, 187,
    194, 248, 256, 270
Fast Food, 136, 137, 138, 147, 249, 250,
    278

G

Germany, 8, 18, 30, 141, 143, 146, 176,
    177, 179, 180, 188, 189, 271
Glaude, Eddie, Jr., 53, 54, 82, 273
Gospel Coalition (The), 34, 35, 39, 112,
    113, 114, 270, 271, 277

H

Hip-hop, 55, 81, 120, 169, 213, 214,
    226–230, 231, 274
Hispanics, 4, 5, 112, 124, 131, 139, 156,
    160, 168, 170
Holistic, 3, 27, 70, 93, 199, 258

I

Ideology, 9, 10, 159, 162, 182
Incarceration, 53, 138, 138, 165, 206,
    233, 273
    rates of, 120
Inner-city (the), 5, 24, 25, 26, 27, 31, 42,
    69, 70, 80, 81, 92, 168, 196–199,
    203, 270

K

Abraham Kuyper, 3, 16, 54, 72, 220
    racism of, 217

L

Latinos, 5, 12, 14, 15, 16, 58, 68, 123,
    124
Leadership, 7, 40, 52, 53, 91, 895, 98,
    115, 125, 146, 149, 154, 159,
    202, 211, 220, 250, 251, 259

M

Mexico, 146, 154, 155, 156, 264
Minorities, 4, 5, 8, 12, 13, 15, 16, 63,
    67, 110, 115, 116, 122, 123, 127,
    144, 152, 188, 202, 237, 276

N

NAACP, 149, 169, 207, 277
Native Americans, 6, 7, 8, 15, 127, 128,
    152, 153, 154, 16, 270
New Testament (The), 49, 79, 85, 91

O

Obama, Barack (President), 12, 30, 110,
    118, 126, 128, 132, 133, 134,
    135, 147–150, 157, 158, 169,
    160, 179, 180, 183, 184, 187,
    188, 189, 190, 192, 196, 197,
    198, 276
Old Testament (The), 49, 59, 60, 85, 91,
    104

P

Pastors, 5, 14, 22, 23, 30, 43, 44, 51, 52,
    55, 60, 62, 63, 76, 83, 87, 90, 91,
    92, 97, 112, 113, 147, 148, 166,
    202, 216, 258, 278
Platt, David, 3, 42, 68, 69, 70
Police, 108, 129, 139, 142, 187, 189, 245
Post-Traumatic Stress Disorder, 25, 253
Poverty, xii, xiii, 4, 5, 7, 69, 70, 71, 72,
    83, 110, 121, 137, 153, 157, 158,
    159, 161, 162, 167, 171, 175,
    176, 179, 208, 214, 220, 271,
    273, 278
Prayer, 22, 23, 30, 37, 39, 60, 87, 182,
    208, 209, 210, 277
Presbyterian, 6, 37, 75, 90, 94, 99, 113,
    116, 227
President (the), 12, 30, 46, 110, 118,
    128, 129, 132, 133, 134, 135,
    147, 149, 156, 157, 158, 159,
    160, 164, 165, 179, 180, 183,
    184, 187, 188, 189, 190, 192,
    193, 196, 197, 198, 201, 204, 276
  Roosevelt, 176
  Bush, George, W., 185, 186, 188
Presidential, 126, 148, 149, 166, 167,
    168
  disappointment in, 183

tracking, 184
  election, 186, 191
Prison, 93, 138, 139, 140, 157, 159, 234
  imprisoned, 216

R

Race, xi, 11- b14, 16, 19, 20, 21, 23, 30,
    31, 34, 37, 38, 44, 50, 55, 71, 80,
    86, 108, 110, 114, 115, 116, 121,
    122, 123, 127, 129, 130, 131,
    132, 133, 134, 135, 138, 149,
    152, 156, 167, 178, 195, 219,
    270, 271, 272, 274, 277
Racism, 8, 15, 16, 25, 46, 67, 119, 121,
    122, 123, 126, 127, 131, 132, 135
  economic consequences of, 152
  white, 204, 217, 219
  charges of, 236, 237, 271
Republicans, 12, 13, 48, 51, 119, 160,
    167, 187, 190, 191
Resurrection (the), 15, 20, 21, 49, 56, 77,
    78, 82, 89
Rhetoric, 4, 12, 71, 72, 87, 106, 110, 141,
    161, 167, 168, 169, 184, 190, 191

S

Scripture, 9, 21, 24, 29, 33, 35–38, 41,
    62, 79, 91, 94, 132, 133, 229, 266
Slavery, 68, 109, 111, 126, 127, 128, 141,
    262
Social justice, 2, 4, 5, 15, 32, 33, 39, 50,
    53, 57, 58, 90, 94, 121, 167, 168,
    272
  understanding of, expectation of the
    church, 61
  of Christians, 70
  rhetoric about, 71
  elements of, 72
  Christian, 73, 85
  culture and, 88
Solidarity, xi, 11, 28, 38, 53, 73, 74, 102,
    114, 115, 118, 135, 173, 218,
    219, 236, 244
Stereotypes, 14, 121, 126, 201

Supreme Court, 8, 130, 131, 165, 183, 187, 188, 270

Twitter, 1, 22, 43, 55, 57, 92, 187, 194, 195, 248, 249, 270, 275

T

Taxes, 149, 157, 158, 159, 176, 178, 191, 192, 193, 277
Theologian(s), 16, 18, 19, 39, 54, 57, 68, 82, 87, 89, 91, 92, 122, 134, 175, 217, 218, 249, 253, 260
Trauma, 213, 253, 255, 276
  childhood, 24
  assessments, 25, 26
  trauma-exposed communities, 27
Trinity (The), 24, 30, 38, 39, 43, 54, 64, 73, 84, 85, 112
Tripp, Paul, 13, 20, 88

U

Unemployment, 144, 145, 149, 150, 156, 157, 160, 169, 170, 180, 206, 279

W

White House (The), 13, 117, 133, 135, 154, 184
Whites, 4–8, 15, 16, 46, 63, 66, 67, 71, 80, 115, 118, 121, 123–128, 131, 138, 139, 151, 156, 160, 168, 170, 236, 237

Scripture Index

Old Testament

Genesis

1:26	73
1:26–27	132
1:26–28	114
3	31
3:14–24	69
3:15	31

Exodus

22	52

Leviticus

19:18	72
20:23	45

Numbers

14–15	91

Deuteronomy

6:1–25	210
6:5	72
7	14, 16, 24, 51
7–13	266

Nehemiah

9:2	218

Job

38–41	260

Psalms

1:1	91
43:2	90
69:29	65

Proverbs

8:4	260
14:31	83
22–23	260
22–23	260
27–30	60

Isaiah

23–29	260
61	258

Jeremiah

11–13	104

Daniel

3:8	36

Joel

1:3	91

The New Testament

Matthew

2:23	91
5:11	36
5:13–16	83, 201, 202
5:44–45	33
6:33	106
18:18	135
18:15–20	36
22:14	105
22:34–40	27
22:36–40	5, 28, 39, 41, 70, 72, 114
22:37–40	32
22:39	40
23:23	70
23:11–12	23
28:18–20	120, 210

Luke

4:4	258
16:1	36

John

3:8	69
4:19	33
4:9–16	85
3:5–6	29
3:5–8	84
3:16	23
10:10	21
14:15–31	106

16:16–17	85
17:17	114
17:6–26	41
17, 85	88
21:25	91

Acts

2:43	62
10:38	83
11:15, 18	84
15:15	59
17:6	132
20:35	91
29:2, 39	75

Romans

1:1	104
1:7	105
1:16–17	135
3:23	217
7:7	56
8:9	84
8:12–25	29
8:16	84
8:19–2	69
8:28–30	105
9:26	105
12:2	216
12:19–10	36
13:1	183

1 Corinthians

1:1	104
1:9	105
1:24	105
1:26	105
1:3–6	97
3:4	23
6:11	84
7:15–24	105
12:2–3	30
12:3, 38	84
12:13	84
13:8	33
13:13	33
15:32	21
16:13	69

2 Corinthians

2:10–13	29
12:9	82

Galatians

1:6	105
1:15	105
3:28	116
4:6	84
5:13	105

Ephesians

1:13–14, 38	84
1:18	105
2:11	105
2:8–10	85
4:4	105
4:30	84

Philippians

3:14	105
4:8	27

Colossians

1:15–23	29
1:3–23	86
3:1–17	45
3:15–20	69
15:2	105

1 Thessalonians

4:5	45
4:11	42
5:21	216, 218

2 Thessalonians

2:13;1	84
2:14	105
3:6	90

1 Timothy

5:18	165

2 Timothy

1:7	69
1:13–14	90
3:8	91

Hebrews

5:13–14	56
5:1–2	56
5:8	81
5:12–14	68
9:15	105
13:17	101

James

1:5	69
1:26–27	52
1:27	87

1 Peter

1:2	84
2:12	46
2:17	183
2:21	105
3:15	50
4:8	36
5:5	69

2 Peter

3:16	90

Jude

3–4	90
14	91

Revelation

3:15–16	81
5:9	67
7:9	39